EMBEDDED

TED GLENN

EMBEDDED

Two Journalists, a Burlesque Star, and the Expedition to Oust Louis Riel

DUNDURN
TORONTO

Publisher: Scott Fraser | Editor: Michael Carroll
Cover designer: Laura Boyle
Cover image: (top) *The Hudson's Bay Company post at Sault Ste. Marie, showing the campsite of Colonel Wolseley's expedition.* Archives of Ontario, 273 Series Donald B. Smith fonds. (bottom, left to right) *Kate Ranoe.* Photograph by William Notman, McCord Museum, Montreal, I-36185.1. *Robert Cunningham.* Archives of Ontario, Toronto, 69 Series, Robert Cunningham fonds. *Frederick Edward Molyneux St. John.* Archives of Manitoba, Personalities, Winnipeg, ca. 1890, N91.
Printer: Marquis Book Printing Inc.

Library and Archives Canada Cataloguing in Publication

Title: Embedded : two journalists, a burlesque star, and the expedition to oust Louis Riel / Ted Glenn.
Names: Glenn, Ted, author.
Description: Includes bibliographical references and index.
Identifiers: Canadiana (print) 20200292722 | Canadiana (ebook) 20200293656 | ISBN 9781459747340 (softcover) | ISBN 9781459747357 (PDF) | ISBN 9781459747364 (EPUB)
Subjects: LCSH: Cunningham, Robert, 1836-1874—Travel—Northwest, Canadian. | LCSH: St. John, Molyneux, 1838-1904—Travel—Northwest, Canadian. | LCSH: Ranoe, Kate, -1903—Travel—Northwest, Canadian. | CSH: Red River Expedition, 1870. | LCSH: Red River Rebellion, 1869-1870. | LCSH: Journalists—Canada—Biography. | LCSH: Entertainers—Canada—Biography. | LCGFT: Biographies.
Classification: LCC FC3214 .G54 2020 | DDC 971.05/10922—dc23

We acknowledge the support of the Canada Council for the Arts and the Ontario Arts Council for our publishing program. We also acknowledge the financial support of the Government of Ontario, through the Ontario Book Publishing Tax Credit and Ontario Creates, and the Government of Canada.

Printed and bound in Canada.

Dundurn
3 Church Street, Suite 500
Toronto, Ontario, Canada
M5E 1M2

To the memory of Kate Ranoe, a true Canadian trailblazer

Whatever may be said of other parts of the route, the Winnipeg was at least a well-known and long travelled highway, presenting remarkable facilities for boats. As a case in point, I may draw attention to the fact that, at the very time the Expeditionary Force was passing, two frail and poorly manned canoes, the one occupied by a very fat newspaper editor, and the other by a gentleman who had his wife with him, passed over all the rapids, portages and whirlpools of the Winnipeg without its occurring to their occupants that they were doing anything extraordinary.

— Simon Dawson, *Report of the Red River Expedition of 1870*

CONTENTS

AUTHOR'S NOTE

In the spring and summer of 1870, Robert Cunningham, Molyneux St. John, and Kate Ranoe filed 89 stories for Toronto's *Daily Telegraph* and *Globe* while embedded with Colonel Garnet Wolseley's military expedition to Red River in what would become the Province of Manitoba. Together, their articles are a first draft, rough and ungainly, of the story of the expedition written from a unique civilian perspective. They also bring a host of long-forgotten characters to life and offer eyewitness insights into the first major crisis faced by a very young Canadian nation.

Embedded: Two Journalists, a Burlesque Star, and the Expedition to Oust Louis Riel is my effort to wrangle their work into — hopefully — a more coherent narrative. I've made no effort to check the veracity of the stories or to correlate them with other contemporary accounts. The book, as such, shouldn't be read as a purely historical chronicle of the expedition to the Red River Settlement but rather for the unparalleled take by three civilians who lived day-to-day with one of the most important military expeditions in Canadian history.

I'd also like to make a few notes on the text. First, I've tried to reduce clutter by removing direct references to the primary source material. For those interested, I've organized the newspaper articles by chapter in the section called "Sources." Other references are noted where appropriate. Second, the text includes a number of dialogues, most between Robert Cunningham and people such as Louis Riel, Reverend George Young, and Chief Henry Prince. These are excerpted from the newspaper articles, with some minimal editing for punctuation and style, but shouldn't necessarily be taken as accurate representations of what the characters were like, what they said, or how they spoke. One case in point is Cunningham's report of his conversation with Louis Riel in January 1870. Riel's hair-trigger temper and mood swings seem to correlate with contemporary accounts, but Cunningham takes considerable licence with Riel's ability to speak English (Riel was fluently bilingual), education (Riel was well schooled in religion, law, and political science), and blasphemy (Riel was a devout Catholic who abhorred the practice). Then, as now, hyperbole sells. Third, some of the cited material includes terms such as *Indian*, *half-breed*, or *squaw*. While considered derogatory today, these were common in 1870 and have been included to preserve historical accuracy.

INTRODUCTION

> The eyes of all Canadians are just now turned with expectation towards the North-West Territory.... A gallant force of Queen's troops and Canadian Volunteers are about to push their way to Fort Garry from Lake Superior.... We have made arrangements to furnish the readers of THE GLOBE with the fullest and earliest intelligence of every event in connection with the Expedition and its object.... No effort will be spared to afford the fullest and earliest details of the most stirring and picturesque, as well as momentous, events which have occurred in Canada of late years.
>
> — Editorial, *Globe*, May 4, 1870

From the day it was announced in the spring of 1870, Colonel Garnet Wolseley's expedition to the Red River Settlement was front-page news. Officially, the campaign was billed as an "errand of peace" to assure the inhabitants of Red River they had "a place in the regard and the counsels of England, and may rely upon the impartial protection of the British Sceptre."[1] In reality, it was a much more complex affair. The mission was the Canadian government's second attempt to safeguard the purchase of Rupert's Land from the Hudson's Bay Company (HBC) and establish a government in the new North-West Territories. The first had failed in the fall of 1869 and triggered the Red River Rebellion. Instability in the territory had also piqued the interest of American annexationists looking to join recently purchased Alaska with the contiguous states south of the 49th parallel. Prime Minister John A. Macdonald hoped the 400 British Regulars at the core of the expedition would dampen their ardour. While these factors made the expedition newsworthy, what really pushed it into the headlines was the execution of Thomas Scott by Louis Riel's Provisional Government. The incident became a lightning rod for English-Canadian indignation with Riel and his band of upstart "French half-breeds," and Wolseley's expedition was seen as the quickest way to exact vengeance.

With a colourful cast of characters, political intrigue, exotic locales, and the prospect of military glory, the Red River Expedition promised to be the story of the year, and Canadian newspaper publishers jockeyed to sell it. The most enterprising were George Brown of the *Globe* and John Ross Robertson of the *Daily Telegraph*. In April 1870, the two arranged to have their reporters accompany Wolseley and the expedition all the way from Toronto to Fort Garry — the earliest example of embedded journalism in Canada, one of the first in modern journalism history.

The *Globe*'s special correspondent with the expedition was Molyneux St. John. He had served as a Royal Marine in the Battle of Canton against the Chinese in 1857 and in the Pig War against the Americans on San Juan Island between Vancouver Island and Washington Territory in 1859 and then retired to Plymouth, England, as a writer and playwright. In 1868, St. John immigrated to Canada and joined the *Globe*'s editorial board before being named special correspondent. Part of the reason he got the job was because John Ross Robertson had just purloined Robert Cunningham, the *Globe*'s first reporter on the North-West beat. Back in December 1869, George Brown had sent Cunningham west to interview Louis Riel. Cunningham got the interview (one of the first "Eastern" reporters to do so), but was thrown in jail, expelled from the settlement, and warned never to return. But return he did — as "Our Commissioner" for Ross's *Daily Telegraph*.

St. John and Cunningham didn't disappoint. Published between May 6 and October 22, 1870, their 89 stories gave Canadians a rich, dramatic, at times funny, and often critical perspective on the expedition and its progress, the only first-hand civilian accounts of the expedition that exist. On these points alone their coverage is worth revisiting. But there is another, more intriguing part of the story that's been buried for well over a century. In a passage written after the expedition was under way in August 1870, St. John reported coming across a "party of squaws" on Namakan Lake in Northern Ontario who were "much taken by the appearance of a lady who was accompanying her husband on this journey." At first, St. John said the Anishinabe women kept their distance, pointing the lady "out one to the other," "amused" by something in the lady's "dress or appearance." Eventually, the elder of the party "came and sat down alongside her white sister, and examined her more closely." One of the men with the expedition offered the woman some tobacco, which she "commenced to eat after the manner of others living in towns and villages." Satisfied with the gift, the woman left. But no sooner was she gone "than another came and sat down under cover of the umbrella which the Englishwoman had raised."

The woman was Kate Ranoe, the husband, St. John. Ranoe was an English-born, Paris-raised burlesque star who immigrated to Canada with St. John in 1868 and quickly became an audience favourite in the theatres and music halls of Montreal and Toronto. Somehow, after St. John was made special correspondent, Ranoe was able to finagle a way into accompanying him on the journey to Red River. And it was a good thing: just out of Thunder Bay, St. John injured his hand and had to rely on Ranoe to ghostwrite his coverage the rest of the way.

The Red River Expedition altered the course of Manitoban and Canadian history as it did the lives of Robert Cunningham, Molyneux St. John, and Kate Ranoe. In October 1870, Cunningham left his position with the *Daily Telegraph* to start a new newspaper, *The Manitoban*. Cunningham used it to advocate for Manitoba's rightful place in Confederation and the rights of Indigenous Peoples, issues he continued to fight for as a Member of Parliament in the last two years of his life. St. John leveraged his time with the expedition to become, among other things, first clerk of the Manitoba legislature, Indian commissioner, publisher of both the *Montreal Herald* and *Winnipeg Free Press*, and Gentleman Usher of the Black Rod. As the only woman on the expedition, Ranoe was able to attract an even larger and more loyal following across Canada for her work both onstage and in production.

So how exactly did these three individuals — an international burlesque star, a Royal Marine turned war correspondent, and an "Eastern" reporter on Riel's watch list — end up embedded on Wolseley's 1,255-mile military expedition to the far-flung Red River Settlement? It's a much longer answer than suggested here and begins with the sale of Rupert's Land in the spring of 1869.

PART I

Insurrection and Expedition

- 1 -

BLAWSTED FENCE

> All the way up, stories have been retailed in the bar-rooms of the hotels of the most ludicrous character. Captain Cameron and his eye-glass comes in for a share of these remarks. It was told that he went boldly up to the stockade the insurgents had thrown across the Fort Garry road, took out his eye-glass, looked through it wonderingly at the impediments, and in a club-house kind of style, said, "take away that blawsted fence," and when some of the half-breeds made their appearance, he took to his heels, and manfully ran for it.
>
> — Robert Cunningham, "The Insurrection in the North-West," *Globe*, January 13, 1870

In March 1869, the Canadian government and the Hudson's Bay Company finally agreed to terms for the sale of Rupert's Land, a vast tract bestowed upon the company by English royal charter in 1670. It stretched from present-day Labrador in the east to the Rocky Mountains in the west to Baffin Island in the north. The nearly 1.5 million square miles featured an extensive fur-based economy that supported 100,000 or so Indigenous Peoples and a few thousand non-Native settlers. It also contained 97 trading posts and a partially built telegraph line. In exchange for the land (and everything else), Canada agreed to pay the Hudson's Bay Company £300,000 cash, grant it nearly 11,500 square miles of land concessions, and guarantee its ability to trade without "exceptional" taxation within its former territory.

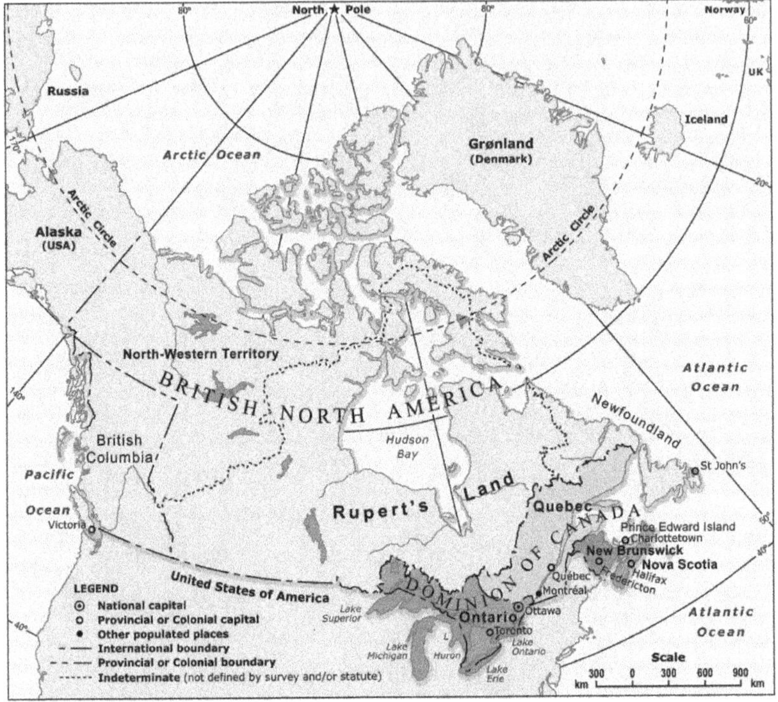

Canada in 1867.

The Parliament of Canada ratified the deal in July 1869 and set December 1, 1869, as the closing date for the transaction. It also passed legislation to establish a temporary government for the North-West Territories "until more permanent arrangements" could be made. Prime Minister Macdonald designated William McDougall, his public works minister and long-time advocate of westward expansion, as lieutenant governor.

On paper, McDougall wasn't a bad choice; he at least had some experience on the file. Earlier in the decade, he'd served as commissioner of Crown land in Canada West, overseeing the department responsible for colonization in northern parts of the province. During Confederation debates, he'd been an outspoken advocate of Canada annexing Rupert's Land, even helping to ensure that a provision for the admission of the territory was included in the British

North American Act, 1867. And in Macdonald's first government, McDougall, as public works minister, was responsible for transcontinental expansion. One of his first acts was to introduce a series of resolutions into Parliament calling on Great Britain to transfer Rupert's Land to Canada outright.

While negotiations with the Hudson's Bay Company dragged on into the summer of 1868, McDougall hired senior Dominion engineer Simon Dawson to map out the "best means of opening a line of communication between Lake Superior and the Red River Settlement." Dawson recommended an old North West Company canoe route he'd run across back in 1857 — "impassable to any vessel larger or stronger than a bark canoe," he said — linked by two new roads to be built at either end, one from Lake Superior to the start of the canoe route at Shebandowan Lake, the other from the western end of Lake of the Woods to Fort Garry. McDougall liked the plan and contracted Dawson to build the eastern road and another engineer, John Allan Snow, the western.

McDougall and the Dominion government billed Snow's part of the project as a "humanitarian mission." The inhabitants of Red River were desperate for food because their crops had been ruined by locusts the previous year and droughts had decimated buffalo herds and game and fish stocks. In October 1868, Snow and his crew arrived in Red River and were initially welcomed by the local population. But quickly the bloom came off the mission. Rather than pay local hires cash for services, Snow and his paymaster, a McDougall appointee named Charles Mair, developed a convoluted payment system involving credit for provisions that were scarce in the settlement. The system became a source of agitation when locals realized Snow's credits had subpar value and could only be redeemed at a store owned by John Schultz, unofficial leader of a small group of outspoken immigrants known as the Canadian Party. Schultz was a strident advocate for Canada annexing Rupert's Land and flooding the territory with English-speaking Canadian settlers. He'd also gained a reputation as an "unscrupulous land-grabber."

Mair's presence didn't help Snow's cause in Red River. Mair was a 30-year-old poet and co-founder of Canada First, a movement dedicated to promoting Canadian nationalism and westward expansion. George Brown, editor of the Toronto-based *Globe*, shared similar politics, and on learning McDougall was sending Mair to Red River, hired him as a correspondent to "inspire eastern interest in the northwest frontier." Mair's columns began running in January 1869 and featured romantic accounts of an idyllic prairie landscape, as well as insulting caricatures of local residents, especially the "indolent half-breeds." Annie Bannatyne, a Métis woman married to prominent businessman Andrew Bannatyne, took particular exception to a January 4 story in which Mair said Métis women had "no coat of arms but a 'totem' to look back to [and who] make up for the deficiency by biting at the backs of their 'white' sisters." Bannatyne and two of her similarly slandered friends accosted Mair in her husband's store shortly after the article arrived in Red River. They pulled his nose, slapped his face, and ran him into the street at the business end of a riding crop. Mair's stories earned the *Globe* significant enmity in the settlement — enmity not forgotten when Robert Cunningham arrived on the scene as the paper's special correspondent in January 1870.

AGITATION GROWS

Over the summer of 1869, agitation in Red River grew. In August, another work crew arrived from Canada, this one to begin surveying Rupert's Land in anticipation of its sale. The crew chief was John Stoughton Dennis, an old schoolmate of William McDougall's, who took up residence with John Schultz. About this time, news of McDougall's nomination as lieutenant governor also reached Red River. Locals, not surprisingly, must have felt betrayed, like "dumb-driven cattle" in Wolseley's later words. They had neither been consulted on the sale of their lands nor involved in choosing their government. The French-speaking Métis were particularly piqued and organized a series of meetings to discuss their options. At one meeting at St. Boniface in late August, a young, eloquent, bilingual man named Louis Riel stood

Louis Riel.

on the steps of the cathedral and denounced Dennis's survey crew as "a menace and a threat" to the Métis and their lands.

Louis wasn't the first Riel to advocate for the rights of the Métis in Red River. In 1849, Riel's father — Louis, Sr. — helped organize Red River Métis in defending Pierre-Guillaume Sayer against charges of violating the Hudson's Bay Company's trade monopoly. Sayer was acquitted and the ruling effectively ended the company's monopoly, leaving the Métis free to trade with whomever they wanted. Twenty years later, Louis *fils* returned from seminary school in Montreal and work in Chicago and St. Paul, Minnesota, to follow in his father's footsteps. Buoyed by his success at St. Boniface in August 1869, Riel helped organize a convention in September where 200 delegates passed a motion to prevent McDougall from entering Red River until Métis rights were guaranteed safeguarded.

Locals weren't the only ones who were agitated in Red River in the summer of 1869. In September, Snow returned from Ottawa with money to finish his road but found his men unhappy with their wages — to the point of walking off the job in protest. Snow gave in to the wage demands, but not before the strike leaders dragged him to the Seine River and threatened to drown him if he didn't pay for lost time, as well. Snow laid charges against the men; four were indicted for aggravated assault and two were found guilty, including a young Orangeman from Ontario who'd drifted into the territory looking for work the previous summer. His name was Thomas Scott.

In October, agitation in the settlement came to a head. One of Dennis's survey crews was working in St. Vital parish, two and a half miles west of the Red River, marking out territory *as per* Canadian practice — on a square-grid section. Local tradition, however, was to divide lots into long, narrow strips from the river's edge to provide greater points of access to water and to the hayfields — *privileges*, colloquially — set back from the river. On October 11, André Nault, a long-time resident, discovered a survey crew on his privilege and went to find his bilingual cousin, Louis Riel, to help him figure out what was going on. Riel returned with 18 Métis and famously stood on

Map showing the routes to Fort Garry via Lake Superior.

the Canadian survey chain. He told the crew, "The territory south of the Assiniboine River belongs to the people of Red River and not to Canada, and the Métis would not allow the survey to proceed any further." The Métis presented no arms, but it was clear trouble would ensue if work continued.

ACCESS DENIED

The same day that Riel stood on the Canadian survey chain, word reached Red River that William McDougall and his entourage had arrived at the railway terminus in St. Cloud, Minnesota. Until the Canadian railway reached Winnipeg in 1883, the easiest way to travel to Red River was by rail from Toronto via Detroit to the railhead at St. Cloud, and then overland 427 miles to Fort Garry by some combination of stage, wagon, or sleigh, depending on the quality of the snow.

McDougall's entourage couldn't be missed. As Canadian Secretary of State Joseph Howe put it, McDougall looked like a "great satrap with a grandeur of equipage and display of pomp enough to tempt the cupidity of all Métis in the country."[1] In addition to his four young children (McDougall's wife had recently died), personal attendants, and various friends and hangers-on (such as Charles Mair and his wife, who were returning from Ontario), McDougall's entourage included Joseph-Alfred-Norbert Provencher (provincial secretary designate and Molyneux St. John's future boss), Albert Richards (attorney general designate), and Captain Donald Cameron (constabulary) and his pregnant wife, Emma. Supporting this cast was a battalion of labourers sufficient to manage the 30-cart wagon train and pitch and keep camp for the party as it journeyed overland to Fort Garry.

Emboldened by news of McDougall's arrival at St. Cloud and the standoff with the surveyors, Riel and his supporters met at Abbé Noël-Joseph Ritchot's house in St. Norbert parish on October 16 and proclaimed the Comité National des Métis. John Bruce was elected president and the not quite 26-year-old Louis Riel, secretary. Through their network four days later, the *comité* learned that McDougall had packed 100 Spencer carbines, 250 Peabody muskets, and 10,000 rounds of ammunition in his wagon train (McDougall was hoping to arm a volunteer constabulary once in office). For the *comité*, Riel drafted a notice to McDougall not to enter the territory without permission and sent an armed patrol to put up a roadblock on the Pembina–Fort Garry road just north of where it crossed the Sale River.

On October 30, McDougall and his wagon train arrived at Pembina, a small village on the American side of the border. Waiting for him was mail from Fort Garry. HBC Governor William Mactavish advised McDougal to remain in Pembina "in view of the temper of the people."[2] McDougall's old schoolmate John Stoughton Dennis told him a fight with the local population wouldn't likely be won and that McDougall should therefore remain where he was. Dennis had learned a lesson about being on the inferior end of superior firepower as commander of the vessel *W.T. Robb* during the Battle of Fort Erie in 1866. His boss at the time, William McDougall, acting minister of the marine with responsibility for gunboats, evidently hadn't.

From Pembina on October 30, McDougall sent Provencher north to gain intelligence on the barricade at Sale River. Cameron set off with his wife and attendants for Winnipeg on his own. McDougall himself left the next day for the Hudson's Bay fort two miles north of the border to set up temporary headquarters. On reaching the American customs post, a Métis courier stopped McDougall and handed him Riel's message:

> Dated at St. Norbert, Red River, this 21st day of October 1869.
>
> Sir,
> The National Committee of the Métis of Red River Orders William McDougall not to enter the Territory of the North West without special permission of the above-mentioned committee.
>
> By order of the President, John Bruce.
> LOUIS RIEL, Secretary

McDougall was infuriated, tore a strip off the messenger, and pushed his way into the territory.

While McDougall took stock of affairs at HBC Pembina, Riel moved to consolidate the Métis position. On November 1, the *comité* confirmed about 400 armed men on muster roll and 100 more available in camp. It also directed Ambroise-Didyme Lépine to take a unit south to escort McDougall, Provencher, and Cameron back across the border to Pembina. Lépine's task was made easier when Cameron drove his team to the edge of the three-foot barricade on the Sale, inserted his monocle, and in his most pompous English accent, demanded the guards "take down that blawsted fence." Instead, the guards seized Cameron's wagon and horses and removed the diminutive captain to Abbé Ritchot's house to wait for Lépine.[3] Provencher had more luck. He was able to negotiate a meeting with John Bruce, president of the *comité*. Once Lépine and his guards arrived on the scene, though, both Provencher and Cameron were escorted back to HBC Pembina and informed they would have to leave the territory with McDougall the next morning. McDougall produced his commission for Lépine but to no effect. At the border the next morning, Lépine told McDougall, "You must not return beyond this line." Without a military or even constabulary force to support his commission, McDougall had no choice but to return to camp at Pembina and cool his heels.[4]

On November 2, Riel continued to consolidate his position. More than 100 armed Loyalists stormed Fort Garry and took control of the food and munitions in storage there. On November 6, Riel issued a notice inviting all inhabitants of Red River to send delegates to a convention on November 16 "to consider the present political state of this country and to adopt such measures as may be deemed best for the future welfare of the same."[5] For two weeks, Riel tried to convince delegates it was in their best interest to support the creation of a provisional government to negotiate entry into Confederation on equal terms with the Canadian government. The English delegates couldn't yet be convinced and the convention adjourned deadlocked on November 24.

COUNTER-RESISTANCE

Exiled at Pembina, McDougall received a steady stream of advice as he stewed. On November 9, HBC Governor Mactavish told McDougall he hadn't received any official direction about the transfer of Rupert's Land to Canada, and in light of the current "peculiar feelings and habits" of the inhabitants, advised him to return home. Joseph Howe reminded McDougall on November 19 that he had no formal authority until the Queen's actual proclamation arrived in Manitoba. Even the prime minister advised caution: "The point you must never forget is that you are now approaching a foreign country, under the government of the Hudson's Bay Company. You are going there under the assumption that the Company's authorities assent to your entering upon their territory, and will protect you when there. You cannot force your way in."[6] And yet that was exactly what McDougall decided to do.

In the absence specific of legal authority or direction from Ottawa, McDougall sent a messenger to Winnipeg on November 30 with a proclamation announcing the transfer of Rupert's Land to Canada and himself as lieutenant governor. Loyalists made copies by hand — the only printing press was controlled by Riel's Comité National — and distributed them around Winnipeg. To enforce his authority, McDougall issued a second proclamation appointing John Stoughton Dennis as "Lieutenant and Conservator of the Peace" with authority to "raise, organize, arm, equip, and provision a sufficient force" to "attack, arrest, disarm, or disperse the … armed men so unlawfully assembled and disturbing the public peace; and for that purpose, and with the force aforesaid, to assault, to fire upon, pull down, or break into any fort, house, stronghold, or other place in which the said armed men may be found." At Stone Fort on December 6, proclamation in hand, Dennis issued a call to "all loyal men of the North-West Territories" to assist in restoring "public peace and order" and upholding "the supremacy of the Queen in this part of Her Majesty's Dominions."[7]

Back in Winnipeg, John Schultz and a group of Loyalists gathered to show support for McDougall and Dennis — and the Comité National responded swiftly. At two o'clock in the morning of December 7, 200 armed troops moved on Schultz's house and trained two cannons on the main door. Riel gave the Canadians 15 minutes to give themselves up. The 45 men and women inside, including John Schultz, Charles Mair, and Thomas Scott, surrendered almost immediately and were marched under guard to Fort Garry and there imprisoned.

On December 8, Riel declared a Provisional Government and issued a "Declaration of the People of Rupert's Land and the North-West." It set out a list of demands based on an earlier "Red River List of Rights" started by the November Convention and expressed the willingness of inhabitants to "enter into such negotiations with the Canadian government as may be favourable for the good government and prosperity of this people." A day later, Riel and his lieutenants,

Louis Riel and his council, 1869. Back row (left to right): Bonnet Tromage, Pierre Delorme, Thomas Bunn, Xavier Pagé, André Beauchemin, Baptiste Tourond, Thomas Spence. Middle row (left to right): Pierre Poitras, John Bruce, Louis Riel, William O'Donoghue, François Dauphinais. Front row (left to right): Hugh (or Bob) O'Lone, Paul Proulx.

Ambroise-Didyme Lépine and William O'Donoghue, hoisted their government's flag in the centre of the square at Fort Garry — a yellow fleur-de-lis with a green shamrock on a white background.[8]

INTO THE MAELSTROM

While McDougall didn't give up trying to assert his authority in the fall of 1869, the Dominion government gave up on him. Spooked by the outbreak of agitation in October, Canada asked London to postpone the transfer of Rupert's Land until "peaceable possession could be guaranteed" (unbeknownst to McDougall). The Cabinet also decided to send emissaries to Red River to communicate the message that "the country is to be handed over to the Queen, and that it is Her Majesty who transfers the country to Canada with the same rights to settlers as existed before."[9] The delay gave Prime Minister Macdonald time to begin preparations to send a military force to Red River in the spring.

As emissaries, the Dominion chose Colonel Charles-René-Léonidas d'Irumberry de Salaberry, engineer Simon Dawson's colleague on the 1857 expedition to Red River; Abbé Jean-Baptiste Thibault, who had served at St. Boniface for the better part of two decades; and Donald Alexander Smith, chief factor of the Hudson's Bay Company, Labrador district. De Salaberry and Thibault set out for Red River in early December; Smith followed with Nova Scotia Member of Parliament Charles Tupper on December 13. Tupper had been dispatched from Nova Scotia by his wife to retrieve their daughter, Emma, from Red River and her husband, Donald Cameron, "the gallant hero of the blasted fence," as St. John later called him. And hot on the emissaries' heels was Robert Cunningham, the *Globe*'s newly named special correspondent in the North-West. He left Toronto on December 23, 1869.

- 2 -

OUR SPECIAL CORRESPONDENT

> Doubtless the Red River difficulty will be the great question in Canada for some time to come, and as so much misrepresentation on one side and so much reticence on the other have jointly contributed to make the whole matter an almost insoluble puzzle, your correspondent, in order to try his hand at solving it, set out for Fort Garry on the twenty-third day of December 1869.
>
> — Robert Cunningham, "The Insurrection in the North-West," *Globe*, January 13, 1870

Robert Cunningham was 33 years old in December 1869. He, his wife, Annie, and their four children had emigrated from Scotland to Toronto the year before where Cunningham found work as a city beat reporter for the *Globe*. It is unclear why — there is no record of Cunningham working as a reporter in Britain — or what exactly Cunningham wrote for the *Globe*; journalistic practice at the time didn't include bylines. All we know is that Cunningham took an interest in the "stark, ghastly poverty" of the Ward, an infamously poor neighbourhood of immigrants in downtown Toronto. In early 1869, he published a short book — *Christmas Eve on Stanley Street* — about one particularly seedy street on the edge of the Ward where "scarcely was there a woman not more or less under the influence of liquor." Cunningham said the "sheer amount of drunkenness" he saw among

Robert Cunningham.

Stanley Street women was "absolutely frightful to contemplate" and clearly the cause of "most of the domestic misery existing in these locations," if not "so much immorality." The sensationalism and hyperbole saturating *Christmas* defined Cunningham's writing at this time, and evidently was exactly what George Brown was looking for to boost sales of the *Globe*'s coverage of the "Insurrection in the North-West."

ON MCDOUGALL'S TRAIL

Cunningham reached the rail terminus at St. Cloud on December 30, 1869, the same day that William McDougall, the almost lieutenant governor, and the lead carts of his entourage arrived back from Pembina. Cunningham said the barrooms were rife with stories of McDougall's deposal, the most entertaining of which featured the "hero of the blawsted fence," Captain Donald Cameron.

On January 1, Cunningham, wrapped tightly in a buffalo coat, fur hat, and robes, tucked into a sleigh and set off on the first part of the overland journey north. Travelling through "sharp wind and drizzling snow," he met two four-horse teams that afternoon with the last of McDougall's entourage. On learning about Cunningham's mission, the councillor-designate Major James Wallace told him feelings against the *Globe* were "so intense" that any special correspondent of that newspaper would "certainly be scalped the moment he entered Fort Garry, if not hung." Cunningham said this put a damper on his spirits.

On January 2, the landscape started to change — "the woods began to disappear, and the prairie began to develop itself. The land opened and stretched away before and on each side, in wide rolling ranges." And then, on January 3, "away, far as the eye could reach — like the ocean — the land stretched, one roll of land succeeding another roll, till, in trying to find a limit to the vista, the eye grew weary, and the heart grew sick. No houses were to be seen, not a living creature in sight."

At Georgetown, Dakota Territory, on January 7, Cunningham met Charles Tupper and his daughter, Emma. Tupper told Cunningham that Thibault and de Salaberry were about to meet with Riel and his *comité*. He also said that 800 Métis had joined Riel's forces and were being paid from the Hudson's Bay safe. Tupper described Riel as "a very shrewd, intelligent, determined man." Cunningham didn't mention Cameron.

COLD RECEPTION

On January 10, Cunningham reached Pembina and left for the Canadian border early the next morning. He said he was nervous —

understandably, given what he'd seen and heard en route — and decided to take his Métis hotelier, Joe Rolette, with him. It was a good decision. It took Rolette a half-hour of negotiating with the armed Métis guard at the border to get Cunningham admitted to the territory. He and Rolette reached a coach house at Scratching River that evening as the temperature dropped to minus 40. Cunningham said the bill for the tiny, windowless room and tough-as-a-board steak was "something more than would have been charged at the Queen's Hotel in Toronto."

Late on the evening of January 12, Cunningham arrived at the gates of Fort Garry. He said the fort itself stood on the west bank of the Red River and was protected on the south and east by a stone wall ten feet high and on the north and west by a strong stockade. Cunningham estimated interior dimensions to be about 600 by 400 feet with "quite a village" set out inside — offices, stores, barrack rooms, hospitals, "gaols," the HBC governor's residence, family dwellings, guardrooms, smithies, et cetera.

At the main south gate, Cunningham presented himself to the guard on duty and declared his intention to speak with "Monsieur le Président Riel."

Old Fort Garry.

"Monsieur le Président is out," the guard replied. "Would *monsieur* go in till his return?"

"*Monsieur* is very tired and would prefer going to a hotel and call on Monsieur le Président in the morning," Cunningham told him.

"*Monsieur* had better go in," the guard declared a bit more forcibly. "In fact, *monsieur* must go in. These are the orders."

"Whose orders?" Cunningham asked.

"The orders of Monsieur le Président," the guard stated. He grabbed hold of Cunningham's horse and led it, the sleigh, and the reporter in through the gate.

Once inside, Cunningham was escorted to the guardroom of a small, one-storey house — nothing more than a low-roofed apartment about twelve feet square with a stove in the centre and 20 or so men around it.

"Will *monsieur* give me his baggage?" one of the men inside asked affably. "I will put it in the right place."

"Will *monsieur* take a seat by the stove?" another man asked, showing Cunningham a chair.

After waiting three or four hours, Cunningham began to doze off by the fire.

"*Monsieur* had better go to bed," one of the guards suggested.

"*Monsieur* is exactly of the same opinion," Cunningham replied. He got up, put on his overcoat and buffalo coat, and made for the door.

Before he could leave, though, the guard said, "But *monsieur* must sleep here."

"Where?" Cunningham inquired, looking around the small, packed room.

"Here," the guard said, leading Cunningham to an adjacent closet. He pointed to a buffalo robe spread on the floor. "That is *monsieur*'s bed."

Cunningham told the guard he'd travelled 1,800 miles and was very tired and would prefer a more inviting bed. "Can I not go to a hotel?"

"I am truly sorry, but Monsieur le Président's commands must be complied with. That is *monsieur*'s bed for the night."

"Then I am a prisoner."

"That is so — by the orders of Monsieur le Président."

The guard turned on his heel and left Cunningham alone in the room, who lay down and fell into a dreamless sleep.

The next morning, January 13, Cunningham got up and returned to the guardroom at about six o'clock. Only a dozen men were left. One kindly offered him a basin in which to wash.

"*Monsieur* is from Canada, is he not?" the guard asked.

"That is so," Cunningham replied.

"Is *monsieur* the *Gazette* man expected?"

"I am," the *Globe*'s special correspondent lied.

"*Monsieur* has come to get news, has he not? To know what we want? To tell the people of Canada why we have taken the front and taken up arms? Is that what *monsieur* has come for?"

"That is exactly why I have come."

"Shall I tell *monsieur* what we want?" the guard asked, turning to his confreres.

"Oui!" came the reply.

"We want to be treated as free men," the guard declared. "Your Canada Government offered to pay £3,000 to the Hudson's Bay Company for the Rivière Rouge Territory. Now, what we want to know, and we will not lay down our arms till we know what they mean to buy. Was it the land? If so, who gave the Hudson's Bay Company the right to sell the land? When the Canada Government bought the land, did they buy what was on it? Did they buy us? Are we slaves of the Hudson's Bay Company?" The guard turned to his comrades and asked excitedly, "Are we slaves?"

"Non!" came the resounding reply from the men in the room. *"Non!"*

"Non," the guard repeated, turning back to Cunningham, "we are not slaves. But remember, and you may tell Canada people this when you go home, that we are not the cruel murderous men we have been described. We do not want to kill anyone in this quarrel. We have hurt no one yet, nor do we mean to do so. Let the Canada Government

come and treat with us as free men, and we will lay down our arms, and go to our homes."

INTERVIEW WITH MONSIEUR LE PRÉSIDENT

Cunningham was given pemmican for breakfast the next morning — "It resembled dried paper pulp, and tasted like singed rags" — and then waited in the room a couple more hours. Around 10:00 a.m., Riel entered dressed in a light tweed coat and black trousers. Cunningham said he looked to be around 30 years old, stood about five foot seven, and was "rather stoutly built." He had dark curly hair and a "very small and very fast receding forehead." With him was a man Cunningham assumed was William O'Donoghue, who was of a "semi-priestly appearance," fair-haired, closely shaven with a "cringing, cunning way" about him.

After ten minutes or so, Riel spoke. "I don't know who you are."

Cunningham presented his credentials. Riel took them, read them, and "coolly" put them in his pocket.

"You know, the people of Canada are anxious to know all about this Red River affair," Cunningham told Riel.

"The people of Canada know all about it already. Look — here, and here, and here." Riel pointed to blotches of ink on the desk. "Some ink has been used, has it not, in writing facts? What more do you want?"

"The people of Canada desire to have the facts of the case laid out before them in a plain, honest way," Cunningham told him. "True, they have read a great deal about the affair, but most of what they have read has come through American channels. All they have read might be good, genuine facts. If so, it would do no harm to allow these facts to be restated."

At this, Riel struck his hand violently on the desk. "We are in the right, we are in the right!" Then the Métis leader got up and walked out of the room with O'Donoghue in tow. They convened in the next room with the *comité* to debate what to do with the *Globe*'s special correspondent. Cunningham said he could hear everything "through the thin walls." The *comité*, Cunningham said, was hung: O'Donoghue argued strongly for expulsion; the Métis maintained he be allowed to stay. Riel didn't weigh in one way or the other.

A short while later, Riel returned and paced the floor, running his hand through his hair, scratching his nose. At turns, Riel would pause and stare and then start off again, "tearing at his hair and scratching at his nose."

After a while, Riel stopped and glanced at Cunningham. "Will you want anything if you have to go back?"

Cunningham said Riel "spoke in the most broken of English" to the point that the reporter didn't exactly comprehend the purpose of the Métis leader's question, which was interesting since Riel was fluently bilingual. "What do you mean?" Cunningham finally asked.

"Goddamn!" Riel thundered. "Don't I speak plain? I ask you want anything if you have to go back!"

"If I have to go back, I would want nothing from you," Cunningham said. "But I hope you think better of it and allow me to remain."

"We are in the right," Riel reminded him.

"If so, then my remaining can do no harm to your cause but the opposite."

Riel furled his brow, "looked thunder" at Cunningham, and stormed off. It was about noon when this occurred.

THE CANADIAN COMMISSIONERS

On the afternoon of January 13, Riel convened the *comité* to hear from Thibault and de Salaberry, the Canadian commissioners. Again, Cunningham said he was able to hear the entire proceedings "through the thin walls."

Riel opened the proceedings with a half-hour speech. He thanked Thibault and de Salaberry for making the long journey and then conveyed other pleasantries. Next, he asked on whose authority they had come and what exactly they were empowered to do. One of Riel's councillors asked to see the two commissioners' credentials. Thibault and de Salaberry responded that they didn't have any and admitted they weren't empowered to do anything — they were merely "visitors here on a friendly mission." This wasn't what Riel or the *comité* were expecting; they were ready to begin negotiations to bring Red River into Confederation. Cunningham said Riel was frustrated and adjourned for lunch.

Later that afternoon, a guard came to Cunningham's room and told him to be ready to leave at first light the next day. Riel came in shortly after, and Cunningham asked if the orders were final.

"Dat is de orders I give," Riel replied. "Goddamn, don't you understand?"

"Well, will you at least allow me to go under guard to see the town of Winnipeg?" Cunningham tried. "I've come some 1,800 miles, and I would feel it rather strange to go back without being able to state that I had seen the town."

Riel refused his request point-blank, but "Major Robinson," editor of the *New Nation* and a member of the *comité*, intervened and made the case that Cunningham be permitted to visit the town after vouching for his loyalty. Riel relented, and Cunningham saw the sights of Winnipeg that afternoon with Robinson and returned to his cell that evening.

The next morning, January 14, Cunningham began organizing his trip south but said the transportation costs were "so glaringly exorbitant" that he hesitated to contract with anyone. He was still in the fort when Riel, "in a furious rage," found him about noon.

"Goddamn my soul!" Riel shouted. "What did you mean taking such a goddamn long time to go out of this!"

Cunningham tried to explain. "I am having difficulty finding affordable transport."

"If you are not out of here in half an hour, I will start you out on the prairie on foot!"

Cunningham endeavoured to show Riel "the unreasonableness of his conduct," but "the creature had wrought himself up into a passion and would listen to no reason."

By two o'clock, Cunningham finally got hold of "an old loyal French blacksmith" who offered to take him as far as Pembina "on something like reasonable terms." As the reporter finished packing, Riel came back one last time.

"Now, I know where you are going to camp tonight, but goddamn my soul if you camp there I will make it too damn hot for you."

"I've no more idea of where I am going to camp tonight than the man in the moon."

"You're a liar," Riel insisted.

"You have chosen a very good time and place to play the braggart," Cunningham said, "but the day might come when we might meet on more equal terms." He then tried for one more favour. "Will you give me a pass downward?"

"Goddamn my soul!" Riel railed. (Cunningham added here: "The poor creature did not seem capable of doing anything original in the oath line.") "I will give you a pass," and he ordered two armed guards to escort Cunningham the 75 miles to the border. The reporter said he travelled through a blizzard and minus 45 degrees Fahrenheit weather, finally reaching Pembina on January 16 — cold, weary, and hungry.

UNRAVELLING THE TANGLED SKEIN

So what did Cunningham learn on his trip to Red River? Did he have any success "sounding the bottom of the muddle" and finding "some clue to the unravelling of the tangled skein"? In a relatively thoughtful and considered analysis, Cunningham said the root of the difficulties in Red River should be traced to the English-speaking Métis and the Scotch. It was they, thought Cunningham, who were the first to meet en masse and denounce "the conduct of the Government for the manner in which the business was being conducted" and advocate for their right "to have some say in the proposed arrangements." These meetings had "stirred up" the French-speaking Métis and set the model to begin organizing "in a quiet and legitimate way."

Cunningham said other factors contributed to the growth of agitation that fall, chiefly "the priests" who were "working the whole thing at present." He said no one really knew what their goal was — perhaps land or confirmation of existing land titles. Cunningham said "everyone agreed" that the leader of "the priest party" was O'Donoghue: "He rules Riel on the one hand, and the half-breeds on the other, and in the meantime rules the whole roost."

The Hudson's Bay Company also played a role. While most people didn't believe that the HBC governor or the company were active participants in "fomenting the disturbance," Cunningham said it was common opinion that "they have been remarkably diligent in keeping the pot a boiling." After repeated requests from the English and Scottish to stand up for "settlers' rights," for example, the governor chose only to "sit on his oars."

Cunningham called out Joseph Howe in particular for helping to "stir up" the troubles. In his trip west three months earlier, Cunningham said Howe repeatedly encouraged the people of Red River to "stand out as the people of Nova Scotia had done, in order to secure a good bargain with Canada." Howe had reportedly said: "The latter had stood their ground and had made a good thing of it; the people of Red River should do the same." Cunningham said no one should be surprised "to see what Joseph's aim was, when the new Governor comes to be named."

As for any possible American role in the troubles, Cunningham reported there was no evidence on the ground of annexation agitators holding any sway. He thought if annexation was "proclaimed as the ultimate aim of the movement tomorrow," before the next day the Métis "would depart to their homes and leave the idea to be realized by those who originated it." Cunningham was adamant that if "there is one thing more certain than another, it is, that the French half-breeds of the Red River Settlement are essentially loyal to the British Crown." And loyalty wasn't some ephemeral matter. Cunningham said the Métis believed Canada represented a much better "market for their produce" than the United States where they would be so far "from the centre of commerce" that they'd "never realize anything like a profitable return for their produce."

And so what about the future? Cunningham thought "a little application of common sense" by a few "sensible men in Ottawa" would be sufficient to "solve the whole question" — i.e., send a bona fide governor "acceptable to the people," empower the governor with a Constitution "somewhat in accordance with the 'Bill of Rights,'" and "utilize the intelligence, which actually does exist in the Red River Territory, for executive and legislative purposes." No one in Red River, Cunningham believed, had any desire for "bloodshed nor separation from Canada." All just wanted to be treated "somewhat different from the way in which they have been treated by the wiseacres at Ottawa." It was thus "untimely," Cunningham thought, to talk of "sending troops to Red River."

The *Globe* reporter concluded by noting that "a great mass meeting of all classes" was scheduled for the following Wednesday, January 19, "to see if some common ground cannot be fixed upon, from which they can approach the Canadian and British Governments."

- 3 -

ERRAND OF PEACE

> The Military Expedition which it is necessary to send will gratify and give confidence to all loyal and well-disposed persons. Her Majesty's troops go forth on an errand of peace, and will serve as an assurance to the inhabitants of the Red River Settlement, and the numerous Indian tribes that occupy the North-West, that they have a place in the regard and the counsels of England, and may rely upon the impartial protection of the British Sceptre.
>
> — Governor General John Young, Address to the House of Commons, May 12, 1870

On January 19, 1870, over 1,000 people gathered on the parade grounds at Fort Garry to hear an address by Donald Smith, the Dominion's third envoy to the Red River Settlement. After standing in minus 20 degrees Fahrenheit for more than five hours, the attendees reconvened the next day and agreed to send 40 delegates — 20 French, 20 English — to consider "Mr. Smith's commission" and decide "what would be best for the welfare of the country." The Convention of Forty set to work confirming a Bill of Rights as the basis for negotiating the terms of union with Canada. On February 7, Smith was invited back to discuss the bill. With no authority to negotiate, though, all Smith could do was invite the convention to send delegates to Ottawa "with a view of effecting a speedy transfer of the Territory to the Dominion."

Donald Smith and Louis Riel, Fort Garry, 1870, original painting by Bruce Johnson featured in the 1969 Hudson's Bay Company calendar. The two leaders address a crowd.

On February 10, Abbé Ritchot, Judge John Black, and Alfred Scott were chosen to go once the Bill of Rights was finalized.

As the diplomacy played out in Red River, the Dominion government began laying the groundwork for a military expedition to the territory as soon as shipping lanes on the Great Lakes were clear of ice in the spring. To this end, Simon Dawson was directed in early January to "increase the force on the Thunder Bay Road" to complete construction of the bridges and the remainder of the roadway "before the opening of navigation." Dawson dispatched his old friend and colleague, Lindsay Russell from Superior City, to oversee the operation; he travelled the 200 miles to Thunder Bay by snowshoe to take on the job. Dawson also chartered two steamers, the *Algoma* and *Chicora*, to ferry men and *matériel* from Collingwood to Fort William and contracted shipyards in Ontario and Quebec to build 140 boats to convey troops from Lake Superior to Red River. And to secure permission for the expedition to travel across Anishinabe land, the Cabinet appointed two envoys to begin negotiations — Robert Pither, Indian agent at Fort Frances, and Wemyss Simpson, the former HBC factor at Sault Ste. Marie, current Member of Parliament for Algoma, and Molyneux St. John's future boss.

Meanwhile, Prime Minister Macdonald lobbied to have Britain participate in the mission. As Macdonald argued, "It is of great importance that a part of the force should be Regular troops as it will convince the United States Government and people that Her Majesty's Government have no intention of abandoning this continent." The prime minister also believed "the insurgents would more readily lay down their arms to a British force than one entirely Canadian — and even in the case of actual resistance, the conflict would not be attended with the same animosity, and after the rising was put down would not leave behind it such feelings of bitterness and humiliation."[1]

On February 11, the Cabinet formally asked Britain to participate. London agreed, but with conditions: the force couldn't be used to suppress the insurgency; British troops — the last remaining in North America — had to be home in Britain by Christmas 1870; and Britain would pay no more than one-quarter of the total cost of the expedition. Canada readily agreed. On February 23, veteran commander James Lindsay was named lieutenant general in charge of organizing the expedition to the Red River Settlement. He arrived in Canada on April 5, but by then the whole point of the mission had shifted.

THOMAS SCOTT

In early February, the Dominion government agreed to meet the Red River delegates, and with this, Riel's success was complete. Not only was he able to unite all parties in the settlement behind a common political and constitutional vision but he also got the Dominion government to agree to that vision as the basis for negotiating Red River's entry into Confederation. It was, in Stanley's words, Riel's *idée maîtresse*.

The achievement still left the problem of the prisoners in the cells of Fort Garry. By February, a few, including John Schultz, Charles Mair, and Thomas Scott, had escaped and made their way to the Canadian enclave at Portage la Prairie, and a few more were released after swearing allegiance to the Provisional Government. On February 10, at the conclusion of the Convention of Forty, Riel agreed to release the remaining prisoners in exchange for English support for a Provisional Government. As a show of good faith, he set three high-profile prisoners free that night — HBC Governor Mactavish, Dr. William Cowan, and businessman Andrew Bannatyne — with assurances the rest would be released over the next day or two. The English delegates agreed, and the Provisional Government was announced. Members included James Ross (judge), Dr. Curtis Bird (coroner), Andrew Bannatyne (postmaster), William O'Donoghue (treasurer), Thomas Bunn (secretary), and Louis Riel (president).

News of the prisoners' release reached the two streets of Winnipeg almost immediately, but not Portage la Prairie 60 miles distant. Since escaping there in January, Scott, Mair, Schultz, and other "refugees" had busied themselves fomenting discontent among the English-speaking Loyalists. On February 12, a party of 60 men armed with clubs set out for Fort Garry behind Major Charles Boulton with plans to forcibly release the remaining prisoners. The group reached Kildonan, east of Winnipeg, on February 14. A couple of hundred Loyalists rousted out by Schultz joined them there on the 15th to settle on a list of demands. These were relayed to Riel on the 16th and involved release of the prisoners and a general amnesty for all, including Schultz who had a price put on his head. The assembly also informed Riel that several of the English-speaking parishes wouldn't recognize the Provisional Government, after all, despite their delegates' commitment to do so just five days earlier.

Riel was furious. He threw the assembly's messenger, Thomas Norquay, in jail, ripped his letter into pieces, and stormed off. Eventually, Riel calmed down, released Norquay, and sent him back with a message informing the assembly that the last of the prisoners had, in fact, been set free the previous day. He also reminded the assembly of HBC Governor Mactavish's request that they "for the sake of God, form and complete the Provisional Government. Your representatives have joined us on that ground. Who will now come and destroy Red River Settlement?" Without common cause — or food or lodging — the assembly disbanded and went home.

With nothing to show for their efforts, the last 48 Portage la Prairie men decided to march home as a unit along the main road that passed directly beside the walls of the still-occupied Fort Garry. Fearing they'd be sitting ducks for the Métis troops inside, though, Boulton pleaded with the men to disperse and return individually and quietly through the countryside. But to no avail — the men insisted on returning home as one, heads held high, the bravery they'd marched to Kildonan with intact. On February 17, the group set off westward single file through the thigh-deep snow. And then, just as Boulton feared, when opposite the north gate of the fort, a troop of Métis guards rode out and took them prisoner. Thomas Scott was one of the 48 placed back into Fort Garry's recently vacated cells.

Riel was incensed — again. He had Boulton put in irons and informed him and three other prisoners, including a belligerent Scott, that they could expect to die the next day for treason. Word of the sentences spread quickly, and a number of Winnipeggers pleaded with Riel for clemency. Donald Smith was ultimately successful on Boulton's behalf — he was able to negotiate a pardon with Riel in exchange for promising to shore up English support for the Provisional Government.

Scott wasn't so lucky. According to witnesses, the Orangeman attacked his guards, hurled racial insults at them, encouraged his fellow prisoners to do the same, and threatened to kill Riel upon release — even to Riel's face. To shut him up, two guards dragged Scott from his cell on February 28 and beat him until someone, supposedly a member of the Provisional Government, forced them to stop. And still, despite more warnings and a personal entreaty from Riel for peace, Scott's rancour boiled. Riel had him placed in irons on March 1 and on the third brought him before a tribunal headed by Ambroise-Didyme Lépine and including André Nault and Elzéar Goulet. The charges against Scott were taking up arms against the Provisional Government and striking his guards. The tribunal heard from Riel

Thomas Scott.

and the guards and then discussed the penalty and eventually voted in favour of a death penalty. The next day, Nault and Goulet went to retrieve Scott from his cell where the Reverend George Young was praying with him. Scott, accompanied by Young, was led through the main gate to a firing squad waiting outside the fort to administer the tribunal's sentence. Five months later, Robert Cunningham wrote the first detailed account of Scott's murder, a rather hagiographic version based on an exclusive interview with Reverend Young.

INDIGNATION

Scott's death ignited a firestorm of rage and indignation across Protestant Ontario — and John Schultz and Charles Mair fanned the flames. Aided

Lieutenant Colonel Garnet Wolseley, Staff, Assistant Quartermaster-General, Montreal, 1866.

by Joseph Monkman and William Drever, Schultz and Mair escaped from Red River sometime in March and made their way to Ontario where George Denison (of Canada First) organized a series of rallies across the province to "express indignation at one of the most cold-blooded murders ever perpetrated" by "that black criminal, Riel," and his band of "black-hearted aggressors." The rallies demanded action "from true and sober Volunteers who will travel to Red River and restore peace and maintain the honour of the country." The first indignation meeting was held in Toronto on April 6. Over 10,000 people packed the square in front of city hall to hear Schultz, Mair, and two other "refugees" regale with tales of being imprisoned "in a room swarming with vermin of no more than twelve feet by fourteen feet. It was more the Black Hole of Calcutta than anything else." The rally in Toronto, like many of the other indignation meetings that spring, ended by adopting resolutions like this: "That prompt and vigorous measures be taken to bring Riel and his lawless bandits to justice, and that every precaution be taken by the government to protect the lives and liberties of the loyal people of the Territory, and maintain the honour of the Empire."

With Canada's second general election looming, the rising tide of indignation across vote-rich Ontario put pressure on Macdonald's Conservative government to speed up plans for the military expedition, at the very least to get the situation in Red River under control, at best to deliver retribution. The government was ably assisted when Lieutenant General Lindsay arrived in Canada on April 5 to get the military logistics under way. His first task was finding a commander and luckily he didn't have to look far.

After fighting in the Crimean War and almost losing a leg, Colonel Garnet Wolseley had served in Canada with distinction since 1861, organizing training academies at La Prairie and Thorold, helping to negotiate the terms ending the Fenian invasion at Fort Erie in 1866, and most recently serving as quartermaster-general. The Dominion government agreed with the appointment, and Lindsay next turned to staffing the force. Canada agreed to contribute 705 soldiers raised in two battalions from militia units in Ontario and Quebec and brought up "to the standard of Her Majesty's Regular Forces" by "strong and drilled" officers "carefully chosen." Regimental orders to this effect were issued on April 21, and the first Volunteers arrived in Toronto on May 2 for inspection and training. To fulfill its contribution to the mission, Lindsay appointed 19 soldiers from the Royal Artillery, 19 Royal Engineers, and 352 infantry from the 1st Battalion, 60th Rifles, most of whom had been stationed at Toronto that winter. And that was where at least the officers of these units fell under the charm of Kate Ranoe, the international burlesque star.

Despite Lindsay's efficiency in getting the expedition up and organized, it couldn't actually leave until negotiations with the Red River delegates were complete. These began on April 25 in Ottawa and finished with the introduction of legislation creating Canada's fifth province on May 2. As per Red River's demands, the Manitoba Act provided constitutional guarantees for the French language in both the legislature and courts, publicly funded Roman Catholic schools, representation in the federal Parliament, and 1.4 million acres "for the benefit of the families of the half-breed residents" to be divided "among the children of the half-breed heads of families residing in the Province at the time of the said transfer to Canada." The Manitoba Act received royal assent on May 12.

As the Manitoba Act was introduced into the House of Commons on May 2, the *Algoma* was readying to depart from Collingwood on the first trip of the Great Lakes shipping season. On board were 150 labourers Simon Dawson had hired to augment the workforce on the road between Lake Superior and Shebandowan Lake, road-building supplies and equipment, 40 horses, a couple dozen oxen, and 150 or so "deck and cabin passengers." These included Dawson himself, Wemyss Simpson, and "two special correspondents from Toronto newspapers" who would spend the next five months embedded with the expedition as it wound its way to Red River — and one international burlesque star neither reporter bothered to mention.

- 4 -

TWO CORRESPONDENTS AND A BURLESQUE STAR

> Mr. Robert Cunningham, our Special Commissioner, left yesterday morning for the Northwest territory. We give his first despatch today from Collingwood, and we are certain that his letters, when he reaches Fort Garry, will be read with the greatest interest by the people of Canada.... As a writer Mr. Cunningham has but few equals in Canada, of which his former contributions to the Canadian Press are evidence.
>
> — "Our Northwest Commissioner," *Daily Telegraph*, May 4, 1870

It is relatively clear how Robert Cunningham was hired to cover the expedition to Red River. When Cunningham went to Fort Garry in January 1870 on assignment for the *Globe*, he wasn't alone; he travelled and was imprisoned with John Ross Robertson, publisher of the *Globe*'s main competitor, the scrappy *Daily Telegraph*. After returning home to Toronto, and as indignation over Scott's death swept across Ontario, Robertson sensed a story brewing that was perfectly suited to the *Telegraph*'s sensational and salacious style. And he knew exactly who to turn to for suitable copy — Robert Cunningham, his fellow prisoner and travelling companion. At the end of April, the *Telegraph* promised to provide "reports of the insurrection [which] will be fuller, more graphic and more trustworthy than [those in] any other journal."[1] On May 4, the *Telegraph* announced, "Robert Cunningham, the gentleman who left

Frederick Edward Molyneux St. John.

for Red River as correspondent of a city contemporary with Mr. J. Ross Robertson, of this paper," had been appointed special commissioner to provide "authentic and reliable and on time information" on events in the North-West. Cunningham's first column, telegraphed from Collingwood, was featured on the front page above the fold of the May 4 edition.

How Molyneux St. John got hired to cover the Red River expedition is a little less clear. It probably had something to do with his prior "service in the tented field," perhaps even more with the influence of his wife's loyal fans.

PIG WAR VETERAN

Frederick Edward Molyneux St. John was born on November 28, 1838, in Newcastle, England, the son of a Battle of Waterloo veteran who had served under the Duke of Wellington. After attending Rossall College at Lancashire, St. John joined the Royal Marine Light Infantry as a second lieutenant in April 1855. His timing was impeccable. In October 1856, Chinese marines seized a cargo ship flying under the British flag and imprisoned its crew within the walled city of Canton. British forces bombarded the city to free the prisoners but were repulsed. They retreated to Hong Kong and spent the next year amassing a joint British-French force for an assault eventually launched in December 1857. Over 6,000 troops, including Second Lieutenant St. John, were successful on January 1, 1858, in taking the city of more than a million citizens with very few casualties — 15 killed, 113 wounded.

A year after the Battle of Canton, St. John transferred to the HMS *Tribune*, then under the command of Geoffrey Hornby, for a posting off Vancouver Island. After a "heavy refit" involving new rigging, hull replacement, and "hooping the mast," the *Tribune*, "awfully lumbered up with 150 marines," started on the 5,151-mile voyage to Vancouver Island on November 27. It arrived in Esquimalt on February 14. Hornby and the Royal Marines spent the winter and spring exploring the area, taking a trip on the Fraser River and visiting Victoria a couple of times.

In June 1860, Hornby received orders to help settle a border dispute that had recently broken out on San Juan Island off the southeast coast of Vancouver Island between the Strait of Georgia to the north and the Strait of Juan de Fuca to the south. Writing 17 years later, St. John said the row erupted "after some Yankee settler on the island tried to annex one of the [Hudson's Bay] Company's pigs." With no other occupants on the island, "the angry claimants of the pig declared war in the name of their respective countries and reported progress to their superiors elsewhere." And that was how Hornby and the marines on board the *Tribune* got orders to "steam up to the island, prepare arms, and prevent the landing of the American troops."

Upon arriving, Hornby sent a message to the American captain that the U.S. soldiers wouldn't be allowed to land. As there was "no use arguing under the guns of a frigate, commanded by an officer who has specific orders, and whose profession is fighting, the American commander took time to consider." Eventually, a settlement was brokered between the belligerents and "the island was jointly and peaceably occupied by the English and American troops, and thus held for years until the arbitration." The result? St. John said he didn't "know who eventually got the pig, but the Americans secured the island."[2] Second Lieutenant St. John remained on San Juan as part of the peacekeeping force until January 31, 1860, when he returned to England aboard the *Tribune*. Sometime the following year, he retired and married Kate Ranoe, the popular singer and actress.

A PERFORMER OF GREAT POPULARITY

Katherine Ranoe was born in 1841. Not much about her early life is known, other than that she was adopted by Louis-Antoine Jullien, the popular music composer, conductor, and impresario. Jullien had gained some fame in London in the 1840s and 1850s teaching "the masses to appreciate compositions of the highest class, and educated the taste of his audiences." He was also generous with struggling musicians, including the very young aspiring singer Kate Ranoe. When Ranoe was about 10 years old, Jullien began featuring her in concerts at Surrey Music Hall. In the mid-1850s, Jullien went bankrupt trying to produce an opera well beyond his means. He escaped demanding creditors by moving to Paris with his wife and Kate Ranoe, whom they had formally adopted. The family lived in a small suite of apartments off rue Saint-Honoré. In March 1860, Jullien died destitute in a French asylum.

Ranoe returned to England shortly after Jullien's death and started performing in various burlesques, at that point in time a form of

Kate Ranoe, Montreal, ca. 1868–69.

humorous parody usually of a serious dramatic or classical work. In September 1860, she debuted at the Plymouth Theatre as Minstrel Graceful in *Fair One with the Golden Locks*, described as "an original fairy extravaganza in one act" based on the popular nursery tale by the Countess d'Aulnoy. The *Plymouth Mail* described Ranoe as a "very pleasing" young actress, obviously the product of a "highly finished musical education" provided by her late adopted father, Monsieur Jullien. Said the *Mail*, "With her natural attractions, fine acting, and influential introductions to the musical world, a high position for her among the favourites of the public is next to certain." The *Western Morning News* also lauded Ranoe, despite the 19-year-old having to contend with "a break-up in her voice" brought on by "overworking of the organ." Still, Ranoe was able to "contrive to win golden opinions from the audience by her intonation and pure style of singing."

She was a hit, and by the spring of 1861 had grown into "an immense favourite with the Plymouth audience." On January 20, 1862, she married Molyneux St. John. There is no record of how or when they met.

Ranoe appeared next in 1867 in New York City, "direct from the principal London Theatres." She made her debut at Wallack's Theatre as William in *The Latest Edition of Black-Eyed Susan, or the Little Bill That Was Taken Up*, a popular burlesque. Ranoe continued through the season playing a variety of roles in other productions such as *Captain of the Watch* (Kristina), *Ours* (Blanche Raye), *Honeymoon* (Zamora), and *The White Cockade.*

St. John showed up in New York around this time, as well, first as the author of the three-installment "New York Theatres" in *Watson's Art Journal* (March 1868) and then as a playwright adopting the French *Paris and Helen, or the Grecian Elopement* for an English-language production at the New York Theatre in the spring of 1868. This burlesque featured the Worrell sisters, "shapely song-and-dance artistes who assumed the roles of Helen, Paris, and Orestes, the first as an imitation of Tostee, the latter two in costumes half-male, half-female." While the billing claimed the show was an original, one critic panned it for "lifting all the music and most of the plot from *La Belle Helene*, larding it with local allusion and slapstick." The *Harvard Theatre Collection* said it was "the first burlesque on the subject of adultery ever seen on the New York stage, and we hope it is the last."

ENTERTAINING THE TROOPS

Sometime after *Paris and Helen* finished its run at the New York Theatre, Ranoe and St. John moved to Canada. In August 1868, Ranoe made her Canadian stage debut as Ophelia in *Hamlet* at Montreal's Theatre Royal. Once again, she was a sensation. By January 1869, the *Globe* reported her enjoying "great popularity in Montreal" playing Blanche Raye in the burlesque hit *Ours*. In February, she played host for a special benefit evening described by theatre critics as "one of the most brilliant and fashionable events of the season." In March 1869, the couple moved to Toronto where Ranoe drew rave reviews for her performance in *Black-Eyed Susan*. According to the *Globe*,

> There is nothing so difficult to place before an audience as a burlesque. People go to the Theatre to see life — or something like life — and when a travesty is put before them, unless thoroughly well done, they are apt to pout and cry "how silly." Miss Ranoe, however, overcame these difficulties last night. In her personification of William she played the rollicking sailor lad in a way that everybody who has seen "Jack ashore" could appreciate, while the artistic element she threw into her hornpipes brought down hearty applause.

Ranoe starred in a number of productions in Toronto that spring, including *Foul Play* at the Royal Lyceum, another benefit featuring *Black-Eyed Susan*, "two roaring farces" at the Music Hall, and then a starring role in Buckstone's *Flowers of the Forest* back at the Lyceum. The season finished with a special Dominion Day performance of Pauline in *The Bonnie Fishwife*, a role "entirely dependent on the refinement and *savoir vivre* of the lady who plays it, and we think it could hardly be entrusted to better hands than those of Miss Kate Ranoe."

St. John was also busy on the Toronto theatre scene in the spring of 1869. In May, he gave his adaptation of *La belle Hélène* another go at the Royal Lyceum, this time to better reviews. The *Globe* said the play "treats, in a ludicrous way, the love making between Paris, the Prince of Troy, and Helen of Sparta, and their flight from Greece." Some time after, St. John joined the editorial staff of the *Globe*. And then in May 1870, George Brown tapped him to cover the expedition to Red River. There is no record why. All we know is that St. John had military experience — as the *Globe* noted, he had "seen service in the tented field" — and his wife had connections. She had become a favourite of the British troops chosen by James Lindsay to anchor the mission to Red River. At a benefit held in January 1870, Ranoe performed "before a house crowded from pit to gallery. The circle looked particularly elegant, filled as it was, by a large number of ladies and gentlemen in full dress." Patrons of the benefit included the lieutenant governor and his wife and the officers of the Royal Artillery, the Royal Engineers, and the 1st Battalion, 60th Rifles — the British heart of the expedition to the Red River Settlement.

PART II

The Long Road to Shebandowan Lake

- 5 -

COLLINGWOOD

> Off for Red River once again. The last time I started on a similar expedition, snows and frost prevailed, and the farther north we went the snows and prevailed the more.... I propose going as far as Fort Garry, and hope to have the privilege of saluting my quondam friend Riel under somewhat different circumstances from those in which I saluted him last time.
>
> — Robert Cunningham, "Manitoba in the Distance," *Daily Telegraph*, May 4, 1870

> We started from Collingwood with considerable éclat. We were not the Red River Expedition exactly, but we were a near relation to it, and though we were none of us soldiers, one of the party wore a military cap with a red band round it, which gave a warlike colour to the affair. We looked like service too, and what we lacked in rank was made up in enthusiasm.
>
> — Molyneux St. John, "The Red River Expedition," *Globe*, May 5, 1870

Around eight in the morning on May 3, 1870, Robert Cunningham, Molyneux St. John, and Kate Ranoe boarded a train at the Northern Railway station at the foot of Brock Street in Toronto bound for the tiny port of Collingwood on Georgian Bay. The train was one of many specially contracted by the Canadian government to carry expedition troops and supplies to Collingwood where they would be ferried to Government Station, four miles east of Fort William on the northwest shore of Lake Superior. With the two correspondents were 150 labourers Simon Dawson had hired to work on the road from Thunder Bay to Shebandowan Lake, the starting point for the inland portion of the expedition. St. John said the men were a mix of French-Canadian, Métis, and Indigenous men, including 21 Iroquois from "Caughnawaga" who had been "engaged for service in the boats."

The trip to Collingwood was relatively short — a quick four hours. The voyage to Thunder Bay would be longer — about 50 hours, not including the time it would take to get through the canal at Sault Ste. Marie. And if the road was in as good shape as Lindsay Russell told Simon Dawson it was, it would only take another two days to reach Shebandowan Lake, the start of the old North West Company canoe route Dawson had mapped out. But from there all bets were off. St. John said no one knew exactly how long it would take to transport Wolseley's army by canoe through the wilderness of northern Canada to Fort Garry. Maybe a month, maybe three.

Collingwood Harbour.

At Collingwood, St. John and Cunningham found that a "whirlwind of activity" had descended upon the tiny village. The expedition trains had been running for days and their cargo spilled along the shore and narrow wharf jutting into the bay. Cunningham said the place was "littered" with wagons, horses, oxen, hay, fodder, and all manner of construction equipment such as wheelbarrows, spades, picks, and axes. And boats. A short spur line between the railway terminus and the waterfront was studded with a long line of cars carrying the 140 boats purchased for the expedition. Some were clinkers, lighter vessels built by overlapping — or lapstraking — the hull planks, and others were the heavier, more rigid carvers whose hull planks were laid smoothly edge to edge and fastened to rigid frames. St. John said the clinkers had attracted a fair number of critics who claimed the rough-and-tumble of the portages would cause irreparable damage. The critics also pointed out that the clinkers couldn't be repaired in the woods the way the carvers could be.

Moored to the wharf were the two steamers Dawson had chartered for the expedition. The smaller of the two was the sidewheeler *Algoma*. It measured 147 feet long, had a beam of 23 feet, and an impressive registered tonnage of 787. For the past year, the *Algoma* had been plying the weekly mail route between Collingwood and Bruce Mines. Beside the *Algoma* was the sleek and graceful *Chicora*. It, too, was a sidewheeler but measured 221 feet long, had a beam of 26 feet, but only a registered tonnage of 740. The *Chicora* had started life as a Union blockade runner in the American Civil War, after which it was purchased by Canadian interests and pressed into passenger service between Collingwood and Fort William. "In point of speed and comfort," Cunningham wrote, "the *Chicora* may be considered the finest steamer on inland waters." Over the next six weeks, six more steamers would be pressed into service, as well, along with four schooners, two gunboats, two tugs, and various barges, rafts, and scows. It would be all decks on hand to transport the expedition's 1,100 troops; 700 voyageurs, guides, scouts, teamsters, and labourers; and thousands of tons of munitions and supplies to Government Station.

The *Chicora.*

How the *Algoma* and *Chicora* were being loaded was evidence of the first major challenge the expedition was about to face. Rumours had been swirling for weeks that the United States would deny expedition vessels passage through its canal at Sault Ste. Marie. Some Americans believed Canada was at a breaking point in the spring of 1870 — financially stressed from the purchase of Rupert's Land, economically challenged by the impending construction of the Northern Pacific Railway across the northern states, and politically weakened from secessionist pressure in the Maritimes. These Americans believed failure to put down the insurrection in Red River would be the straw to break Confederation's back. And with that the United States could annex Rupert's Land and thereby join recently purchased Alaska with the rest of the country. Like an apple ripe from the tree, Canada would fall into American hands. On May 3, Hamilton Fish, the pro-annexation American secretary of state, ordered officials at Sault Ste. Marie to deny canal passage to any foreign military vessel or vessel with military *matériel.* While the U.S. government wouldn't meddle directly in Canadian affairs, annexationists weren't going to sit idly by, either.

As a workaround, expedition officials decided to send only labourers and construction equipment north on the *Algoma* on May 3. The thinking was that at least Dawson and his crew could go through the canal and proceed to Thunder Bay to get the road finished in time for the troops' arrival. The *Chicora* would depart four days later with munitions and other military supplies. Hopefully, that would give diplomats in Ottawa, London, and Washington enough time to figure out how to gain access to the canal.

TO THE SAULT

St. John said it took longer than expected to get everything and everyone aboard the *Algoma* and properly secured. In addition to Dawson's crew, 150 "regular passengers" had to be brought on, along with supplies and mail destined for "the survivors of the six-month Lenten period" cut off from civilization by the winter freeze-up on, the Great Lakes. At around 5:00 p.m., the steamer finally cast off into Georgian Bay. Three hundred people crowded the deck to wave farewell to the well-wishers on the shore. Those on board included Simon Dawson, Wemyss Simpson, "two special correspondents from Toronto newspapers," and "a half-dozen more waifs." And the international burlesque star.

At around 11:00 p.m., the *Algoma* "touched" at Owen Sound to land Mr. Wilkes, the proprietor and editor of the *Owen Sound Advertiser*, and tie up for the night. The ship got under way the next morning and pulled alongside the jetty at Killarney in the early afternoon. St. John described Killarney as a small village made up of a few fishing huts and a "store-*cum*-post office." The terrain was largely rock, with a number of fishing nets stretched on the larger ones to dry. As the first steamer of the year to arrive, the *Algoma* was "heartily received" by the locals who seemed, to Cunningham at least, to be mostly Indigenous women, some Métis men, and a few "non-descripts." Leaving Killarney, the *Algoma* passed Little Current, a village the same size as Killarney but where Cunningham heard both the "white man and fire-water" had gained a footing "so effectively that prostitution, debauchery, and misery are rampant." Just like Stanley Street in Toronto.

The *Algoma* passed Spanish River later Wednesday night and reached Bruce Mines early the next morning — a "long, straggling village" built on the rocky shore. While the captain tended to postal duties, a number of passengers went ashore to hunt for the area's renowned copper-streaked rocks. For St. John, the prospect of nifty souvenirs couldn't outweigh the destitution of the place: "If there be an inhabited spot on the route that looks more uninviting than another, it is the Bruce Mines."

The next part of the trip made up for the wastelands at Bruce Mines; St. John called it "the most beautiful view of the trip." Proceeding north on the St. Marys River toward the tip of Sugar Island, they passed Echo Bay and the entrance to Lake George to starboard. St. John said the lake was nestled between two ranges of hills running inland where they met at the far end in a single mountain. It was a dramatic backdrop "situated at such a distance that its colour and apparent density varies from that of the foreground. The openings at the remote end of the enclosing hills admit the light, and cause beautiful gradations of light and shade." The *Algoma* slipped to the far side of Echo Bay, and the sun sank toward the horizon into the western sky and turned a fiery red. The colour transformed "all around the western side of the lake and the adjoining land" into "a succession of fantastic shapes in colours varying from pale sea green to deep gold-fringed purple." And then as the sun dipped lower and lower, the mountain at the far end of Lake George caught the reflection of the richer tints, and "the last remaining light of the day lit up the farther slopes of the receding hills, the inward face of the western range had subsided into the gloom of the evening." At that moment, St. John said a loon rose to the surface beside the ship, and looking at the "vessel in the sharp indignant-like way peculiar to its kind, rose and took his way into the lake, where uttering his dismal cry, he seemed to call attention to the solitude of his home."

As the sun went down, the *Algoma* continued past Sugar Island and the International Raspberry Jam Manufactory, the "epicentre of an extensive raspberry trade" run by Philetus Church. At about 11:00 p.m., the steamer docked at the Canadian village of St. Marys — about

The *Chicora* passing through the Sault Ste. Marie locks.

40 or 50 houses, Cunningham estimated, where once again the locals gathered to welcome the first steamer of the year.

Cunningham said no one really slept that night, since they were all eagerly engaged in a debate over the "great question" of whether the Americans would allow the passage of expedition vessels through their canal. Early the next morning, on May 5, with locals assembled on both sides of the rapids, the *Algoma* steamed through the half-mile waterway "unmolested." Question answered, the ship set immediate course for Michipicoten Island to drop supplies and was under way to Fort William by mid-morning as if the imbroglio never happened. The *Chicora*, by contrast, would have an entirely different experience a few days later. Cunningham elected to "remain over at the Sault" to keep readers apprised of the situation; St. John stayed on board the *Algoma* and reached Thunder Bay early on Sunday morning, May 8. It would be almost a month before the two would meet up again.

- 6 -

ISOLATED BACKWOODSMEN

> Soon after one o'clock the fire burst through the inner edge of the forest and spread along the partially cleared land of the settlement, seizing upon every trunk, shrub, log and stump along the line of clearing.... Rushing along to the edge of the water it was met by a number of men who had got round an outlying shanty in which lived a half-breed woman attached to the station, and her children. Great efforts were made to save the shanty but to no purpose, the fire attacked the ground logs, sprung upon the roof and raced round the edges; water seemed only to heighten its fury, and in a few minutes the poor woman's home was a smouldering ruin.
>
> — Molyneux St. John, "The Red River Expedition," *Globe*, May 30, 1870

Passengers and crew aboard the *Algoma* sighted Isle Royale off Thunder Cape late Saturday afternoon, May 7. It took until two in the morning for the ship to reach Fort William, just upstream on the Kaministiquia River. There it dropped mail and steamed back four miles east along the northern shore of Thunder Bay to Government Station. The captain sounded the whistle as he rounded the bend back into the lake proper, and by the time the Government Station pier hove into sight, the locals were all down on the shore eager to help unload.

The *Algoma* passing Thunder Cape. From a painting by William Armstrong.

Most were members of Dawson's crew who had wintered there; all were grateful for fresh news and supplies.

The waters off Government Station were too shallow for the *Algoma* to tie up directly to the wharf, so it was anchored 300 yards offshore. Despite the hour, the men got down to work, since the captain was keen on returning to the Soo in case the *Chicora* didn't make it through the canal and the *Algoma* was needed to help ship supplies. A tow line was run the 300 yards back to shore along which a flat-bottomed scow soon ferried freight.

When the sun rose, St. John said a "small but pretty" village revealed itself on the shores of Thunder Bay. At the centre was a British ensign flying from a pole, with 10 or so wooden houses scattered around. One served as government headquarters, another four as government stores, and four or five were private houses. One of these, "a shanty," served double duty as a boarding house for individuals "unconnected with the Government" and who, like St. John, were "disinclined to commence cooking operations on their own account." The *Globe*'s special correspondent was impressed with the "multifarious groceries" available at the main store; he said it included everything required for the backcountry, from tents to eau de cologne. To the west of Government Station were the tents of Dawson's camp.

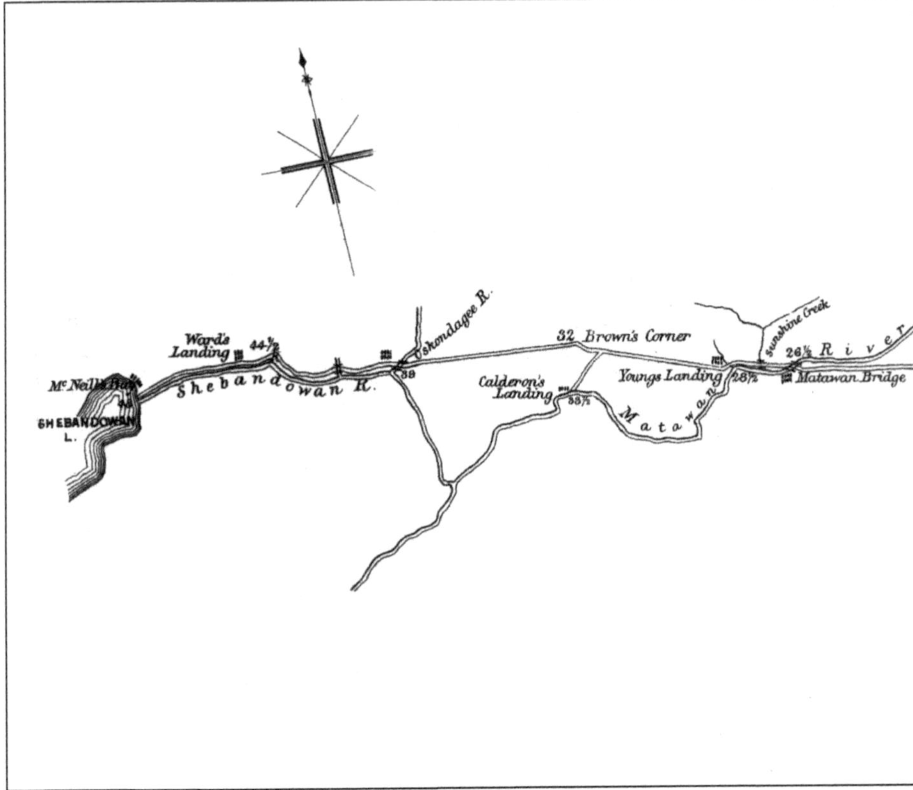

Plan of Simon Dawson's road from Thunder Bay to Shebandowan Lake.

It took the bulk of the day to unload the *Algoma*. Early Monday morning, the captain raised anchor and set course for the Soo, while Dawson's men marched up the road to get on with their work. St. John was left with the few employees and residents of Government Station. All believed the *Algoma* would return in the next few days and that perhaps the diplomats would resolve the crisis and the *Chicora* would arrive, as well. But it wouldn't be until May 26 that Thunder Bay would be connected to the outside world again. Until then, St. John and the others would live as "a party of isolated backwoodsmen."

STATE OF THE ROAD

With nothing else to do, St. John joined Lindsay Russell, "the civil engineer in charge of the party," to see first-hand the state of Dawson's

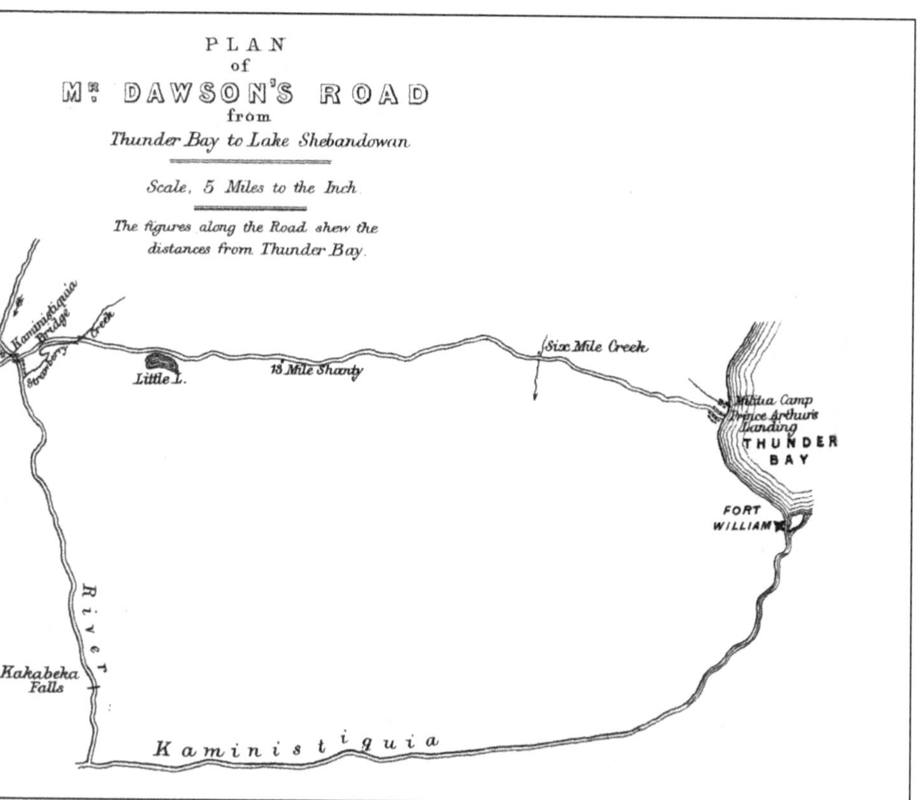

famous road. They set off in a "four-wheel buggy" on the morning of Wednesday, May 11. St. John said the first section of the road to the Kaministiquia Bridge at Mile 21.5 was the most developed. From the shore, the road rose gently over a mile and a half to the base of a 100-foot hill known as "the Sandhill," an "unpleasant one for heavily laden teams." The next 20 miles to Strawberry Creek was a "succession of level stretches, and easy gradations of ascent and descent." In some places, Dawson's men had removed groves of trees and blasted stumps. In other low-lying areas, they had built "fascine or a corduroy of logs" covered with earth. West from Strawberry Creek at Mile 20, the road wound down "a long winding hill" into the Kaministiquia Valley and across a "bridge over which heavy wagons and artillery can pass." St. John estimated the troops could march from Thunder Bay to the bridge over the Kaministiquia here "between breakfast and supper without difficulty."

The road then went over a "long red marl hill" from the Kaministiquia Bridge to the Matawan Bridge at Mile 26.5. The next mile to a bridge at Sunshine Creek was over "soft, marshy soil." A "working party was busily engaged" here laying corduroy and draining a number of small rivulets and marshes. St. John said the crew finished the section when it returned next day, "leaving very little to be done to make the road as good as that which we had passed over in the section nearer the bay."

At Sunshine Creek, the road crossed a temporary bridge and entered "the woods for eleven miles when it strikes the Oskondaga" at Mile 39. Parts of this section were "good, and some are as yet in the first stages." St. John said most of the ground was "covered in moss; it is in fact in a state of nature — the trees only having been removed."

The Oskondaga River was as far as the road reached on May 11. A crew of "Iroquois from Caughnawaga" had just started removing trees on the last seven miles to Shebandowan Lake. These, said St. John, were "capital axemen and a week's work will leave a large field for the gangs that may then be unoccupied." While details of this final section had yet to be sketched out, St. John thought only four miles of road would actually have to be constructed; the expedition could travel on the Shebandowan River for the last three miles to the lake and "not lose much time." There were no portages on this section of the river, "although there is a strong current."

From Shebandowan, St. John said Dawson had dispatched a crew to "make roads across the longest and most difficult portages between Shebandowan and Lac des Mille Lacs." When finished, they would continue on to French Portage, the halfway point to Fort Frances.

Russell and St. John left their buggy at Mile 32 near Brown's Corner and rode the last eight miles to the Oskondaga River. St. John thought they could have taken the buggy all the way "had it not been for one or two places still in a rough state." He expected the stretch between Sunshine Creek and the Oskondaga River to be finished "before this is in print," leaving only the section from there to Shebandowan Lake to be finished. And then "ten thousand men can, if necessary, march from Thunder Bay to the embarking point of the long water-journey in two days." Unless "long or heavy rain" turned the road to mud, or massive fires consumed the bridges and ravaged the countryside. Or both.

THE FIRE RAGING

On Monday, May 16, some of Dawson's crew came into Government Station with news of a "fire raging in the woods." They said it had already consumed "one or two of the smaller bridges and culverts." Early the next day, St. John left with Lindsay Russell to inspect the damage. They got as far as Six Mile Creek when "the roar of a fire became audible and vast columns of black smoke" rose leeward of the bridge and drove "hawks and other birds before it." A gale-force wind had picked up from the west, and very quickly the road was blocked with thick smoke. "Discretion," said St. John, "required an early movement from the bridge."

The two men turned back toward the bay but made it only a mile or so when from a short hill they saw that a second fire had started "from a point about ten miles to westward" of Government Station. From their vantage point, they could see this second fire was in the process of joining the first and was "spreading quickly to windward of us." Rather than make a break for it through a quickly closing window between the two fires — "a miscalculation at such a juncture would have been a serious matter" — Russell and St. John decided to proceed by way of the brûlées, or already burned patches of forest.

A mile or so on, Russell and St. John found refuge in a clearing made by "an old Frenchman" who was huddled with his wife and five children outside their single-room shanty. Their eyes were "swollen and streaming from the effects of the smoke." St. John said the man "built some hope on the fact of there being a swamp between his home and the fire." His wife and children, though, "seemed to know that the thickly wooded belt on which he trusted would not stop the fire for a second." Russell and St. John pushed on, anxious to reach Government Station, knowing it would "shortly be attacked by the fire."

At the next brûlée, the men came across a French couple anxiously watching the fire "rush before the wind, howling as it went, rushing along the undergrowth, leaping from tree to tree, and encircling as it darted up the banks to set the tops in a blaze." All around, groves of beech were ablaze, giving off "thick rolling clouds of parti-coloured smoke" until "it was impossible to discern anything except in the immediate vicinity or to form any opinion as to where the fire was or was not burning." Russell and St. John made a dash for it, passing another beech grove engulfed in flame until they were forced to stop. The smoke was "so thick" that they were "unable to see one another though hardly a yard apart." Breathing was also difficult and "feeling the rush of hot air from the fire on either side, we judged it wiser to turn back while we were able, and regain the clearing." Here they found another settler who had dug "a large hole wherein to bury his goods." The man said the fire had crossed the road above them and was now "running down the wind toward his swamp." The only safe spot in the vicinity was on top of a nearby hill that the fire had already passed over. As "the stumps and fallen trees were still burning, and the smoke from them unbearable, the prospect was not a very inviting one."

Russell and St. John picked their way through the brûlées toward Government Station. Eventually, they found their way back on the road, and from there they could see "over a breadth of several miles" how the fire had burned "shanties, bridges, and even earth-covered culverts, and rushing on had joined the fire from the Matawan." They continued past charred trees and stumps that were still burning rapidly, dodging falling trunks as they went. All the while, in the woods to their leeward, "the fire travelled at a fearful rate, crashing through the woods, causing trees to fall in quick succession, and rushing through at such a rate that it seemed as if it had not time to consume all in its path."

THE STATION IN DANGER

By the time Russell and St. John reached Government Station, "the men were all turned out, and a line of points drawn at which the fight with the fire was to be made." The horses had been removed from their stables and picketed as far from danger as possible. St. John said "the poor animals were, like all their kind, uneasy at the approach of fire, and tried to break from their fastenings, but none were lost." The men drew water from the bay by the cask. Depots were filled all along the boundary of the woods, and buildings — particularly the stables and houses — were drenched as the raging fire hemmed them in on three sides. "Every exertion" would now be necessary "to save home and property, if not life itself."

Just after one o'clock in the afternoon, the fire burst through the edge of the forest and "spread along the partially cleared land of the settlement, seizing upon every trunk, shrub, log, and stump along the line of clearing." Where there was grass or undergrowth, the flames were able to lick right to the water's edge. The men were too late saving one woman's small house — the flames "attacked the ground logs, sprung upon the roof, and raced round the edges; water seemed only to heighten its fury, and in a few minutes the poor woman's home was a smouldering ruin."

At some point, the wind shifted and long "tongues of flame" reached for the centre of the tiny village, testing "the worth and endurance of each man to the utmost." For three hours, the men fought through "blinding and choking smoke." As soon as they were successful in one spot, the fire sprang up in another "as if by invisible hands." Cordwood stacked on the wharf caught fire, and sparks from it set ablaze "everything that was made of wood" around the central buildings. It was here that the men made a last stand, marshalling "the greatest exertions necessary to save the houses themselves. Men went into the black smoke to cast water on the fire, little knowing whether they would come out of it again, and others threw themselves on the ground to get a breath of air." At one point, Russell ordered all gunpowder at Government Station to be thrown into the bay alongside all the tool chests and personal effects already dumped there.

Eventually, with the wind's help, "the fire was at last got under." The exhausted crew watched it roar off down the bay. A short time later it lay siege to the buildings of a silver mine 10 miles along.

St. John rode back up the road a couple of days later to assess the damage. Overall, he said the fire had consumed "the greater part of the country" between the bay and Shebandowan Lake, "between forty and fifty miles." All the smaller bridges along the road, even many of the earth-covered culverts and corduroy sections, had been destroyed.

THE *CHICORA* AT LAST

After the fire, everyone became preoccupied with the status of the *Algoma* and *Chicora*. St. John said some imagined the former "must have broke her machinery"; others said the latter was still stuck on the wrong side of the canal at the Soo. All had come to believe "the world in general had forgotten Thunder Bay and all on its shores." St. John wrote, "All day long, the idlers of the village turned wishful glances to seaward, scanning the horizon with the eagerness of men cast upon a desert island." Occasionally, a mirage would "trace some indistinct form against the distant sky, and experienced eyes would at once discern the boat, and even the particular class of vessel to which she belonged."

THE GENTLEMAN WHOSE PATIENCE WAS EXHAUSTED

Kate Ranoe must have been getting antsy, too. In his last story written before the *Chicora* arrived on May 25, St. John described a trip to Thunder Cape with "a gentleman whose patience was exhausted." While there is no definitive proof, the "gentleman" is possibly a ruse for Ranoe.

St. John said the "gentleman" was in "constant transition from the depths of despondency to the bliss of perfect confidence" over the absence of the steamers — and "business engagements overdue at Montreal and New York." The gentleman, he said, was also equally determined to resolve the situation, at one moment fully committed to waiting patiently for the steamers to arrive, the next adamant about taking a canoe and making for Superior City. To "kill the time," St. John said he persuaded the "gentleman whose patience was exhausted" to take a three-day trip to the silver mines across the bay at Thunder Cape. On their way back on Wednesday, May 25, their guide "called attention to a thin streak far away on the eastern horizon." The couple "sprang up in the seats of the boat in a way which certainly would have upset any less beamy craft."

- 7 -

CAMP SAULT

Rules of the Camp, Detachment Order Book, Red River Expedition:
The camp at Sault Ste. Marie being formed for the purpose of guarding and forwarding the stores of Red River expedition, all ranks of force are for the present confined to camp.... The usual bugle sounds will be called. Reveille at 4 a.m.; breakfast, 7; dinner, noon; tea, 4; retreat at sunset; 1st post at 9 p.m.; and tattoo at 9.30 p.m., and lights out at 10 p.m.

By order, W.J. BOLTON
Com'r detach't, & D.A.A.G., Sault Ste. Marie
— Reprinted in the *Daily Telegraph*, May 24, 1870

Denied passage through the American canal, expedition officials had to come up with some way to transport troops and *matériel* either over or around the Sault Rapids. Cunningham estimated the waterfall there to be about 1,700 feet wide and 1,300 feet long, with a total drop of 18 feet. Even with the extra water from spring runoff, the drop made the rapids too shallow to float loaded barges. That left the overland route via Portage Road the only viable option for moving expedition supplies onward.

Writing on May 5, Cunningham said the first mile and three-quarters of Portage Road — from the main wharf at the Canadian village of St. Marys to the Hudson's Bay Company fort — was "in tolerably good shape." The remaining three-quarters of a mile was "yet in the workman's hands." The ground was so wet in some spots that wagon wheels cut in seven or eight inches and wouldn't roll. And where the river washed in at another section, about 50 feet in length, the road had to be planked over on a series of supports. To add to the challenge, the bay on the Superior side of the rapids was too shallow for the steamers to tie up anywhere near the shore; as at Government Station, a scow would have to ferry men and supplies from a wharf at the north end of the road out to the steamers anchored 400 yards away. Dawson contracted a man named Graham and a crew of Soo men to finish the road and build the wharf.

The *Chicora* arrived at noon on Wednesday, May 11. As it took on coal, Captain McLean, his purser, Wemyss Simpson, and the intrepid Cunningham rowed over to the U.S. Fort Brady to see if the steamer would be granted passage through the canal. Cunningham said the fort was a large square occupying about 100 acres and was bounded by the river in front and a six-foot-high wooden palisade on the other three sides. Inside was a typical collection of military buildings — barracks, stables, an armoury, officer's residence — in the centre of which, from the top of an enormous pole, flew a mammoth star-spangled banner. The party made its way to the canal superintendent's office where Simpson requested a "definite and official statement as to how matters stood." In the "most courteous way," E.H. Carleton, the superintendent, handed the Canadians this note and said he couldn't let them through:

> Capt. McLean,
> SIR, — Until further instructions, I cannot permit you to pass through the St. Mary's Falls Ship Canal with the Chicora.
> Very respectfully,
> Yours, &c.,
> E.H. CARLETON, Superintendent

The foursome rowed back to Canada, and Captain McLean gave the order to unload the *Chicora*. Dawson reassigned the 120 voyageurs and labourers to Graham to finish work on Portage Road, and Cunningham reported this accomplished by Saturday, May 14.

FENIANS

Just as officials got a handle on the first challenge of the expedition, news of a second cropped up: the Canadian government received intelligence that Fenians were organizing once again up and down the Canada-U.S. border. In Michigan and Minnesota, reports had Fenians at Duluth and Superior City about to move against the expedition at the Soo and Fort William and a force of 300 was reported at St. Paul preparing to march north to support Louis Riel at Red River.

The news put expedition officials in another bind. One steamer's worth of supplies was lying unguarded along Portage Road and another was on the way. (In addition to the military wares, Cunningham counted 1,300 half-barrels of flour, 400 barrels of pork, 400 barrels of biscuits, 300 packages of tea, 300 cases of preserves, 220 bags of beans,

On board the *Chicora*, May 9, 1870.

and 150 half-barrels of sugar.) And soldiers with any real military experience — those with the 60th Rifles — were still in Ottawa and weren't scheduled to depart until the last week of May. Wolseley had no choice but to activate four companies of the untried Volunteers assembling at the Crystal Palace in Toronto. On May 9, he ordered Captain Henry Cook's No. 1 Company and Captain Daniel McMillan's No. 4 Company of the 1st (Ontario) Battalion of Riflemen to establish a temporary garrison at the Soo under the command of Lieutenant Colonel W.J. Bolton, Royal Artillery, then at Toronto, as well. These 100 men left Toronto on the morning of May 14, boarded the *Chicora* at Collingwood later that evening, and reached the Soo the next day.

As the Volunteers disembarked in the afternoon, Cunningham watched them form up on the shore and march "smartly" to a meadow beside the Hudson's Bay fort, two-thirds the way up Portage Road. In front was a small bay near the bottom of the rapids behind "a clump of spruce and pine trees," and a short distance away the ruins of an old North West Company fort. As the officers claimed one of the Hudson's Bay buildings for their quarters, the enlisted men pitched tents in the meadow and started dinner (pork and tea) with all "the usual amount of grumbling indulged in." The next day, two more companies of Ontario Battalion Volunteers — Captain William Smith's No. 2 Company and Captain Thomas Macklem's No. 3 Company — arrived aboard the little *Waubuno*. (Cunningham also catalogued the following on board: 100 barrels of flour, 258 bags of feed, 375 bags of oats, 20 cases of preserved potatoes, 15 wagons, nine yoke cattle, and two beef cattle.) It, too, was a sidewheel paddler but measured only 135 feet in length and had a registered tonnage of 193. Its usual route was running freight and passengers between Parry Sound, Collingwood, and the Soo.

Cunningham said he was a regular visitor to Camp Sault. One Sunday morning, he arrived as the men were turning out and preparing breakfast over two large fires at either end of the camp. The aroma from the beefsteak was "most pleasant." The Volunteers ate without ceremony: they filled their tin plates, sought out "the most eligible spots" on the various rocks and logs, and commenced to eat with their

The Hudson's Bay Company post at Sault Ste. Marie, showing the campsite of Colonel Wolseley's expedition.

jackknives. Cunningham thought a few were suffering from "a little too much indulgence in the soldier's pleasure" the night before. After breakfast, Reverend Wilson, a clergyman on his way to Fort William, delivered the Sunday service. The sermon, which went on a little long for Cunningham's taste, was repeatedly interrupted and punctuated by exclamations coming from the portage workers close by: "'Get up, you brute — gee — woe — get up, won't you' and other eloquent phrases from the vocabulary of the equine language." After the service, Cunningham was invited to lunch with the officers in Captain Cook's tent. The meal consisted of roast beef and potatoes, the former looking to Cunningham as if it had been dragged through an extensive coal pit. Lunch was served on a three-foot-square table converted for cards and stories post-meal.

FULL SPEED AHEAD

It took the British ambassador threatening to close the Welland Canal to American vessels, but the Americans finally relented: on May 16, President Ulysses S. Grant announced that Canadian vessels would be allowed passage through their canal. The ban on soldiers and munitions would remain in place. The Canadian government immediately chartered as many vessels as it could to get the expedition back on track. These included the Canadian steamer *Francis Smith* (the largest available on the Great Lakes), the Canadian tug *Okonra* towing the schooners *Nemesis* and *Snow Bird*, and the American steamers *Brooklyn, Arctic, Clematis,* and *Union.* These were in addition to the vessels already under contract, including the Canadian steamers *Algoma* and *Chicora,* the Canadian tug *Shickluna* towing the schooners *Pandora* and *Orion,* and the Canadian gunboats *Rescue* and *Prince Alfred.* All told, these vessels made 19 deliveries to Government Station between May 25 and June 26 when the last of the supplies were brought up.

The first vessel through the canal after May 16 was the *Brooklyn* on Friday evening, May 20. On Sunday morning, the *Shickluna* arrived with the *Pandora* and *Orion* in tow. And on Monday, the most anticipated vessel came in — the *Chicora* with Colonel Wolseley, his staff, No. 1 Company of the British 60th Rifles, and the barge *Clifton* in tow. The *Chicora* docked next to the *Pandora* and *Orion* at the main wharf, and as military supplies were unloaded (as well as 64 horses, 24 teamsters, and another 75 voyageurs) U.S. Colonel Robert Offley came across the river, boarded the *Chicora,* and had a "cordial meeting" with Wolseley and Captain William Smith. Offley told them the *Chicora* was free to pass through the canal, just not with troops or military supplies. After Offley departed, Wolseley mounted up with Lieutenant Colonel Bolton and Captain Nagle and rode to Camp Sault where the colonel spent the afternoon inspecting the road and complimenting the officers. Cunningham said Wolseley was "particularly pleased" with Graham's work, especially the "completeness of the road and the transport arrangements."

Sometime that afternoon, the intrepid Cunningham called on Wolseley and was received "in the most courteous manner." Cunningham said Wolseley "expressed pleasure" that a *Telegraph* correspondent was going to accompany the expedition, and even though Cunningham would have to "paddle his own canoe," the colonel promised to do "everything he could in the way of affording information forwarding mails, &c." Wolseley ended the interview by telling Cunningham not to have the "least hesitation in calling upon him on any business connected with the TELEGRAPH."

To Cunningham, Wolseley "seemed affability personified with not the slightest particle of the *haw* style about him." Appearances might have been deceiving. Wolseley had written the year before that the only value reporters had on the battlefield was in disseminating counter-intelligence to the enemy. In his opinion, "Travelling gentlemen, newspaper correspondents, and all that race of drones, are an encumbrance to an army; they eat the rations of fighting men, and do no work at all."[1]

As Cunningham and Wolseley were meeting, the *Francis Smith* arrived with the rest of the 60th Rifles. At 4:00 p.m., Wolseley, his staff, and the whole battalion of 60th Rifles were ferried out to the *Chicora*, which, along with the *Shickluna*, had passed through the canal and was now anchored in the bay. Then the scow took Ontario Battalion Companies No. 1 and No. 4 to the *Shickluna*. At 6:30, the *Chicora* (towing the *Clifton*) and the *Shickluna* (towing the *Pandora* and *Orion*) set course for Thunder Bay, the Regulars to work on Dawson's road and the Volunteers to transform Government Station into a new village that Wolseley would soon christen Prince Arthur's Landing.

ON TO THUNDER BAY

Over the next few days, Cunningham said the Soo was flush with activity — the *Clematis*, *Union*, *Snow Bird*, *Prince Alfred*, *Rescue*, *Arctic*, and *Okonra* all proceeded through the canal, and whatever military *matériel* they had was brought up via Portage Road. But then "things settled down" — all the supplies landed at the wharf were transported across the portage, the teams and wagons had been put aboard the ships, and the village became "almost as dull a place to live in now as it was five hundred years ago." Cunningham complained the only way of knowing "an army is in the neighbourhood" was to walk the couple of miles up Portage Road to see it. The only excitement anyone had was trying to keep up with the latest rumours "being daily propagated" about the Fenians. After the battles at Eccles Hill on May 25 and Trout River on May 27, the U.S. soldiers at Fort Brady were put on alert on June 1 with news that 1,400 Fenians had amassed at Duluth along with "a considerable number" at Marquette. None of these rumours amounted to anything.

For Cunningham, relief came on Thursday, June 2, when the *Chicora* arrived back from Thunder Bay with orders for the reporter to "start for Fort William" on its next trip north, scheduled for Saturday, June 4. Cunningham was over the moon, but had a lot to do. First, he bought a "fine new bark canoe" and provisions. Then he sought "to obtain the services of a couple of Indians" to man and guide the canoe. The first fellow he found was Joe Sagers, supposedly the son of a Chippewa chief "of considerable importance." Sagers "caught at the suggestion at once" of exploring the Red River Territory. On Sagers's recommendation, Cunningham then hired George Waubussy, "the most genuine type of a full-blood Chippewa" he'd ever seen, with "long, lank hair" and "almost as dark as a negro."

As they prepared to leave Saturday morning, Cunningham glimpsed a touching moment when Sagers bid farewell to his family. Sagers's wife handed her husband their baby boy, and he took the infant and held him for a few minutes "with something like a tear dimming his eye." Next, Sagers hugged the child, handed him back to his wife, "took out all the money he had in his pocket, and gave it to her." Without uttering another word, Sagers then shouldered the canoe with Waubussy to the water's edge.

By the time the *Telegraph*, its crew, and passenger were ready to depart, the *Chicora* had already crossed to the U.S. side of the rapids. Cunningham's inaugural trip "in the frail bark" was thus over the rough waters of the Sault Rapids. While the boat "danced lightly," Cunningham had a premonition he "might fall right through" the bark hull, which he estimated to be only an eighth of an inch thick. He "mentioned the difficulty to Joe, who in turn mentioned it to Waubussy — who speaks only Indian — and the two had a hearty laugh at my expense."

- 8 -

CONDITIONS ON THE GROUND

> The *Chicora* arrived this morning, bringing Colonel Wolseley and his staff, one company of the 60th Rifles, Mr. Joley, Mr. Dawson, and a party of men for the road, together with twenty horses, a like number of boats, and a quantity of stores. Her appearance was a source of gratification that in some cases was too profound to find expression in words.
>
> — Molyneux St. John, *Globe*, May 30, 1870

The *Chicora* arrived at Thunder Bay on May 25, and Wolseley wasted no time trying to get a handle on the state of Dawson's road. He and Lindsay Russell rode up to the Oskondaga River but found the road pretty much as St. John had described it two weeks earlier — the last four miles were still under construction, more than half the next section was "only cut through the woods," and the last five miles to Shebandowan Lake hadn't even been "marked out through the woods." Work hadn't progressed because the crews had been busy repairing the extensive damage caused by the fire, i.e., rebuilding the bridges, culverts, corduroy sections, and crib work built to hold back the cut-through hillsides. While St. John said most of this work was completed by the time Wolseley arrived, it came at the cost of any progress on construction.

Wolseley was in a bind again. He had orders to leave Fort Garry with the British contingent no later than August 20 in order to ship back to Britain by Christmas. The imbroglio at the Soo put that timeline in jeopardy. And now delays on Dawson's road meant the expedition might not even reach Red River by fall, and an early freeze-up could mean British troops wouldn't get home until spring.

The pressure on Wolseley to "greatly expedite the forward movement" could literally be seen building on the shores of Thunder Bay. Between May 26 and June 3, eight vessels disgorged over 700 troops, scores of voyageurs and teamsters, tons of stores, supplies, and *matériel*, and dozens of horses and oxen. (To get a sense of how "inconveniently crowded" the *Chicora* was on June 3, Cunningham said its manifest read as follows: 318 barrels of flour, 107 barrels of pork, 282 barrels of biscuits, 100 barrels of sugar, 200 barrels of beans, 100 boxes of tea, 50 cases of preserved potatoes, 25 barrels of potatoes, 30 tons of general merchandise, three tons of camp equipage, 285 bags of oats, five tons of hay, six barrels of coal oil, 17 lumber wagons, one engine, one boiler, 15 expedition boats, 40 horses, and 12,000 feet of lumber.) In the course of just one week, the tiny outpost of Government Station mushroomed from a "motley collection of wooden buildings and canvas tents" into Prince Arthur's Landing.

On June 3, Wolseley came up with an idea to help relieve the pressure. He proposed sending a flotilla of eight boats up the Kaministiquia River to see if it was feasible to bypass the road and reach the bridge at Mile 21 entirely by water. Captains Young and E.I. Fraser were put in charge of a small team from the 60th Rifles — "and what man can accomplish Captain Young will do," St. John judged. Simon Dawson, one of "two competent authorities at Thunder Bay," opposed the experiment point-blank as a reckless danger to both men and boats.

While Young and Fraser laboured to move their boats up the Kaministiquia River, particularly around the daunting Kakabeka Falls, Dawson's transportation service began moving supplies to the base camp at the Matawan Bridge (Mile 26.5). Progress was slow as "alarming numbers" of the horses fell ill. On June 9, St. John said 20 of the 50 horses available were out of commission with many more "rapidly approaching the same state." One issue was the horses purchased by the Canadian government were artillery horses "accustomed to limited food and light work." They were simply overworked pulling the heavy wagons, especially through mud at times up to their bellies. Another issue was that the government had outfitted the horses with "ill-fitting harnesses," resulting in severely chafed or "galled" shoulders. And on top of this were three days of heavy rains that made the road beyond the Kaministiquia Bridge impassable to the wagons. Lindsay Russell told St. John that the combined effect of the fire, rain, and horses likely meant "no part of the expedition will leave Fort Garry this winter." The only good news was that Young and Fraser had been able to get boats to the "smooth water" beyond Kakabeka Falls by June 10. Wolseley deemed the experiment a success and ordered a second detachment of boats under Captain Francis Northey to depart up the Kaministiquia River the next day.

A NEW PLAN

To deal with "conditions on the ground," on June 10 Wolseley announced a series of changes to expedite the plan to get the expedition to Shebandowan Lake.

First, rather than take supplies directly from Thunder Bay to Shebandowan in one shot, Wolseley decided to stockpile everything at the Matawan Bridge. This would take advantage of the relatively decent state of the road that far and allow crews to finish the road beyond without any traffic on it. To this end, Captain Ward's company of Regulars was moved up to supplement Dawson's crew.

Second, based on their success on the Kaministiquia River, Wolseley ordered Young and Fraser to see how far they could float their boats up the Matawan River beyond the Kaministiquia Bridge. St. John said little was known of that river, but Wolseley hoped "and indeed seemed to take for granted that no insurmountable obstacle would be met."

Third, Wolseley settled on using the Shebandowan River for the last three miles of the journey to Shebandowan Lake. As St. John predicted on May 11, it was simply more efficient to move men and supplies via the shallow-hulled "Ottawa boats" for the final stage rather than by wagon overland.

A fourth change involved the final approach to Fort Garry. Up to June 10, the plan had been to march the expedition overland on John Snow's road from Lake of the Woods to Fort Garry. On news from "Indians of the interior" that Snow's road was both incomplete and too wet to be crossed by a force as large as the expedition, Wolseley decided to proceed from Lake of the Woods via the Winnipeg River to Lake Winnipeg and then south to Fort Garry on the Red River. Wolseley had had enough of unfinished roads. He also confirmed orders that the British contingent of the force would assume lead position "on the line of march" so that as soon as the Canadian battalions arrived at Fort Garry they could begin their return home.

- 9 -

DECEITFUL APPEARANCES

In the hope of sport, Major Streatfield and your correspondent, a few days ago, started in a canoe, determined to find this fabulous wealth of trout, and after paddling for eleven or twelve miles reached a diminutive creek, the appearance of which was so disappointing that Major Streatfield immediately designated it "Minnow Drain." Here we camped for the night, and in the morning rose early, in the hope that appearances, which are proverbially deceitful, might be so in this case.

— Molyneux St. John, *Globe*, June 5, 1870

I am beginning to think better of the Indians than ever before. On the authority of traders I had been taught to regard them as utterly untrustworthy — without even the idea of such an emotion as gratitude — and utterly and essentially selfish. This I think is a mistake. Let the Indian be treated as a man.

— Robert Cunningham, *Daily Telegraph*, June 15, 1870

At Prince Arthur's Landing on June 3, Sagers and Waubussy found a spot on the edge of the Ontario Battalion camp to pitch their tent. The two took an axe into the woods and returned with "a few poles and a large quantity of pine brushwood." They fixed the poles in the ground, secured the canvas on top, and laid down a "thick floor of pine twigs." Cunningham said he was "exceedingly struck" by the "elegance and comfort" of his new home — Waubussy had even made a candlestick "from a piece of birch bark and a sharp pointed stick." Cunningham thanked his "two friends" profusely. After a meal of fresh-caught trout, the men turned in for the night, their first together under the same canvas. Cunningham said he was a bit nervous "going to bed alone with two wild children of the wood" but quickly discovered there was nothing to be afraid of beyond prejudice and stereotype. Waubussy, "as wild looking a man as ever trod the forest," went into one corner of the tent, folded his hands, and "for a full three minutes" engaged in prayer. Waubussy, it turns out, was a Methodist, Sagers a Catholic: the latter took to the other corner of the tent and "with equal reverence and earnestness performed the Catholic prayer ritual." Cunningham said he fell asleep feeling "as safe in the hands of my two friends as I would with my own brothers."

In the weeks that followed, Prince Arthur's Landing mushroomed. The *Chicora* returned on June 14 with the last two companies of Ontario Volunteers; the *Arctic* brought the first three companies of the

Unloading stores at Prince Arthur's Landing.

Quebec Battalion on the 15th, the *Algoma* arrived on the 19th with supplies and horses to replace those fallen ill, and the *Arctic* returned on the 22nd with the last four companies of the Quebec Battalion. The *Chicora* delivered the last military supplies on June 26.

The look of the new town evolved, as well. By mid-June, Cunningham said the mix of wooden houses, stores, and canvas tents had become "very gay and pretty," with many tents sporting "green curtains and rustic tables" to facilitate toiletries and meals. A lot of the troops had built poplar fences around their tents and strung up "a very numerous assortment of flags." One of these sported a red ensign surrounded by a frying pan, a symbol "meant to designate the locality of the regimental kitchen." St. John said streets were marked off between the tents — Control Road was flanked by Control Department buildings, Bakery Lane led to the field ovens, and Ordnance Road was home to the Royal Artillery and Royal Engineers, while Shoo Fly Avenue boasted "the principal comic vocalist of the upper camp." Shoo Fly, of course, referred to "Shoo Fly, Don't Bodder Me!," the popular burlesque ditty "just about everyone" was whistling and dancing to in the late 1860s and early 1870s.[1]

Up the road, Wolseley's troubles continued. The transportation service to the Matawan Bridge at Mile 26.5 was in full swing with 52 wagons moving supplies continuously from the bay to the depot there, despite no fewer than 60 horses being listed as sick. And even though most of the boats poled, tracked, and portaged up the Kaministiquia River received some damage, progress was being made on that front, as well. But at the Matawan Bridge everything ground to a painful, frustrating halt. Young and Fraser reported their second experiment to move boats up the Matawan River to be a failure after encountering a long set of rapids that could neither be poled and tracked across nor portaged around owing to the "high perpendicular bluffs" on either side. And despite the assignment of "gang after gang of men" to work on the road past the bridge, that section wasn't ready yet for "continuous heavy traffic." On June 20, St. John declared that the expedition "practically stopped" at the Matawan Bridge.

Characteristically, Wolseley wouldn't admit defeat. On the Matawan front, he assigned an additional company of Regulars to cut a road around the rapids that Young and Fraser had encountered. The result allowed boats to be loaded with supplies at the Matawan Bridge, rowed the few miles to the rapids, portaged back to the main road, then down another side road to regain the river and rowed the rest of the way to Oskondaga River at Mile 29. On June 22, four companies of Regulars — 200 men — worked alongside Dawson's 250 between the Matawan Bridge and Shebandowan Lake.

"THE GOOD DOCTOR"

On Wednesday, June 22, St. John made a fourth trip up Dawson's road to "better understand the existing difficulties and the methods adopted to overcome them." Accompanying St. John was a "Dr. McDonnell." No such doctor appears on the expedition's rolls or is mentioned by the expedition's chief surgeon, E.W. Young, in his final report.[2] There is good reason to believe that "the good doctor" was another ruse for Kate Ranoe.

St. John said the road from the bay to the Kaministiquia Bridge continued to be in decent shape (this was where St. John counted 52 wagons plying the route). But he didn't recognize the next section, from the bridge over the Kaministiquia River to the one on the Matawan River. Gone were the pine forests that had lined the road "mile after mile, stretching away as far as the eye could see." They were replaced by acre upon acre of brûlées "blossoming with strawberry plants, thick clusters of wild roses, and variegated heaths." Beyond the Matawan Bridge, "bad would hardly convey an idea of the road's real state." St. John said it had been "churned up until mud ponds and boulders combined to stop the way." The road was found to be in a similar state past the Oskondaga River. The first mile and a half had been cleared but still hadn't been "touched by spade and shovel." The last half-mile remained "in a state of nature."

At Mile 45, where the road ended at the Shebandowan River, St. John and "the good doctor" met up with Captain Ward of the 60th

Rifles. He offered to take the pair the final three miles to Shebandowan Lake in his canoe, which was manned by three Iroquois. All aboard were expected to "work the oars" to beat the current and series of shallow rapids, but, St. John said, "as two of us are new to the work, and Dr. McDonnell declared that someone had always to sing in the canoe and he'd do the singing, the bulk of the labour fell upon the Indians."

"The good doctor" also dodged hard work at one set of rapids where the canoe had to be tracked. St. John recounted the episode with notes of domesticity:

> The doctor made a great show of aiding the Iroquois, and zealously handed your correspondent the role to lead on, while he remained at the most difficult point near the canoe. It turned out that the lead meant pioneering [the way] under the boughs and trunks of trees hanging over the water's edge, springing from rock to rock, walking over slippery stones, and eventually, in sheer desperation, walking boldly into the stream; while the difficult work near the boat was watching others to see where to step and using the rope as a steadying aid. In our case the proper labour of the so-called difficult point was performed entirely by the Indian in the bow of the canoes, and the tracking by two of the three that went ashore.

After surveying the lake — a long stretch of water with the "usual bays and promontories" connected by narrow passages to two additional lakes — the party returned to camp at the Oskondaga River at seven in the evening. Ward invited St. John and "the good doctor" to spend the night, but "certain considerations" induced them to return to Prince Arthur's Landing in the dark. Around two in the morning, the couple reached Matawan Camp and then struggled on through the darkness, St. John leading the horse around the mudholes, "the good doctor" remaining on the buckboard to drive. At some point, the torrential rains started again. Not until four in the afternoon did the two finally arrive back in camp. St. John said they had "long-exhausted an extensive repertoire of comic songs" and looked "more wet, more weary, and more miserable than the pony."

JACK "THE MAJOR" MALONEY

It is unclear exactly what convinced St. John and "Dr. McDonnell" to travel back to Prince Arthur's Landing in the dark, but it might have been the much-anticipated boat race scheduled for Saturday evening, June 25, between the Ontario Battalion's No. 5 Company and the Royal Engineers. The No. 5 Company crew had recently defeated No. 7 Company for the honour of being the first Volunteers to square off against the Regulars.

The start time for the race was set for 7:30 p.m., and Cunningham said the shores of Thunder Bay had never before "presented so gay and animated an appearance." In addition to the officers out in full uniform, "all the ladies for ten miles round were invited to see the contest." While Cunningham admitted there weren't many "ladies about," those who showed up were "very pretty and exceedingly interesting."

At 7:30, Wolseley fired his pistol to begin the race. The Royal Engineers got off to a strong start, but with a series of "splendid spurts" and "gallant oaring," the No. 5 Company crew kept even to about the one-mile mark. At that point, "the steady stroke of the Ontario men told" and the No. 5 Company boat pulled steadily ahead over the last half-mile to a distance of more than two lengths by the finish line. The judge, a fellow named Lieutenant Colonel John McNeill, declared the winning time at eight minutes, 47 seconds. Not bad for a bunch of Volunteers in a heavy, unwieldy military boat.

The thicket of spectators cheered the crews as they returned to the starting area, and Wolseley complimented each of the Royal Engineers when they stepped ashore: Sergeant Fowler (stroke oar), Captain Herchmer (coxswain), Corporal Jackson, and Privates Austin, Yates, and Thurston — and a seventh person whom Cunningham identified as Jack "Major" Maloney. Cunningham said the "major" was "quite a character," having done more to "give vivacity and good temper to the camp than any other *man*.... *His* native wit is something prodigious ... *his* sallies are oftentimes irresistible. You just require to look at *him* to see the kind of a *man he* is; for great round massive smiles are settled on every feature" (italics added). Ahem. There was no major named Maloney on the expedition, not even a Moloney. Cunningham's "major" was perhaps yet another subterfuge for Ranoe.

Once the crews were welcomed back on the shore, Cunningham said the "major" mounted a rostrum and addressed the troops after shaking hands with Wolseley.

"Fellow patriots — you ought to be very proud of the crew of number five boat this night," Maloney began.

"Why, Major?" someone in the crowd asked.

"Now, don't be in such a hurry," Maloney continued. "Wasn't I just coming to tell you all about it? But I can assure the owner of that voice that said 'why' that judging from the voice itself and judging from the face and judging from his part history and judging from his inevitable future history, that it will be a very long time indeed, before any gentleman in such a public and gallant assembly as this will have the hardihood to rise and tell such a thundering lie, as to say that anybody will ever and can ever be proud of him."

This sally received considerable applause, and "the major" smiled benignly all around and then continued.

"Yes, gentlemen, I say and I will say it a thousand times if you please, even though I am one of the victims, that you should be proud of us for licking the Engineers!"

"That's so, Major!" said a rather young and small private.

"Maloney" transfixed him with one of the most genial smiles that ever shone on a human countenance and exclaimed, "Brethren, the child's name is Johnny!"

The private then collapsed in laughter.

"And now, gentlemen, I have nearly done, and all that I have to say further is that the crew of No. 5 Company are ready to row with any seven men in the brigade, so you had better go to bed, like good boys, say your prayers, always take care in every circumstance in which you may be placed, to behave yourselves like gentlemen, so that you may do honour to your Queen, your country, and your mothers."

After charging the Crown for three cheers for the Queen, Lieutenant Colonel Samuel Peters Jarvis, the Royal Engineers, and the No. 5 crew, the "major" gave up the rostrum and vanished into the crowd.

- 10 -

HARRY WITH THE ROAD

It would seem as if Noah had been there not long ago, and even yet it would be rather difficult for the dove to find a resting place for the role of her foot.

— Colonel Garnet Wolseley, quoted by Robert Cunningham, *Daily Telegraph*, July 8, 1870

By the last week of June, the expedition was in full motion from Thunder Bay to Shebandowan Lake. All the troops and supplies had arrived, as had scores of extra teamsters, labourers, horses, and oxen to make up lost time. The total civilian force peaked here at over 700 men, 150 horses, 36 oxen, 50 wagons, and 30 carts. Boats continued up the Kaministiquia River batch by batch and up the road, weather permitting. Company after company marched up to help with construction: Captain Francis Northey and two companies of Regulars moved up past the Oskondaga River on June 25 and four companies of Volunteers took another eight boats up the Kaministiquia on the 26th. By June 28, St. John said the "long wished for start" of July 10 appeared finally to be "near at hand."

And then it rained again, this time to the point that Wolseley ordered the wagons off the road for a couple of days so it wouldn't get "cut up" and become impassable as it had a week earlier.

Into this gloom, Lieutenant General James Lindsay arrived aboard the *Algoma* on June 29. He had intended to ride up Dawson's road with Wolseley when he disembarked but was forced to postpone and wait out the storm within the comfortable confines of Fort William. On the afternoon of June 30, the easterly winds blustered to gale force and at nightfall thunder boomed in regular succession off Thunder Cape and Mount McKay — "like noise dancing in the air." From time to time, St. John said, "the black canopy above gave way to a vivid sheet of light, which lit up for a moment every peak of the land, every inlet of the bay, every tent and building in the camp, so that the forms inside the canvas were seen distinctly, and then passed away, leaving everything darker than before."

Early the next morning, those troops still in garrison at Prince Arthur's Landing rose to wring out soaked clothes and bedding and prepare for inspection by Lindsay and Wolseley. At 10:00 a.m., the Quebec Battalion marched down to the beach. After inspection, Wolseley had Major Acheson Gosford Irvine put the men through part of a platoon exercise. Then Lindsay addressed the troops:

> Under circumstances like the present, I am able to judge of a battalion only by comparison. And so I asked Colonel Wolseley, how does the appearance of the regiment compare with that presented by them at the former inspection? I am glad to say that Colonel Wolseley observed a marked improvement.
>
> There are a few points I would like to mention here today.
>
> The duties of a soldier are various and working parties always form large, if not agreeable, portions of the duties of a camp. It is, therefore, necessary for a soldier to apply himself as cheerfully to this duty as to any other.
>
> And the great secret of getting the work well done is that the officers should set an example by taking up a pick or shovel, when they find men doing their work badly, and do some of the work themselves.
>
> Nothing tends to maintain discipline more than cleanliness; and it is a mistake to suppose that this was

> unattainable on service. Regular troops are expected to keep themselves and their accoutrements as clean in camp as in barrack — and you have done that.
>
> I am pleased to see the battalion in good order, and trust you remain so throughout your term of service.

The general then proceeded to Headquarters Camp to visit the bakery and other commissariat departments.

In the afternoon, Lindsay inspected the companies of the Ontario Battalion remaining in the base camp, watched them parade, and then "repeated the remarks he made in the morning to the Quebec regiment," as St. John related. Then it was the Royal Artillery's turn for inspection. They split into four crews, broke their guns down, and waited for orders. On command, they reassembled their guns on the carriages, sponged, loaded, and fired. St. John said the fastest crew was able to get its round off in 17 seconds. The reporter said Lindsay appeared impressed.

NEW ORDERS

Lindsay, Wolseley, and Captain George Lightfoot Huyshe mounted and trotted up Dawson's road on the afternoon of July 1 — and didn't like what they saw. In the "emphatic language" of one excited official, the heavy rains had "played Harry with the road." Some of the portages were up to six feet underwater, two of the smaller bridges at Sunshine and Six Mile Creeks had been carried away by the high waters and were destroyed, and the wagon train had ground to a halt.

Wolseley sent Huyshe back to the base camp early on July 2 with orders to "impress upon the officers in his force the great urgent necessity there is for pushing on the completion of the road by every means that lie in their power. There is a scarcity of tools, but the men are advised to make themselves useful by picking up the fallen trees, making corduroy work, and filling up the bad places." The last two companies of the Ontario Battalion started up the road in the morning of July 2, a company from the Quebec Battalion took eight boats up the Kaministiquia River in the afternoon, and the last of the 60th readied to start at daylight the next morning for road duty.

On July 3, Lindsay and Wolseley returned to Prince Arthur's Landing and Wolseley reluctantly issued orders to push departure off until Wednesday, July 13. He also prepared letters for dispatch to Winnipeg to "get the road from the North-West Angle made by the Red River people in time for the arrival of the troops." St. John thought Wolseley was buying himself another option for the final approach to Fort Garry in the event the settlers didn't see the expedition as the errand of peace that Governor General John Young promised. The letters were given to Donald Smith, the Dominion government's envoy, for delivery. He had arrived at Thunder Bay on June 26 on his way to attend the Hudson Bay's Company Council at Norway House on the northern shore of Lake Winnipeg.

- 11 -

UP THE KAMINISTIQUIA

> As I write, a perfect plague of sand flies settles on my hands by the score; they get into my neck and my ears; go for my nose; and if the plague of flies which was set upon the Egyptians, the poor wretches must have suffered horribly, even more than from the other anthropophagical insects that visited them.
>
> — Robert Cunningham, "Kaministiquia," *Daily Telegraph*, June 30, 1870

The day Lieutenant General James Lindsay arrived, Cunningham left Prince Arthur's Landing for Shebandowan Lake with Sagers and Waubussy. They got to the mission above Fort William on the evening of Monday, June 27, and spent the next day giving the canoe, now christened the *Telegraph*, "a thorough overhaul." At five the next morning, they paddled out into the Kaministiquia River.

Cunningham said the river at that early hour was "as calm and placid a looking stream some could wish to look at." And then a clap of thunder let loose and rain "as I never had the pleasure of enjoying before" poured down all day and the next — the same storm that waylaid Lindsay at Fort William. Fifty yards on, lightning struck a huge pine, "a giant of the forest," and it splashed into the river just ahead of the *Telegraph*. Sagers and Waubussy rowed on, and Cunningham set to bailing water in an effort to keep the canoe afloat. Despite his efforts, the rain got to "everything on board" — the biscuits and flour stashed under the tarpaulin, the tent and bedding, the powder, the paper, the matches.

At 11:00 a.m., Sagers and Waubussy steered the *Telegraph* to shore and prepared a lunch of hardtack, bacon, and tea, the same they had had for breakfast and the same they would have again for supper. The men then paddled all afternoon and pitched camp for the night, Sagers and Waubussy foraging for a "quantity of beautiful ripe strawberries, glistening with very freshness."

Wednesday was much the same as Tuesday, Sagers and Waubussy paddling, Cunningham bailing. By evening, everything on board was wetter than it had been the day before, if that were possible. After a quick dinner, the men turned in at 7:00 p.m., "resolved to drown our miseries in sleep." But then a new misery descended. Mosquitoes. Cunningham said he had encountered the little buzzing beasts before, had even seen one "occasionally," but never could he have imagined "the plague" that swarmed into the tent that night. The three fought valiantly but could only find sleep "in snatches." Cunningham said he woke in the morning "looking for all the world like a man labouring under a severe attack of smallpox. My whole face being literally one mass of eruption."

The three were tired, miserable, bitten, and soaked — and paddled into the river again resolute on escaping their tormenters. The only problem with the plan, though, was that the rain had raised the level of the water "seven or eight feet" and the canoe was now "dancing to the current" in the middle of a swollen watercourse. After Waubussy swam out and retrieved the canoe, he and Joe paddled to the first set of rapids on the Kaministiquia just downstream from the famous Kakabeka Falls. Cunningham suggested waiting a day or two for the water level to subside; Sagers and Waubussy laughed and took to poling the canoe along — Sagers standing in the bow with his pole, Waubussy in the stern with his. Cunningham thought it "almost madness" to continue, given the velocity of the river — 10 to 12 miles per hour, he guessed — and the fragility of the bark canoe. Sagers and Waubussy just laughed.

Slowly, steadily, the seasoned guides cajoled the *Telegraph* up the rapids, sticking close to the shoreline here, riding the edge of a manageable eddy there. With all the runoff, Cunningham judged the width of the river at between 300 and 700 yards, swamping large portions of the forest on either side as a result. At times, the men's poles bent and quivered to the point that it seemed they might snap. But then one of the guides would scan the river and banks and send the canoe across to a sheltered nook, "dipping and skimming like a swallow."

Just before noon on Thursday, June 30, the *Telegraph* reached the largest rapid in the set, the crest of which Cunningham eyeballed at six feet. The men elected to portage rather than track. After relaunching on the other side, their way was immediately blocked by a massive tree trunk and they had to vacate the river again for another portage. When they were about to disembark once more, Waubussy in the stern lost traction with his pole and the *Telegraph* was drawn immediately into the middle of the current, hurtling toward the six-foot rapid. All three men paddled "with almost superhuman effort" to get back to shore. But to no avail — the current was too strong. Waubussy, at this point,

Robert Cunningham, reporter for Toronto's *Daily Telegraph*, and Indigenous men beside a canoe.

"gave a war whoop" and stood up "with his teeth set, his eyes flashing, and his long dark hair floating behind him, looking like an inspired maniac." He then jammed his paddle into the river beside the canoe and used it like a rudder. And "in a tenth of the time it takes to read it," the *Telegraph* dashed over the rapid. Cunningham said he closed his eyes as the bark "took the leap," and when he opened them, they were in the middle of the "surging, boiling, raging" rapids where Waubussy quickly steered them back to the safety of the shore.

GRAND PORTAGE

After falling from a height of nearly 45 yards at Kakabeka, the Kaministiquia River rushes two miles downstream through a channel at a "terrible velocity" to the set of rapids the *Telegraph* had just ascended. To get the boats up this section, Young, Fraser, and the other Kaministiquia boat parties had beaten a path along the bank from which to track the boats. The heavy rains, however, had raised the water level well above the height of the path. Not that poling was an option, given the current height of the river — the poles simply couldn't touch bottom.

The solution happened upon was for Cunningham to tie one end of a rope around his waist, another around the *Telegraph*'s bow, and work his way up the path as best he could while Sagers and Waubussy used their poles to navigate around the stumps and rocks along the swamped shoreline. Cunningham said the water was in places up to his knees, at others up to his waist, and in one place "clean over his head and ears." Lucky thing for the life preserver. Not making much progress, the men elected to portage the canoe and supplies through the woods to a "little green dell by the river" where they pitched camp for the night. Across the river was a rocky cliff "thick with pines and ash and birch," which the "dipping sun" was lighting the tops "with a gorgeous tinge." And beside them the "mighty falls" roared like thunder and sent up clouds of spray that "fell like dew" on Cunningham's writing paper.

At four the next morning — Dominion Day 1870 — Sagers, Waubussy, and Cunningham set off on the "grandiloquently named"

Grand Portage. To transport their supplies, the men employed eight-foot leather "packing straps" three inches thick in the middle, tapering out to a half-inch at each end. To prepare for transport, the ends of the straps were tied around a barrel or a pack and the load hoisted onto the back of the carrier. The broad middle was then drawn over the head and across the forehead "thus sustaining most of the weight." Cunningham said Sagers and Waubussy were able to "trot along" with 300- or 400-pound loads, but he could manage only 120.

The first section of the Grand Portage around Kakabeka was "a great rack" of nine-inch logs spaced a foot and a half apart and about 200 feet long. The path to it was "almost perpendicular." In between the logs were great, muddy "bog-holes" that Cunningham said were about "nine or ten inches deep." And so between the diameter of the logs and the depth of the holes, each step had a "perpendicularity" of about 18 inches. With his legs "not of the longest," Cunningham said this part of the march "was the toughest I ever made." At times, Cunningham feared his pack would cause him to "execute a back somersault." The next section of the portage was outfitted with "great logs" set two feet apart over which the boats could be rolled on nine-inch logs. Reaching the top of the portage, Cunningham declared the Kaministiquia to be "a failure as a navigable river."

DASHED TO ATOMS

Much to Cunningham's chagrin, the Grand Portage wasn't the end of the work — or the excitement. Five hundred yards on was another set of falls requiring another "portage almost as grand as the last." And after that came another two-thirds of a mile on. This one required trekking over a small island — "a rock really with a few stunted trees on it" — where the men came upon three detachments of troops. They were trying to figure out the best line to a narrow point of land a couple hundred yards off from which a large tree jutted into the river. Getting there was a bit of a trick, since a "rushing roaring rugged fall of about eighty feet" lined one side of the island and on the other was "a similar cataract." The idea was to peel off from the island and make a dash between the currents of the two rapids for the tree where the boats could be lashed before being drawn out of the river and hauled to the next portage.

Cunningham, Sagers, and Waubussy watched the first few boats get out into the current all right, but then one with the Ontario Volunteers missed the tree and the boat was sent "whirling towards the fall" on the right side of the island. The men on the shore shouted for the crew to backpaddle. Some of the crew "lost their self-possession," threw down their oars, stood up, and started shouting frantically, as if "they were about to jump into the current." The boat got to within nine feet of the precipice. Cunningham said it was a "moment of awful intensity of feeling" — those on the shore yelling frantically, those in the boat yelling at one another. Cunningham said he was paralyzed, expecting to see "the poor fellows dashed to atoms in the boiling gulf beneath." Luckily, other members of the crew kept their heads and were able to push the boat out of the current "but only to get into the other." Anticipating the line of descent, Waubussy rushed to the rocky jetty and held out his hand. One of the doomed crewmen stretched out his paddle, which Waubussy gripped on to "like grim death" and drew the boat to shore, saving all seven men. The crew tried again and this time made the tree. The *Telegraph* followed suit, and after resting overnight, they reached camp at the Kaministiquia Bridge the next morning.

- 12 -

AND THEY'RE OFF

> The first move from Shebandowan is the breaking of the ice, and the event for which we have all been wishing and striving for the past two months.
>
> — Molyneux St. John, *Globe*, July 29, 1870

Over the first two weeks of July, the expedition stretched out along Dawson's 48-mile road. On July 6, most of the Ontario Battalion was stationed between the Matawan Bridge and Six Mile Creek, headquarters was moving up to the Matawan Bridge (Mile 26.5), and most of the 60th Rifles were finishing work on the section between there and Ward's Landing (Mile 45). On July 8, the last tenants of Prince Arthur's Landing — the Royal Artillery, the Royal Engineers, and a couple of Quebec Battalion companies — were packing up and getting ready to leave (except for Captain L.C.A.L. de Bellefeuills's No. 1 Company, which remained in garrison), and the entire Ontario Battalion had advanced past the Matawan Bridge. On July 10, the first two companies of the 60th Rifles reached Shebandowan Lake, and on July 11 the last troops at the Matawan Bridge prepared to depart on the 12th. On that day, Wolseley pushed departure back to Saturday, July 16, and announced the order of battle: two companies of the 60th under Lieutenant Colonel Randle Joseph Feilden together with the Royal Artillery and Royal Engineers would depart first in three brigades of six boats each, followed by the Ontario Battalion and then the Quebec Battalion bringing up the rear. Accidents aside, St. John said

Wolseley hoped to "get the whole force off in thirteen brigades" by the beginning of August.

Cunningham and his crew left camp at Oskondaga Bridge on July 12 and reached Shebandowan the next evening. St. John and Ranoe arrived three days later, having travelled in one shot — "from daylight to dark" — all the way from Prince Arthur's Landing.

THE START

The expedition was due to launch at 10:00 a.m. on Saturday, July 16. As the hour approached, though, "preparations were still incomplete," since many of the boats still required repairs — rowlocks and oars, tillers and rudders, et cetera — from the dings and knocks endured on the rapids and portages from the bay. And then there were the hijinks: one soldier tried to appropriate the gear from another, someone else complained that his boat had fewer barrels of pork or flour than others, and then the inevitable fight broke out concerning which belonged to whom or who had more or less than the other.

As morning bled into afternoon, the pressure to launch increased. The officers' orders became more "peremptory," the "general bustle" greater. St. John said control officers marched around "with memorandum books in their hands," and the regimental officers barked "for sergeant this or corporal that." At several points it seemed as if the boats were ready to go, and then some complication or other arose. Late in the afternoon, Wolseley arrived and made it clear he expected the detachments to start that night. Regardless.

Finally, at 8:30 p.m., the first boats shoved off from the little wharf at the southeast end of Shebandowan Lake. St. John said it was a beautiful evening — the winds had died down, the lake was calm "like a mill pond," the sun had just set in a cloudless sky, leaving the western border of the lake painted with a "mellowed tinge of purples and reds."

The stillness was broken by shouts of encouragement and goodbyes from the well-wishers onshore.

"No more rapids!" exclaimed one.

"No more poling!" cried another.

"Off we go for Red River!" repeated many.

St. John said everyone was in great spirits with the "long, dragging, wearisome journey from Thunder Bay" now behind them. As soon as the first brigade got under way, the second, with the Royal Artillery and Royal Engineers, followed suit. It took another 17 days before the rest of the expedition left.

FINAL ASSESSMENT

Before departing Shebandowan Lake, St. John wrote about the challenges the expedition had overcome to complete those torturous 48 miles of the journey to Red River. In his estimation, Dawson's road would probably have served to move the expedition up to Shebandowan on its own if the weather had held and the horses had been "equal to the work for which they were intended." As it turned out, the heavy rains, the fire, and the "unexpected manner in which the horses fell sick" made transport to Shebandowan by land alone "impossible." Hiring better horses, those accustomed to heavy work, feeding them more and better, and purchasing proper-fitting harnesses could easily have solved most of the horse-related challenges.

But even with "all the horses available," St. John said the precarious state of the second half of the road wouldn't have withstood "the transport of all the boats and provisions." And moving more men up to aid with construction wouldn't have helped, since the wagons required to carry additional provisions would have only added to the wear and tear on the road. Thus was Wolseley's determination to find an alternative "exceedingly fortunate." As dangerous and toilsome as the river route was, it proved to be a useful "auxiliary" to the road. To Dawson's point, though, the water route couldn't have been used on its own owing to the "severe trial" the rapids and portages on the Kaministiquia River presented to both men and boats. For St. John, in other words, the road and the water route "together have enabled the expedition to pass over what is described as being the most difficult part of the journey." Decades later, most historians would agree.

Before leaving Shebandowan Lake, Cunningham added his two cents, as well. He said the cost of the first 25 miles of the road was pegged at $114,000. At $4,560 per mile, that was $182,400 for the entire 48 miles. Or roughly $3.5 million in 2019 Canadian dollars. Quite a bargain!

In the first story written after leaving Shebandowan, St. John admitted to "a temporary inability to hold a pen in any other way but that in which one holds a spoon." On August 3, he said, "owing to a disabled hand I had been unable to write." On August 21, he confessed that his "crippled arm, and the remnants of a lengthened attack of fever and ague," had forced him to dictate his stories from his bed. And then, on August 24, St. John revealed that Kate Ranoe was the one taking his dictation: "My crippled arm prevents my writing, and though my wife sits patiently writing from my dictations, the joint effort is to us at least hardly satisfactory … it is no easy matter to arrange and dictate the mass of interesting and uninteresting events that pass before one, when sickness comes to impede one's efforts."

In other words, at least from when they departed Shebandowan Lake on July 16, the *Globe*'s coverage of the Red River Expedition was jointly produced by Kate Ranoe and Molyneux St. John, "R-SJ" for short.

PART III

Off We Go for Red River!

- 13 -

INTELLECTUAL CHARACTERS

There never was a river with a greater disinclination to go in a straight line for ten yards together, and mile after mile was passed with only a few hundred yards gained. The stream, too, was choked with fallen trees and snags, so that at several places it became necessary to hew through large trees before the canoe could pass.… The only comfort derived from this was a dinner of pigeons that I shot from the canoe, and which my travelling companion curried.

— Kate Ranoe and Molyneux St. John, *Globe*, July 25, 1870

The industry of these women is most remarkable. At daybreak this morning four of the canoes were dancing over the lake in various directions, and in the evening they returned, one with beans, two with a few fish.… If such industry could be taken hold of and directed into other channels, how much comfort might accrue from it, and how much squalor and misery and wretchedness might be banished from the face of the earth.

— Robert Cunningham, *Daily Telegraph*, July 26, 1870

The first part of the journey from Shebandowan Lake to Fort Garry was 208 miles to Fort Frances. This followed the old North West Company canoe route through an area called the Lake Region. It began

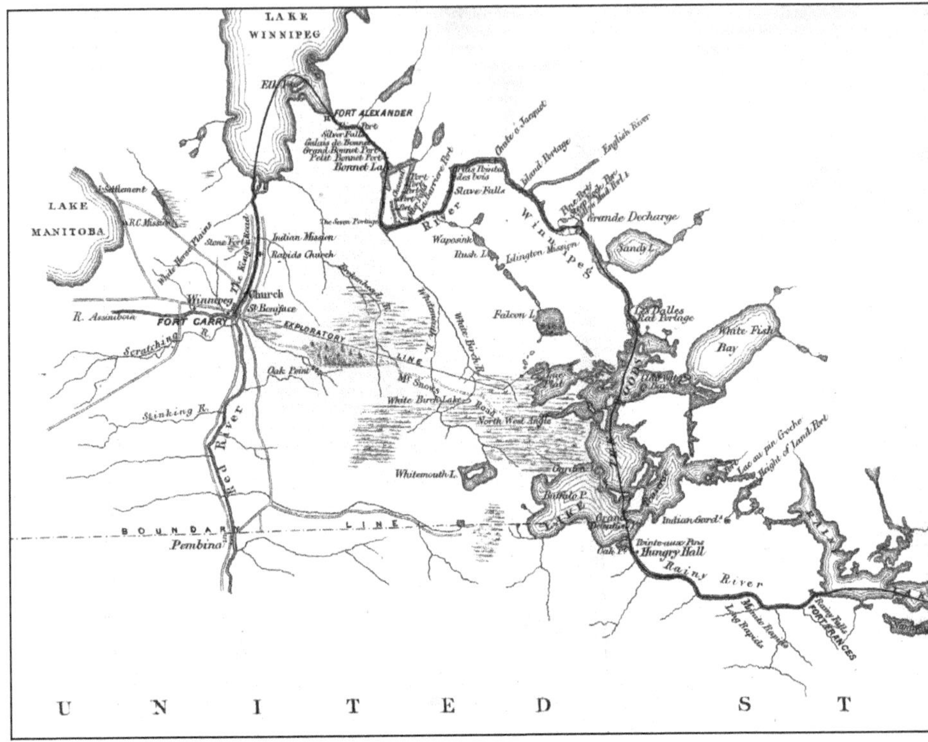

Plan of route from Lake Superior to Fort Garry.

with 20 miles of paddling across Shebandowan, then three-quarters of a mile across the Kashabonne Portage, paddling eight miles across Kashabowie Lake, then across the one-mile Height of Land Portage and into Lac des Milles Lacs. On a map, this part of the journey was one of the hardest, since the Height of Land Portage represented the high point of the watershed boundary between Hudson Bay and the Great Lakes. Together, the first two portages made up one-quarter of the length of all 46 portages between Shebandowan Lake and Lake Winnipeg. The rest, said the map, was all downstream. "Downstream" from Lac des Milles Lacs, however, involved another 15 portages totalling one and a half miles. These stitched together a long succession of lakes, rivers, streams, ponds, marshes, and bogs before getting to Fort Frances, roughly the halfway point to Fort Garry.

If the expedition seemed extended across Dawson's 48-mile road during the first two weeks of July, that paled in comparison to the 160 miles it stretched out on August 2. The first boats with the 60th Rifles got under way on July 16, the last on July 21. The Ontario Battalion departed on July 23 and finished five days later. Then came the Quebec Battalion bringing up the rear, the last of which left McNeil's Bay on August 2.

The main reason the boats were spread so far was to prevent clogging at the portages; built for canoes, only one expedition boat with its dozen men and three and half tons of supplies could get across at a time. By this point, the only thing connecting the expedition was the inter-canoe mail service. As R-SJ described, "Four small canoes are stationed at portages between Shebandowan and Fort Frances and carry the mail bag from one point to the next, where it is taken on by the canoe waiting. The time of departure and arrival is so calculated that under ordinary circumstances a weekly mail service will be in operation between Thunder Bay and here, and by and by, further on."

St. John and Ranoe set off from McNeil's Bay on Tuesday, July 18. Cunningham was delayed a day after Waubussy found the pork supply had gone rancid, forcing the reporter to travel back down to the Matawan Bridge depot to buy more. All three were keen to stick as close to the lead boats as possible because they wanted to "enter Fort Garry with the van." And given the pressure on Wolseley to get the Regulars started back home before freeze-up, the very real possibility existed of the first two detachments pushing on from Fort Frances "without stopping for other detachments." Neither correspondent would see a Canadian soldier again until after they began arriving at Fort Garry on the evening of August 27.

PORTAGING

At the end of Shebandowan Lake, the gruelling labour of the first portage began. The experienced voyageurs used tumplines to haul the heaviest barrels and boxes — some over 300 pounds — the 1,200 yards to Kashabowie Lake. The "less hardy" carried lighter supplies such as biscuits, tea, and camping gear in whatever manner they could, including the modified hand-barrow method where two men transported one barrel between two eight-foot poles, with one man at the rear and the other in the lead. (A few portages on, the barrow method was dropped in favour of tumplines, despite the "perspiration flowing in great drops, and every nerve and muscle quivering as if under the action of a galvanic current.") Once across the portage, the men went back to skid the boats over greasy green poplar logs placed at three-foot intervals. Here, the Regulars had the advantage of experience: they had learned how to portage the boats on the Kaministiquia and Matawan Rivers, and most of the voyageurs, "many of whom are lads," had been assigned road duty since arriving at Thunder Bay.

The *Globe* canoe reached the Height of Land Portage on Thursday, July 21, and started into Lac des Milles Lacs later the same day. Almost

20 miles across, R-SJ said the lake was "so dotted" with islands, "intersecting points and promontories," and numerous straits formed by "the jutting land" that only three or four miles of open water could be seen at any one time. Not surprising, the topography made the map "incomprehensible," and the *Globe* correspondents were soon lost in a landlocked cove they nicknamed Blunder Bay. And they weren't the only ones. As it turned out, the guides weren't familiar with this route (most knew the more northerly Dog Lake one), and a number of the Regulars' boats — those of Lieutenant Colonel W.J. Bolton and Captain Francis Northey — got lost, as well.

SNOW FLAKE

By Monday, July 25, things were looking up. Lac des Milles Lacs and the Baril and Brule Portages were to stern, and both the *Globe* and *Telegraph* canoes were in Windigoostigwan Lake with the lead brigades of the expedition — Cunningham near the van, St. John and Ranoe bringing up the rear. In the late afternoon, the lead boats reached the western end of Windigoostigwan where it emptied into the French River over a series of small rapids "not seven feet in width" followed by a fall of about 40 feet. After Sagers and Waubussy sussed out a satisfactory line, the *Telegraph* went first, shot the rapids, and waited in a small pool at the head of the falls for the next boats. Lieutenant Colonel Randle Feilden's canoe came next. When it reached the pool, the troops unloaded, portaged down past the falls, and pitched camp for the night a bit downriver.

While the *Telegraph* held at the foot of the rapids, Cunningham and crew received company — seven canoes full of Anishinabe. In the first was "Snow Flake, a chief of the Chippewas," and seven "younger Flakes." Cunningham said "old Flake" was smoking so "vociferously" on his pipe that he wondered exactly how much tobacco the man and his family actually smoked in the course of a year. The "young Flakes" had long raven hair arranged "quite touchingly" into neat long braids that fell over their shoulders. The other six canoes were "freighted with as hungry-looking crews as ever sailed on water."

The Anishinabe canoes surrounded the *Telegraph*, and a grand powwow, as Cunningham called it, began with Waubussy at the helm. Everyone spoke at once, Waubussy managing to "keep them all going" with a "wonderful, really incredible versatility." At one point, Snow Flake motioned that he wanted to talk with Cunningham privately. Through Sagers as interpreter, the chief said he was responsible for many people who were starving and wanted Cunningham to give him food. Waubussy and his conversationalists stopped talking to listen in.

"Chief Snow Flake, I am very glad to see you," Cunningham said. "I hope that you will shake hands with me."

The chief shook Cunningham's hand warmly.

"I hope that all your people are in good health," Cunningham continued.

Through Joe, Snow Flake said they were.

"As to your question of food," Cunningham said, "I am sorry to find that our stock of provisions are getting fearfully low. Somehow they are diminishing with a celerity that fills me, not only with alarm but with much amazement. In short, I cannot spare anything. If a plug of tobacco, however, would serve in any way to mitigate your and your people's hunger, you may have it."

Snow Flake expressed "a thousand thanks," took the tobacco, and shook Cunningham's hand once more.

At this point, Lieutenant Colonel Feilden emerged from the portage trail to find out how the boats were proceeding down the rapids. Snow Flake asked Sagers who he was, and Sagers told him the officer was also a chief, whereupon Snow Flake told Feilden through Sagers that he and his people were hungry and needed food.

"I don't have much to give anybody, but may be able to manage a little," Feilden said.

And then "such a scamper took place." The canoes shot across the little inlet "like arrows" and exited the water. The men emptied the canoes, turned them downside up, and scurried off down the portage trail, leaving the women to do the bulk of the work — "packing up the bark and bedding, putting on their packing straps, leaded themselves with a bundle which would have made any ordinary men gross, and each crowning the thing by making the papooses describe a somersault in the air and landing on top of the bundles away they trotted to get something to eat."

That evening, the *Globe* canoe reached the end of Windigoostigwan where "shouts and laughter from the soldiers ahead" could be heard through the trees. Despite the darkness, the *Globe* boat shot the rapids, "bumping ominously" once or twice against the rocks. Then the crew portaged around the falls, re-entered the river, and paddled a short distance around a bend until they came upon Feilden's camp. The river there was "filled with bathers' heads and bottoms," the shore and woods lit bright by the "blaze of camp fires," shouts and laughter echoing off the rocks and trees. The *Globe* crew found a place to pitch camp for the night and settled into preparing dinner over the campfire. Afterward, pipes were stuffed and smoked and the day's run "computed and discussed" until the embers of the fire died down and the night breeze "freshened sufficiently" to keep mosquitoes away. And then everyone sank into the kind of "deep, steady, and refreshing" sleep that can only "succeed a hard day's voyaging."

MRS. FLAKE

The next day, Tuesday, July 26, Cunningham and the *Telegraph* canoe set off down the tree-clogged French River (Dawson's men hadn't cleared it yet). As they proceeded, wood pigeons flapped up from the riverbank, and Cunningham and mates "kept popping away at them in the most persevering manner." And they weren't the only ones — shots could be heard coming from ahead, as well.

Rounding a bend in the river, "the culprits" came into view. Five bark canoes, each containing one "squaw with papoose" and "at least one dog," were pulled up along shore, evidently on a break. Cunningham said the women were smoking in the "most nonchalant fashion," enjoying their reflections "mightily." As the *Telegraph* boat drew near, Waubussy, "with his best foot forward," greeted the women and in a minute or two was at the centre of another grand powwow.

Cunningham thought one of the women was the elder of the group. She was "exceedingly clean and tidy," had a massive string of beads around her neck, was dressed in a "kind of waistcoat," and was crowned with a "gentleman's rowdy hat" that had seen better days. Joe introduced the woman as Chief Snow Flake's wife.

"I am delighted to see you and most happy to make your acquaintance," Cunningham said, presenting her with a small gift of tobacco, which Mrs. Flake accepted "with delight."

The *Telegraph* got under way again, and Cunningham assumed the visit with the women was finished. But no sooner had the *Telegraph* found the current than the five canoes "wheeled to the right" and "came on in line in the rear."

Waubussy was "in ecstasy" and kept up a conversation with Mrs. Flake in the lead boat of the flotilla as they paddled along. Cunningham said he felt "a little uncomfortable" leading a convoy of five Anishinabe women but remembered they were in their own territory and "each carried a musket in her canoe." These, the reporter calculated, made the odds against the *Telegraph* "considerable."

At one point, Cunningham asked Sagers if he thought the women were good shots. Sagers gave him a "sarcastic smile" and said something to Mrs. Flake, who laughed likewise, drew up to the bank, and sent her dog into the bush. Not two minutes later, the dog flushed out "quite a flutter of pigeons and partridges." Each of the women seized a gun and brought down a pigeon. Through Sagers, Mrs. Flake told Cunningham that he was welcome to join in. The reporter did and ended up "bagging four off one tree!" For this, Cunningham gave Mrs. Flake a few beans and then bid farewell once more.

APPARITION

Ranoe and St. John caught up with Cunningham and the *Telegraph* in the late afternoon at a "pretty little campsite" on a sandy beach. After pitching their tents side by side, the men set a table for dinner on one of the tarpaulins while "my travelling companion" — Ranoe — "curried" some of the pigeons they had shot earlier in the day. Cunningham judged the meal "capital" and the dinner party "very pleasant." (While the reporters mentioned this dinner in their respective articles, Cunningham made no reference to Ranoe and R-SJ neglected to say Cunningham was present.)

As the sun set that evening, the reporters enjoyed a pipe around the campfire and then turned in for the night. Not long after, Cunningham said he was awakened by "an apparition" peering through the flap. The figure looked human "but not entirely." The mouth and chin were definitely human, the hair, as well, but not the eyes, nose, or cheeks. These were painted a "deep horrible black." Cunningham jumped up in fear but said something in the eyes stopped him — they seemed timid, tired, and sad.

The reporter screwed up his courage, threw back the tent flap, and found a young Anishinabe girl about 12 years old standing nearby. In her outstretched hand, she offered a tin of blueberries. Feeling as frightened as she appeared to be, Cunningham took the berries and gave her a coin. She didn't move. In the moonlight, Cunningham said she looked so hungry, "so pinched was her cheek," that he went back into his tent and came out with some hardtack.

While the girl ate, Cunningham went to find Sagers and Waubussy. Through Sagers, Waubussy said the girl was an orphan whose parents had recently died. The black face paint was "an Indian custom" used to "signify her sorrow." Waubussy also said Mrs. Flake had adopted the girl out of the goodness of her heart, which Cunningham said moved him to send over a "modicum of tea."

MOST REMARKABLE INDUSTRY

At daybreak the next morning, four of the Anishinabe women "danced out over the lake" in their canoes to catch fish for breakfast while a fifth remained in camp, fetching water to boil the fish and begin packing. Cunningham marvelled at the women's "most remarkable industry." When the others returned, the fish was cooked and dished out with a wooden fork, "chunks to this one and that," until all were served. Cunningham didn't find the meal at all appetizing to look at but did say it had one consolation — "a scientific one" — that fish "by far" is

Deux Rivières Portage, on the Red River route.

the "most effective nourisher of the brain," making these women "very intellectual characters, much above the average brain power."

As the *Telegraph* crew packed up their own camp, Cunningham turned to Sagers. "Why has Mrs. Flake not cooked the beans I gave her yesterday?"

"She dare not."

"What do you mean?"

"She cannot eat the beans until Mr. Snow Flake arrives," Sagers explained.

"But couldn't she cook them and eat them without Snow Flake knowing anything about it?"

"The papooses would tell," Sagers replied, closing the matter.

NEWS FROM FORT FRANCES

On Friday morning, July 29, the *Globe* passengers made their way over the "difficult and severe" Deux-Rivières Portage (750 yards) and launched into Sturgeon Lake just behind Wolseley and his officers, Captain George Huyshe and Lieutenant Frederick Denison. The men had their coats off and were blazing the route, using axes to strip bark off strategically located trees to mark a trail for the boats to come. It was a lesson Wolseley had learned the hard way on Lac des Milles Lacs. Not long after the *Globe* canoe arrived on the lake, a boat came up from the west carrying Wemyss Simpson, the MP for Algoma, and Robert Pither, the Indian agent based at Fort Frances, the Canadian government's envoys to the Indigenous Peoples of the Northwest. The two had left Fort Frances the day before to update Wolseley on the state of negotiations with the groups prior to his arrival.

Simpson said the chiefs from the tribes around Rainy Lake were adamant that their permission was required for the expedition to pass through their lands and for all subsequent immigrants who were bound to follow. Pither said some of the chiefs threatened to withhold their consent, but he told them, "They might as well try to stop the waters of the river as prevent the troops coming through." Pither said this was enough for the chiefs to withdraw their objections. Simpson said the matter of permission for the immigrants was left unresolved. They agreed to come back to the issue in formal treaty negotiations to follow in the spring.

Simpson also delivered a letter from Henry Prince, chief of the Saulteaux and Swampies, which R-SJ included in their August 15 story:

> LETTER FROM AN INDIAN CHIEF
> INDIAN SETTLEMENT, RED RIVER
>
> May 26th, 1870
> To the General Commander-in-Chief of the Red River Expedition.
>
> Sir, — Newspaper reports have reached us that an expeditionary force is sent by our great mother the Queen across the great waters to restore peace and order in our hitherto quiet settlement. We condemn all the proceedings that have taken place against the representative of our great mother who was turned back from Pembina, and heartless and brutal murder

of one of the innocent Canadians, and the imprisonment and ill treatment of our fellow British subjects, both foreigners and our countrymen.

We have suffered in many ways. Anxious for our families, unable to pursue our usual avocations, poverty and want stared us in the face all winter, endeavouring to maintain our loyalty. We shall be greatly relieved when you arrive in our midst, where we are not only ready to receive you with open arms, but shall be most happy to render you what assistance we can, should you require our services. We have done it last winter to Col Dennis, and will always be ready to do it to any of our great Mother's representatives.

We say nothing at present with regard to our lands: we have every confidence in the Imperial and Canadian Governments to treat us fairly as soon as can be done. It is well known we were never treated for our lands, either by the late Earl of Selkirk or the Hudson's Bay Company.

We long to see you come. Come with all possible speed. We shall hail the day that you arrive with your force. You have nothing to doubt or fear from any one tribe of Indians, as well as the Protestant part of the population of the settlement. We ask you to make strict enquiries for the loyal French. A large number have maintained their loyalty at all risks and hazards.

We enclose a copy of the reply we have received from the Vice Consul of the U.S. with regard to the Fenian movement. We have since heard with deep regret that a body of them are waiting on your route to obstruct your way. We hope it is a false rumour.

We will heartily welcome you and your force. Wishing you every success.

> Signed, on behalf of the loyal settlers, Saulteaux and Swampies,
> I beg to remain,
> Your humble and obedient servant,
> HENRY PRINCE,
> Or MIS-KOO-KE-NEW
> Chief of the Saulteaux and Swampies

To R-SJ, Prince's reference to "a settlement for lands taken on the Red River" was "perfectly just and justifiable," and similar claims would continue to be made until settled "in some equitable manner." In a twist of fate, St. John himself would soon be working alongside Simpson and Pither on the negotiation of Treaties 1 and 2.

AN ENGLISHWOMAN AND HER HUSBAND

Finished their briefing, Simpson and Pither pitched in to help Wolseley and his crew blaze trail back to Fort Frances. With tricky sections coming up on Lac La Croix and the eastern end of Rainy Lake that promised to rival Lac des Milles Lacs, Wolseley was glad of the assistance.

On Sunday afternoon, July 31, Wolseley and the lead boats of the Red River expedition reached Maligne River between Lac La Croix and Rainy Lake. A few hundred yards on, they pulled ashore and the guides and soldiers got out to survey the rapids downriver. The military men thought it best to portage around the first couple of sets, but the young Iroquois guides felt confident they could be run, so the boats were unloaded on the shore. Two guides jumped into the first boat — Simpson's large "north canoe" — and poled into the rushing water, followed by two more guides in the *Globe* canoe. The larger vessel disappeared down the run easily enough, but the bowman in the *Globe* stopped the vessel mid-rapid and swung it around, struggling to regain his line in the heavy water. Everyone on the shore thought the canoe "would be lost," but the guides were able to get "the paddles at work against the rocks" and back the canoe over to the better line. Then, with a "loud Ojibway shout of triumph," the *Globe* rushed through the foam and into the small pool of water below. The two boats were brought ashore there, and the rest of the military boats were moved down the rapid in a similar fashion.

The second set of rapids was smaller and was "passed with complete success." On the third, one of the military boats "engineered across the corner of the rapid in some peculiar manner and came to grief," but the soldiers were able to repair the vessel "in time to go on that night."

The fourth set of rapids presented a challenge of a different order. The chute there had a "heavy fall of water" that ended with a "bank of water that rushed along in an angry curl." It wasn't a problem for the high-sided military boats to navigate, but for the canoes with their low gunwales, the curl presented a "rather formidable matter to compete with." The guides walked the length of the rapid a couple of times, "eagerly scanned the rushing, roaring sheet of water," and eventually decided "with the canoe lightened, they could take her down safely." Two guides shoved the *Globe* into the river where the bark vessel "took the current immediately" and shot over the waterfall. It was lost to sight for a few seconds "in the whirl and spray behind," but then emerged right next to the angry curl, which did indeed spill over the side. Other than "having shipped a quantity of water," the canoe was untouched. R-SJ were impressed: "When an Indian, after mature consideration, says he can do a thing of this kind, [we] have confidence in his ability to perform that which he undertakes."

At the end of the river, the little flotilla crossed into the eastern section of the Rainy Lake system where dozens of "interior Indians" — men, women, and children — had gathered on the rocky shores to "see the troops." All three reporters were struck by the people's "chronic state of hunger" and said how difficult it was to make them understand Wolseley's orders forbidding the troops from giving away provisions. And then, just before the entrance to Namakan Lake, the boats came across "a party of the interior Indians" who were "much taken by the appearance of a lady who was accompanying her husband on this journey." At first, the Anishinabe women kept their distance, pointing the lady out to one another, "amused" by something in the lady's "dress or appearance." Eventually, the elder of the group "came and sat down alongside her white sister, and examined her more closely." Pither offered the woman some tobacco, which she "commenced to eat after the manner of others living in towns and villages." Satisfied with the gift, the woman left. No sooner was she gone, though, "than another came and sat down under cover of the umbrella which the Englishwoman had raised."

The encounter put R-SJ in a reflective mood. They said many of the Hudson's Bay men believed the interior Indians "incapable of work" and "entirely unamenable" to any instruction, education, or advice. R-SJ thought this "ridiculous," since the Hudson's Bay men were well known not to have "any great desire to improve the natives of the interior." If they did, the results would "now be different" because whatever the people's faults, "a want of intelligence is not one of them." To R-SJ, the problem boiled down to the fact that the HBC needed Indigenous people to remain in a state of "semi-serfdom." Any effort to educate or train the people would only serve to impair their utility as "cheap hunters" or "out-door servants." R-SJ were hopeful that the sale of Rupert's Land and the forced transition of the HBC into a competitive trading market would remove some of the obstacles to betterment, since "there is very little of which an Indian is not capable if properly taught and governed."

- 14 -

RIGHT-OF-WAY

> It appears that the arrival of Colonel Wolseley and the expedition was looked for by the Indians, not only from a desire to see the soldiers, but for the most interested motive of explaining the price to be paid them for the right-of-way through their country.
>
> — Kate Ranoe and Molyneux St. John, *Globe*, August 4, 1870

The *Globe* and *Telegraph* canoes arrived at Fort Frances on Thursday, August 4, with the first three brigades of the expedition — the *Telegraph* around 6:00 a.m., the *Globe* about five hours later. For months, everyone had looked forward to reaching Fort Frances because it marked the halfway point between Thunder Bay and Fort Garry. Getting this far meant nearly 300 miles of portaging, paddling, insects, and storms were behind them with only a couple hundred miles to go.

As a Hudson's Bay post, Fort Frances was typical — a collection of wooden one-storey houses inside a wooden stockade with some outlying storage huts scattered around. The fort sat on the right bank of the Rainy River with a set of 20-foot falls below. The area surrounding had been cleared and featured "luxuriant grass," a "good field of wheat, barley, and potatoes," and "cattle feeding and lowing near the water." Along the portage from the river to the lake were a dozen or so "Indian lodges" or "wigwams" housing several families of people related to the chief known as Crooked Neck, a very old man, thought Cunningham,

Hudson's Bay Company post at Fort Frances.

"excessively dirty, with his head a little to one side." Nearby was a cemetery with wooden caskets resting on frameworks about seven or eight feet off the ground. R-SJ said these were "the bodies of chiefs and their families." From the fort, a few miles of western and southern expanse "could be appreciated."

On landing, the troops were given a few hours to rest. R-SJ said they "scattered themselves over the place" and bought up "everything that could be found" — fresh milk, bread, vegetables, et cetera. Then they hit the wigwams and bought up as many "stone pipes, bead purses, and similar articles" as would fit in their luggage. After a quick lunch, the lead boats, minus Wolseley, set off down the Rainy River to begin the last stretch of their journey.

INTELLIGENCE, OF SORTS

Wolseley had business to attend to in Fort Frances, the first order of which was to meet with Captain William Butler concerning events in the Red River Settlement, specifically what the expedition could expect upon arrival. Back at Thunder Bay in June, Wolseley had sent Butler ahead to assess Fenian activity in the northern U.S. states and the political and military temperature in the settlement. Butler arrived at Fort Frances just before the boats did on August 4. He told R-SJ he had travelled overland from Thunder Bay to St. Paul and then boarded a steamer to Fort Garry. At Pembina on July 21, Butler said he saw a messenger "gallop off across the prairie" and assumed the man would alert authorities that a British officer had crossed into the territory. Deeming it "wise," Butler and a man he met on the journey — William Drever, John Schultz's friend — jumped "just short" of Fort Garry into knee-deep mud and made for Lower Fort Garry 20 miles away. Butler said he "escaped just in time" and evaded a dozen men dispatched by Ambroise-Didyme Lépine, Louis Riel's adjutant general, to apprehend him. Drever and the luggage weren't so lucky — the former was taken prisoner, the latter confiscated.

At Lower Fort Garry the next day, Butler was told it "wouldn't be safe" for him to remain there, so he moved to "the Indian Settlement nearby." The day after that, July 23, HBC Governor Mactavish's son, John, rode up and told Butler that Riel was "much offended" at him for "having avoided the fort" and asked him to return. Butler said he wouldn't visit the fort "until the rebel flag was hauled down," Drever was released, and his luggage returned. Mactavish said he could make that happen and would send a buggy for Butler the next day.

Butler travelled back to Fort Garry on July 24 but found the "rebel flag" still flying above the fort. He again refused to meet Riel and went instead to the governor's house where he played billiards in the recreation room. At some point, Riel came in, but Butler paid him "no account" and continued his game, "making occasional remarks about it to Riel and others in the room." Butler told R-SJ this drove Riel into "a huff" and Riel stormed out. Luckily, HBC Governor Mactavish intervened, showed Butler's billiard opponent out of the house, and left Butler alone with Riel to talk.

Butler said Riel spoke about his "love of peace" and his "good intentions" and made it clear he was "only keeping the fort until the troops arrive." At some point, Père Lestang, "one of the most active of the rebel instigators," walked in, keen to discuss the possibility of amnesty for the rebels but made it clear they would "welcome the soldiers without it." Butler said he left shortly after "thinking that possibly the peaceable sentiments of Riel might subside and that he himself might be detained as a hostage for the personal safety of the Provisional President."

Captain Butler wasn't the only one waiting at Fort Frances with news from Red River. The Canadian government had hired Joseph Monkman (a "half-blood who'd lived all his life in the North-West country") to provide intelligence, as well. According to R-SJ, Monkman said residents were living "very much as if there was a chance of a private war amongst themselves." As a result, their "intercourse is guarded" and their "ordinary pursuits" weren't being carried on as normal. Monkman said most settlers were afraid that if St. Boniface Bishop Alexandre-Antonin Taché were to allow a man such as Père Lestang "to threaten resistance to the troops, it is not beyond the bounds of possibility that Riel may be permitted to put these threats into execution."

RIGHT-OF-WAY

While Wolseley was meeting with Butler and Monkman, R-SJ said Crooked Neck and his people spent most of August 4 trying to figure out exactly who to talk to "about the price to be paid them for the right-of-way through their country." They debated between Colonel Wolseley ("evidently a great man"), Assistant Controller Matthew Bell Irvine (with his "vast quantities of pork and flour"), and Captain Huyshe (with his "gold-laced cap"). The group decided Wolseley was the "Shemogeneche Gitchie Okey," and at around 8:00 a.m. on August 5, arrived at the front door of the main building ready to negotiate. Eighteen delegates entered single file behind Crooked Neck and took up positions opposite Wemyss Simpson, Robert Pither, and Colonel Wolseley and his officers. Joseph Monkman and the government's "interpreter" followed. R-SJ said the delegates were adorned in their ceremonial best — ornamented leggings, colourful shirts, a "profuse ornamentation" of beads and feathers about their heads, and a blanket over one shoulder or folded around the body.

The room was a large square space sparsely furnished with two high-backed settees, a simple cupboard, a stove, and a few wooden chairs. Strewn across the plain wooden floor were newspapers, writing pads, pens and ink, caps, satchels, glasses, and other military paraphernalia. R-SJ said that one of the delegates — not Crooked Neck — had been elected spokesman, and he sat down in a chair pulled into the centre of the room opposite Wolseley. The rest of the group squatted on the floor or sat on the settees and proceeded to smoke their pipes. The group watched Wolseley and the interpreter "severely, as if to see that their spokesman's words were given aright, and that their effect was not lost upon the white chief."

R-SJ related the gist of the powwow, which went on for some time. Wolseley opened the proceedings by walking around the room and shaking hands with each member of the delegation. He then returned to his chair opposite the spokesman and addressed the room.

"Although I am very glad to see my Indian friends," Wolseley began, "I am sorry to be unable to provide any presents of provisions. We are hurrying through to Red River and have brought barely sufficient provisions to feed my own men. Mr. Simpson and Mr. Pither, however, have gone down to Canada just yesterday where I have instructed them to make arrangements for some presents to be brought up this fall or next spring."

When the interpreter finished, the spokesman rose and crossed the room to shake hands with Wolseley and his staff again. He then returned to his seat and launched into his own speech in a "loud voice, and accompanied by frequent and violent gesticulation."

The interpreter subsequently translated the spokesman's words. "He says he is pleased to see the Great White Chief, and he desires to express to him the views of his people on the question of payment for a right-of-way through their country. He has seen Mr. Simpson and told him what is required, but he desires to repeat it to the Shemogeneche Gitchie Okey man himself."

The interpreter continued. "With regard to the expedition passing through, this man says he has nothing to say, beyond that his people expected to receive presents this fall on account of it. Their business now, he says, lies with permission needed for emigrants and others to go in. His people are prepared to grant a right-of-way, but the payment for this must be ten dollars a head for each person — man, woman, and child."

At this point, in order to "prevent the possibility of mistake on the score of children," the spokesman lowered his hand "to within a foot of the floor."

Then the interpreter carried on. "As for presents and provisions, this man says it is another thing. Of course, his white friends should send these, but in addition to anything of that kind he says his people require ten dollars a head — not three, as Mr. Pither had offered — but ten dollars a head for man, woman, and child." Here the spokesman's hand went down again to emphasize the point that "the size of the child was not to be taken into consideration when the time arrived for his allotment of dollars." "This man," the interpreter resumed, "says his people are much concerned about the purpose of the expedition. They have many relations in the Red River Settlement and say it would grieve them very much if the troops were to fight with these men."

Next, Wolseley interjected, "Tell this man I can assure him that the expedition is a peaceful one and we will make no aggressive movement on their friends' relations at Fort Garry. And as regards the question of settlers and the right-of-way, I can say nothing as I am concerned only with the expedition."

Wolseley once again apologized for how he was unable to provide any food as presents and added, "As I am compelled to go up the lake, I trust you will excuse me." He shook hands with the group and the meeting ended.

Later that morning, the *Globe*, its crew, and its passengers started down Rainy River for Lake of the Woods. Wolseley followed a few days after the first Ontario Volunteers arrived on August 7.

- 15 -

ON TO FORT GARRY

> We danced over the water and down into the troughs of the sea, keeping pace with the boats that were running under two large square sails, and at midday had passed the Grand Traverse, and many miles, as well, without incurring the fate that had been prophesied for us.
>
> — Kate Ranoe and Molyneux St. John, *Globe*, August 12, 1870

> After leaving the mouth of the Winnipeg River, which entered the lake a mile below the fort, we entered into the southeast corner of Winnipeg Lake itself.... And to look back and see the forty-five boats with all sail out and all in Indian file tripping it gracefully over the somewhat rough sea was a sight worth looking at, and certainly the like of which these waters never saw before.
>
> — Robert Cunningham, *Daily Telegraph*, August 22, 1870

The route from Fort Frances to Fort Garry had four stages: Rainy River, Lake of the Woods, Winnipeg River, and Red River. The first stage, Rainy River, was relatively straightforward — a "languid and lazy" paddle down to Lake of the Woods, about 70 miles. To Cunningham's eye, the river was a relatively "broad stream" varying in width between 300 to 400 yards, with the edges crowded thickly with "reeds, bulrushes, and wild grasses," and had only three portages. The

Hungry Hollow Station for tugs at the mouth of Rainy River.

lead boats of the expedition, with the *Globe* and *Telegraph* canoes close behind, reached the end of the Rainy on Sunday, August 7.

LAKE OF THE WOODS

The second stage of the route involved getting across massive Lake of the Woods — 75 miles long, 70 wide, four and a half times the size of Rainy Lake, the largest body of water the expedition had navigated so far. Since Thunder Bay, the challenge of crossing the great open body of water loomed large in the troops' minds and was amped up at Fort Frances where Anishinabe guides said the crossing would be difficult, since most of the time the boats would be "out of sight of land, with wide stretches of water to the north, south, and west, and the breeze coming on in a moment, raising waves like trees." They said it would be near impossible for the lighter canoes.

Early on the morning of August 7, the lead boats and the *Telegraph* and *Globe* canoes struck out from the dilapidated American trading post Fort Louisa in "a moment of fine weather." Within an hour, though, the vaunted breeze came up and stiffened by the minute until it was blowing so hard that "had we then been ashore we should not have started." But they weren't, and the *Globe* crew tried to capitalize by setting a good-sized sail and "a large umbrella." This carried the canoe "over the tops of waves in a marvellous manner," flying out ahead of the "long, heavy columns" of water rolling up behind and occasionally shipping over the bow and rear gunwales. As they flew along, R-SJ remembered a second umbrella Wolseley had loaned them and quickly set it "as a studding sail." The light barque craft now fairly "danced over the water and down into the troughs of the sea, keeping pace with the boats that were running under two large square sails." Four days of fair sailing allowed the boats to traverse Lake of the Woods to its most northern point at Rat Portage "without incurring the fate that had been prophesied for us."

To help with the intricacy of the lakes, islands, falls, and false passages, Simon Dawson, the Dominion engineer, brought in special guides from the Red River Settlement with local knowledge. These men arrived during the evening of August 8 — but quite by surprise. Cunningham said that a small canoe came around a point slightly downstream from the boats and "without any apparent reason" quickly turned around, paddled back upstream, and disappeared around the point again. The canoe caught the troops' attention. It wasn't like the other Anishinabe canoes they had encountered thus far, since it was filled with men both "red and white."

It was the troops' worst fear — "Riel's advance guard were upon them."

The Regulars pulled hard on the oars in quick pursuit. They rounded the point and spotted the canoe speeding back toward two larger boats. The strangers saw them, too, and began "shouting and discharging their firearms." A couple of officers drew their revolvers, and one of the expedition boats made off to shore to unload pork, flour, and tea in order to get at the arms chest.

Just as quickly as the threat came on, it dissipated. As it turned out, the "firing and shouting were only a salute and welcome" from the guides Dawson had brought in from the Red River Settlement.

THE WINNIPEG RIVER

The third stage of the route from Fort Frances to Fort Garry was the 164-mile-long Winnipeg River, by all accounts the most difficult stretch the expedition would navigate. R-SJ said that calling the Winnipeg "a river" was "a mere matter of fancy on the part of the geographer who did it." In reality, the watercourse was a succession of lakes — some larger than those east of Fort Frances — connected by various chutes, falls, and rapids that descended a total of 340 feet from start to finish. In all, the map said there were 27 portages studding the river; R-SJ expected the number was probably closer to 30 because they had heard that "three of the rapids are so much like falls that they are very seldom 'jumped.'"

The first day of the journey down the Winnipeg on August 11 was for the most part through "smooth water" with only "some short rapids" at Les Dalles, which were run. On the second day, the portaging and rapids shooting began in earnest. At a place called the Grande Discharge, the river narrowed through three deep, heavy chutes. The *Globe* canoe fell behind the others here and ended up taking the wrong chute down. It came through into a "broad sheet of water" ending at an even larger rapid that one of the *Globe* guides refused to shoot. R-SJ tried reasoning with him, pointing out that "even the lady in the boat was not afraid to go." The guide wouldn't budge, so the crew had to find a way back to the main route.

On August 14, the head of the armada arrived at Island Portage, one of the largest on the Winnipeg. Here, the guides held a "great consultation" concerning the "feasibility of the boats running the chute." The chute in question was short and fast, winding through a narrow passage that squirrelled alongside the larger rapid. One of the younger Iroquois guides volunteered to run it and off he went down the rush of water, emerging unscathed, "if not a little wet," from the roiling waters at the bottom. Not to be outdone, some of the braver soldiers stepped forward to take their boats through, as well, with "everyone on shore congregated on the rocks" to watch and raise a shout as each "swept out of the rush into the eddy."

From Island Portage, the route became drudgery again, one portage after another, at some places the water stretching for several miles, at others only 100 yards before the boats had to be hauled out just after they were put in. At one point on Sept Portage, an officer missed a turn and ended up with his boat stuck against a large rock in the middle of the rapid. When he was unable to dislodge his craft either by pole or paddle, the strong current threatened to stave in its hull. The officer tried to lighten the boat by dumping overboard the pork, flour, tea barrels, tin cans, and whatever other articles he could get his hands on, while his crew scurried to retrieve the bobbing contents from the eddy downstream. Just as the officer clutched the arms chest, a boatload of guides drifted up from behind and shoved him off the rock, much to everyone's relief.

FORT ALEXANDER

On Wednesday, August 17, the lead boats and reporters' canoes reached Fort Alexander on the southeast shore of Lake Winnipeg. The men's first priority, as at Fort Frances, was to ransack the Hudson's Bay store. R-SJ reported that "every available article was quickly purchased" — handkerchiefs, knives, sashes, nightcaps, hats, and "a hundred things besides." Cunningham thought the frenzy was "not so much that the articles were absolutely required" but merely "on account of the luxury of spending a little money."

The British soldiers arrived in succession over the next three days and enjoyed "the relaxation granted them here wonderfully." For the first time in almost six weeks, the men could get up in the morning, "loll on the green sward," and not have to think of reloading the boats with barrels of pork, flour, tea, and everything else. All revelled in the fresh beef, new potatoes, and buttermilk. Only men who had been in the bush for six weeks and on rations could appreciate and savour every bit of these provisions. Cunningham said that the men were in great spirits and good health, not one accident having occurred to them, "excepting one of the Red River half-breeds." At one of the portages, this unfortunate voyageur was hauling a pork barrel when he slipped on one of the skids. The barrel "fearfully crushed" the fellow's leg and he was "left behind with a man in charge of him."

For Cunningham, the "greatest attraction" at Fort Alexander was the "immense number of dogs" that congregated there. These weren't stray curs who had wandered in to steal food from the fort; they were trained dogs "employed in winter for drawing sleds" that spent their summers doing nothing except "loafing, fighting, howling, and stealing" to pass the time until seasonal work began again. And they weren't quiet. Inevitably, at night, one of the "brutes" would start up the nightly concert with a "dismal howling," keeping at it until "all of them have taken up the wail" in the fashion of their "Esquimaux ancestors." The concert didn't detract from the affection the men felt for the mutts, nor the mutts for the men, since "some of the favourites" had become "perceptibly fat already." The mutts, not the men.

By Friday, the steady arrival of troops (six companies by then) lent Fort Alexander a more military appearance — "something of a respectable and somewhat more lively aspect," wrote Cunningham. That afternoon, the officers had the men parade and gave them a thorough inspection. While most of the "arms and accoutrement" were found to be shipshape and generally in decent condition given the "amount of knocking about they have gone through," the troops' uniforms were showing signs of wear. Some articles — shirts, jackets, pants — had been "torn to shreds by stumps and barrels." It wasn't a big deal, but some of the men did think it unfair that the clothing given to them was the same "had they remained in garrison."

The Regulars kept coming in throughout Saturday, August 20 — Captain Francis Northey's company first in the late morning, and then around 5:00 p.m., "a large canoe hove in sight." Cunningham said "the greatest excitement prevailed in camp." If it was Wolseley, it meant they would be under way to Fort Garry in a matter of hours. Slowly, the canoe "crept in range of the glasses" and then cries of "It's the colonel!" resounded all around. When Wolseley pulled himself onto the wharf, the Regulars gave him three loud cheers.

After a short conference with his officers, Wolseley issued orders for the Regulars to start for Fort Garry the next day at 3:00 p.m. With only 65 miles to go, Cunningham thought there was "every probability that Fort Garry will witness the arrival of the 'Army of Peace' in two days." R-SJ said that Wolseley held off leaving until Sunday afternoon because he had promised the first two companies of Ontario Volunteers (those of Captains Cook and Scott) that he would wait at Fort Alexander "half a day after the arrival of the last of the 60th" for them to catch up and accompany the Regulars into Fort Garry. All the Regulars, including Wolseley, were impressed with the Ontario Battalion's "pluck and soldiery ability" and thought its participation in the final advance would "add much to the moral results of the entry — looking at it from a Canadian point of view — and probably would prevent a taunt which may be thrown in our face many days hence."

At 10:00 a.m. on Sunday, August 21, the bugle sounded for church parade. Four hundred and fourteen Regulars, "neatly got up in their regular military attire," formed a quadrangle with Wolseley and his staff on the east side. Prayers were read by Father Finn, the resident priest, and Reverend Joseph Phelps Gardiner from St. Andrew's Parish, who had arrived with the Hudson's Bay guides on August 8. Gardiner preached "an eloquent sermon" on the theme of "To him that overcometh," and at the conclusion, an "excellent band, partly vocal and partly instrumental," sang hymns "to the delight of all."

After a quick lunch, the men of the 60th Rifles began preparations to embark on the last phase of their journey: "The boats were loaded — cooking utensils and clothes were packed — last of all the tents were struck." R-SJ said that Wolseley held off leaving until the last moment, but with no Ontario Battalion boats in sight, and the pressure of his timetable increasing by the hour, the Regulars' boats slid off the shore and into Lake Winnipeg at 4:00 p.m. Cunningham said that the dogs were the saddest for the departure and "made their feelings known with loud howling." Near the head of the armada, Cunningham looked back and saw the 45 expedition boats "with all sail out and all in Indian file tripping it gracefully over the somewhat rough sea." The Regulars, together with the *Globe* and *Telegraph* canoes, paddled 14 miles to Elk Island and camped there for the night.

- 16 -

CHIEF HENRY PRINCE

Throughout the day we observed picturesque groups watching the course of the expedition, and here and there a wild-looking Indian in his blanket and leggings would be seen standing next in succession to a young lady whose dress might just have come from Paris.

The ample edifice of the pasture of St. Andrew's gives place in the scene to the whitewashed hut of his half-breed neighbour. A field succeeds a garden, a prairie a field, till houses again take their place in the moving scene, and trimly built, well-finished residences sit side by side with the poor unfinished houses of the Indian farmer.

— Kate Ranoe and Molyneux St. John, *Globe*, August 23, 1807

At dawn on Monday, August 22, the lead boats rounded the southwest corner of Elk Island and pulled hard for the Red River estuary. At this point, a smudge of poplars could be made out far along the southern horizon. These eventually gave way to "low, stagnant marshes and mud banks" marking the estuary. At around 10:00 a.m., the boats entered the Red River proper and set ashore for a quick meal. Our correspondents didn't record much of the day's journey, save for R-SJ noting that "the boats made their largest advance of any single day, a grand total of 44 miles."

The troops pitched camp that night on what Cunningham thought was "the dirtiest, muddiest, and most uninviting spot along the banks of the Red River." As they did, Chief Henry Prince and a delegation of Saulteaux came in to meet with Wolseley. Dispensing with the usual "high-flown compliments and expressions of devotion to the Great Mother," Wolseley got down to business by asking, "Chief Prince, what is it you want?"

Through the interpreter, Prince replied with what Cunningham described as notable calmness. "If the chief was visiting England, he should have considered it his place to have explained his visit. And so, under these circumstances, the chief will be silent and wait to hear the Gitche-okey-man speak."

Cunningham thought that Wolseley was impressed. "Well, if you put it in that light, tell Chief Prince I have received his letters of loyalty and am very pleased. I would be delighted to hear anything further the chief has to say."

"The chief has a great deal to say but will only say now that his soul has longed for the day of meeting with the Gitche-okey-man to explain his desire with which he has been waited for, and the loyalty her red children feels for their Great Mother."

Wolseley was tired and tried to end the conversation. "I have travelled far this day and would like to eat and rest. I would, though, take an early opportunity of meeting the chief again and would make a special appointment for that purpose. In the meantime, I hope that the chief and his young men would also eat before they retire."

The colonel then ordered one barrel of pork and one of flour be provided to Prince and his delegation. "I wish the chief would instruct his people that they should not ask the Volunteers for provisions — they do not speak the language and would not understand the matter." And with that the conversation ended, Chief Prince and his followers returned to their settlement across the river, and Wolseley retired to his tent.

EXCLUSIVE

Always with an eye for a scoop, Cunningham grabbed an interpreter and followed Prince across the river to his village — a collection of about 100 wigwams "laid out in regular order" — to pay his respects to the chief of the "celebrated Swampies." Cunningham said that he found Prince in his wigwam dressed in striped pants and a red woollen shirt. The chief was seated beside his "Queen," who was clad in a "blue calico with yellow spots — the pattern of 50 years ago." When Cunningham and the interpreter entered their home, Prince rose, "wiped his right hand on his trousers," and shook the reporter's hand. Cunningham was impressed — "Prince is one of the finest men, physically speaking, I have ever looked at. He has a noble head, large vivacious eyes, a chest like an ox, and the muscle of a prizefighter."

Prince invited Cunningham and the interpreter to take a seat on the mat with his wife and children. They were tucking into the pork and potatoes Wolseley had presented. Cunningham said that he and Prince talked "a great deal," mostly about "the land question."

"The chief would like to know how much Canada is going to give the Indians for the land," Prince said through the interpreter.

"What particular land is the chief referring to?" Cunningham asked.

"The chief says the whole of the province of Manitoba."

Cunningham replied that he was "staggered" by the answer. "Tell the chief I haven't the slightest idea of to what extent Canada might be inclined to fork out, or whether she means to fork out at all or not."

The reporter signed off for the night by saying from what he had been able to gather, the Métis and Saulteaux "not only lay claim to the territory" but also regard the Hudson's Bay Company as "having acted quite illegally in giving grants to anyone." Cunningham said he would have to "learn more about this afterward." He took the commitment seriously. In 1872, Cunningham ran for Parliament on a promise to force the Dominion government to "come to prompt and generous arrangements with these tribes. Any delay on this head would be dangerous and shabby economy would be folly."

STONE FORT

On Tuesday, August 23, with 30 miles to go, the expedition pulled up stakes from their muddy campground and started "a little before four o'clock" on the cold, chilly morning. The soldiers were on tenterhooks — "more nervous by the mile as they approached the great unknown at Fort Garry." Their apprehension began to subside as the rising sun promised a "warm, dry day" and the muddy banks filled with settlers, Saulteaux, and Métis who had "come down to the edge of the water to fire salutes and wave signs of welcome to the troops." Children waved, women shook their kerchiefs, and men fired off volleys in salute. At some places, R-SJ said, whole villages of 40 to 50 Saulteaux turned out to sit on the banks of the river in front of their wigwams, "dressed in blankets of every colour, with leggings of an equally bright appearance, and such bead and feather ornaments as each one possessed." The women and children generally squatted on the ground, while the men "stood draped in their blankets, as if models for a sculptor." R-SJ thought it all had a quieting effect — the soldiers relaxed and "evinced the pleasure with which they witnessed these greetings."

As they passed by, Wolseley and his troops tried in vain to gather intelligence about what to expect at Fort Garry. No one seemed to know anything other than that "Riel was carrying provisions in large quantities out of the Fort [including] one hundred and sixty-five bags of pemmican." Similarly, the locals seemed surprised that the expedition was so near. Chief Prince, in fact, had made the point the previous day that "he did not know we were in the river until he saw us round the point."

At around 10:00 a.m., the expedition reached Lower Fort Garry — a.k.a. Stone Fort — where a large, welcoming crowd of "Indians, French and English half-breeds, and pure-blooded British and Canadians" had gathered to give the troops a "right royal welcome." Flags flew "from every elevation," and the church bells rang. Cunningham said that the reception was welcome tonic for the weeks and weeks of travelling through the wilderness: "We had at last come once more in contact with civilization and Christianity."

At Stone Fort, the enlisted men lit their fires and started breakfast, while Donald Smith, the Dominion government's envoy, invited the officers to dine up in the main hall. After they "demolished a substantial and luxuriant breakfast," Wolseley and his officers spent the next few hours reorganizing the battalion for the final approach to Fort Garry. Most of the provisions — the pork, flour, and tea — were taken out of the boats and put in storage at the fort. The force was also converted into various landing parties: an "advanced guard" was created from one of the brigades, B Company was "transformed from voyageurs into riflemen" and sent on ahead along the west bank of the river, a third unit was established as a mounted troop in Red River carts, and a fourth was turned into a mounted unit of 30 men under Captain Nesbit Willoughby Wallace's command. This last featured a mounted signalman and bugler. A fifth unit — composed entirely of Wolseley's intelligence officer, Captain William Butler — was sent off with a 16-shooting repeater "somewhere doing something for our security," wrote R-SJ.

Wallace experienced "some little difficulty" in organizing his *"corps d'observance,"* mainly because it was unclear who could ride. Said R-SJ: "One man, when asked whether he could ride, said yes in a prompt and decided manner, but, being given a horse, endeavoured to scramble up on the wrong side and became involved in difficulties with the tail and crupper; another, hardly less confident, said that he had never tried to ride, but that he had no doubt he could. His efforts were scarcely more successful."

Eventually, all was ready and the force moved upriver, the land-based "gallant protectors" out front, careening behind house and garden, reappearing farther up the road. As they proceeded, Wallace's population of ponies grew as "fresh captures were made" and "fresh men mounted." R-SJ said that most of the little ponies were mares and nearly all had foals "running at their heels" so that "one saw swinging across the prairie a long straggling animal running with her foal, and a rifleman with his rifle on his back holding on to the saddle."

At St. Andrew's parish, the 50 boats came to a small rapid that everyone tried to run at the same time. Cunningham wrote that there was an abundance of "shouting and a noise of poles and oars driving against the rocks and shingle, and a whirr of the water, and the clamour of many voices uttering and repeating inharmonious orders." On the banks above, the good people of St. Andrew's watched the proceedings, the women and children waving their kerchiefs, "a token of welcome to those who have come so far to relieve them."

And so the expedition continued upstream, field succeeding garden, prairie replacing field, "till houses again take their place in the moving scene." With so many hours spent organizing at Stone Fort, though, darkness came quickly and the battalion was forced to come ashore seven miles short of Fort Garry to pitch camp one last time. Wallace's troop established a picket and posted sentries, with orders to detain anyone attempting to pass through their line. Cunningham said about 50 "nocturnal visitors" were apprehended. R-SJ said that these were "really held as prisoners" and remained in custody until morning. So much for Governor General Young's mission of peace.

- 17 -

TAKING FORT GARRY

The morning was raw and wet and chill, but, somehow, everybody's spirits were wonderfully up — for Fort Garry was all but in sight, and the reward of our arduous labours was about to be reaped.

— Robert Cunningham, *Daily Telegraph*, August 27, 1870

For a few minutes the hope was high that Riel would fight. The gate which the force approached was shut, a large gun was mounted *en barbette* over it, and not a sign of a man could be seen. Riel rose in the estimation of the men. They had feared, during their long months of daily toil, that when Fort Garry was reached there would be nothing for them to do. The sight, therefore, of the closed gates, the gun, and the marked silence that reigned around led them for a moment to believe that Riel had been maligned and that there was more in him than people thought.

— Kate Ranoe and Molyneux St. John, *Globe*, August 24, 1870

As midnight approached on Tuesday, August 23, a "drenching storm of rain and thunder" came on and "saturated everything most effectually" in camp. Cunningham judged it "by far the most severe storm" they had encountered since Thunder Bay. Throughout the night, lightning flashed brilliantly, thunder shook the muddy ground like an earthquake, and rain fell torrent upon torrent. The storm was relentless.

At 4:00 a.m., the bugles sounded to start the final day, but since the camp was "going the amphibious pretty successfully," Wolseley pushed departure off till 7:00 a.m. Fortuitously, the rain stopped briefly, permitting the troops to gulp a quick breakfast and pack up camp. Then they loaded the boats one last time.

The rain began pounding again as the force pulled upstream. R-SJ said that everyone was "in a state of mystery" as to what to expect at Fort Garry. All were confident of entering "as conquerors, but ignorant as to whether they were to fight or take possession peaceably."

At 8:30 a.m., Wolseley ordered the boats ashore two miles north of Fort Garry at Point Douglas. The troops disembarked and assembled in battle formation on the brow of a hill just above the river, which Cunningham said they ascended "knee-deep at every step." Wallace's advance guard, now converted to skirmishers, "loomed ahead in the mist." Next was Wolseley and his staff, "dripping from every seam of their waterproof coats" and mounted on what horses Wallace was able to scrounge. Then came the main body of the battalion and the Engineers and Artillery with two carts limbering cannons. Captain Francis Northey brought up the rear with a small guard. To the right of the force gathered "a number of horsemen having some indirect connection with the expedition," and scattered all around were a number of "hangers-on," including Hudson's Bay men clothed in their standard-issue "blue-clothed, brass-buttoned capotes."

When all was ready, Lieutenant Colonel John McNeill galloped off to "close the skirmishers" and the main body marched forward "in fours from open column." With all the rain, the road was near-impassable — "thick black mud, ankle-deep at every step," wrote R-SJ. Near Winnipeg, about 600 yards north and just east of Fort Garry, a number of "spectators and followers" had come out to offer encouragement and guesstimates about where Louis Riel was and what he was doing.

At this point, Wolseley ordered the battalion into open column with "the hope high that Riel would fight." All could see that the north gate of the fort was shut, "a large gun was mounted *en barbette* over it, and not a sign of a man could be seen." For a moment, R-SJ said it seemed "Riel had been maligned and that there was more in him than people thought."

The soldiers marched stoically toward the fort, encouraging one another on with cheers of "He's going to fight!" A couple hundred yards off, Wolseley ordered a halt and sent John McNeill, William Butler, and Frederick Denison to ride forward and put eyes directly on the fort. They galloped off around the perimeter and everyone held their breath, but Denison returned just as quickly with news that the south gate was wide open and there was no sign of activity within. Wolseley ordered Wallace's skirmishers to establish a perimeter around the fort and not let anyone in or out. When the perimeter was set, Denison, Butler, and McNeill rode back around to the south gate, followed by the rest of the force.

As the soldiers marched, R-SJ said they "cast glances up and down as if to seek the best spots for storming." But there would be no fight

Fort Garry, Rupert's Land.

Inside the walls at Fort Garry.

today. Writing later in the day, R-SJ commented that witnesses saw Riel and 60 of his men leave the fort and cross over to St. Boniface about 15 minutes before the troops entered, roughly the same time as when the force met the crowd of well-wishers near Winnipeg. The thick mist shrouding the fort and prairie that morning had camouflaged Riel's escape from the advancing army.

The soldiers rounded the last bastion and the band "struck up a quick-step" as they passed through the south gate and formed into companies on the main quadrangle. Once assembled, Captain George Huyshe, with McNeill and Butler, hoisted the Union Jack from the flagstaff while the band played "God Save the Queen." The ceremony ended with a 21-gun salute. It was the same spot where Riel and Donald Smith had addressed the inhabitants of Red River just seven months previously.

WHERE'S RIEL?

The question on the minds of everyone, of course, was "Where's Riel?"

With the flag raised, Wolseley ordered the fort searched for "arms and men." R-SJ accompanied one of the search parties and reported the fort to be in a "dreadful state of mud and dirt." In the main dining room, they found "the undeclared remnants of the Riel's breakfast" on the table. Next door, in a room used for a study, a variety of papers was found littering the table — "Canadian statutes, encyclopaedias, and other books, together with printed proclamations of Riel's, and the proclamation sent into the settlement by Colonel Wolseley." Cunningham followed another group to Ambroise-Didyme Lépine's room and discovered the table in "complete breakfast array, only some of the coffee cups were half empty while some of the plates had only been tackled with and nothing more."

Within a couple of hours, Lieutenant James Alleyne of the Royal Artillery finished taking stock of the guns and munitions found. Cunningham reported the inventory as follows: 40 side arms, 47 muskets, two one-pounders, six six-pounders (iron and brass), seven three-pounders, four three-pwounders carriage-mounted, and one nine-pounder. All the guns were loaded, "some to the muzzle," and Cunningham said that Alleyne thought they had been loaded within the week. In addition, 300,000 rounds of ammunition and 100 barrels of powder were discovered. Cunningham believed that if Riel "had had the courage and system to use, he could have blown the whole 60th into the water." He said "some of the artillerymen" were of the opinion that had the "brass guns alone been planted outside the walls, loaded with canister and fired off, the battalion and all belonging to it might have been blown into the river."

Other than their breakfasts and papers, the soldiers found no sign of Riel or his lieutenants. R-SJ confirmed two days later, "on reliable authorities," that Riel and his men had "crossed the bridge over the Assiniboine" just as the expedition was "passing between the town and the fort." They said Riel watched "the Union Jack being hoisted from Bishop Taché's front porch and the firing of the salute" and remained there for the remainder of the day and the next.

The search for Riel and his men ended in the middle of the afternoon, August 24. At that point, Alleyne had his artillerymen hauled two of the captured brass six-pounders outside the walls, fired a second "royal salute," and gave three cheers for the Queen and three for Wolseley. As Cunningham wrote, "And so ended the taking of Fort Garry."

PART IV

Reign of Terror

- 18 -

INTERREGNUM

> With this Bill in one hand, and the flag of our country in the other, we can enter, not as conquerors, but as pacificators, and we shall satisfy the people there that we have no selfish object of our own to accomplish, that we go there for their good as well as for our good.
>
> — Adams Archibald, Debate on the Manitoba Bill, May 1870

While Molyneux St. John was fighting fires on the shores of Thunder Bay back in May, Adams Archibald, Member of Parliament for Colchester, Nova Scotia, was named lieutenant governor of Manitoba and the North-West Territories. Archibald had distinguished himself in debate over the Manitoba Act with calls for compassion and tolerance in the Red River Settlement. He agreed that law and order needed to be re-established and the "supremacy of the national flag" vindicated. But rather than establish military rule, as many indignant Ontarians were righteously demanding, the lanky and likable Nova Scotian argued that the Dominion had a "stern duty" to show all residents "their fears are unfounded, that their rights shall be guaranteed, their property held sacred, and that they shall be secured in all the privileges and advantages which belong to them." The speech impressed many, including George-Étienne Cartier. In the wake of the debacle of William McDougall's appointment as lieutenant governor, Cartier believed the new man in that position had to

Sir Adams Archibald.

be independent from local affairs. Governor General John Young swore Archibald in at Niagara-on-the-Lake, Ontario, on July 27. Two weeks later, he and Young travelled by special train to Collingwood where they and 60 "excursionists" boarded the *Chicora* for Thunder Bay. Just before departing, Young addressed the "townspeople and farmers of Nottawasaga" and described Archibald's task as "indeed an arduous one." But he said he felt the new lieutenant governor's "calm judgment and tried ability" would guarantee "the unhappy differences of the past will be forgotten and that all classes will unite in the furtherance of the common good, and in the innocent rivalries of peaceful industry." On August 12, Young saw Archibald off from Shebandowan Lake for Fort Garry, 10 days behind the Quebec Battalion.

Until Archibald arrived, Wolseley's orders regarding civil authority in the settlement were clear: the laws of Rupert's Land, and the authority of the Hudson's Bay Company to administer those laws, were to remain in force. Wolseley's own authority was limited to command of the expeditionary force. And so Wolseley asked Donald Smith at Fort Alexander to assume the role of acting governor of Assiniboia until Archibald arrived. Riel's departure and evident collapse of the Provisional Government simplified this decision: to him, there was no other authority to turn to.

Almost immediately, the fragile arrangement was put to the test. As Lieutenant Alleyne's men searched Fort Garry for arms and men on August 24, R-SJ said that a group of "loyalists" arrived and asked Wolseley to issue warrants for the arrest of "Riel, O'Donoghue, and others on charges of false imprisonment." Wolseley deferred to Smith, who issued the warrants "under the older form of the judiciary," but was unable to execute without willing and able magistrates. Cunningham said that as fast as Smith swore in special constables, they resigned "one after the other, as fast as they are called upon to act." Cunningham ascribed the resignations to "a fear of Riel and his friends."

This was the first symptom of what R-SJ described as "an entire absence of all law and executive" in the period leading up to Archibald's arrival. In Cunningham's words, "as far as law, order, and government is concerned, [Wolseley] is trusting to luck and getting on as best he can."

WINNIPEG SANDWICH

Some time after taking control of Fort Garry on Wednesday, August 24, the soldiers, voyageurs, scouts, and guides were paid. With cash in hand, a large number went into Winnipeg to drink and debauch. As Cunningham wrote, "It was so long since the men had tasted liquor that all who could, troops or voyageurs, went off to make up for lost time." In short order, the "Winnipeg liquor" succeeded in "overturning the strongest head and demoralizing the steadiest legs" and the muddy

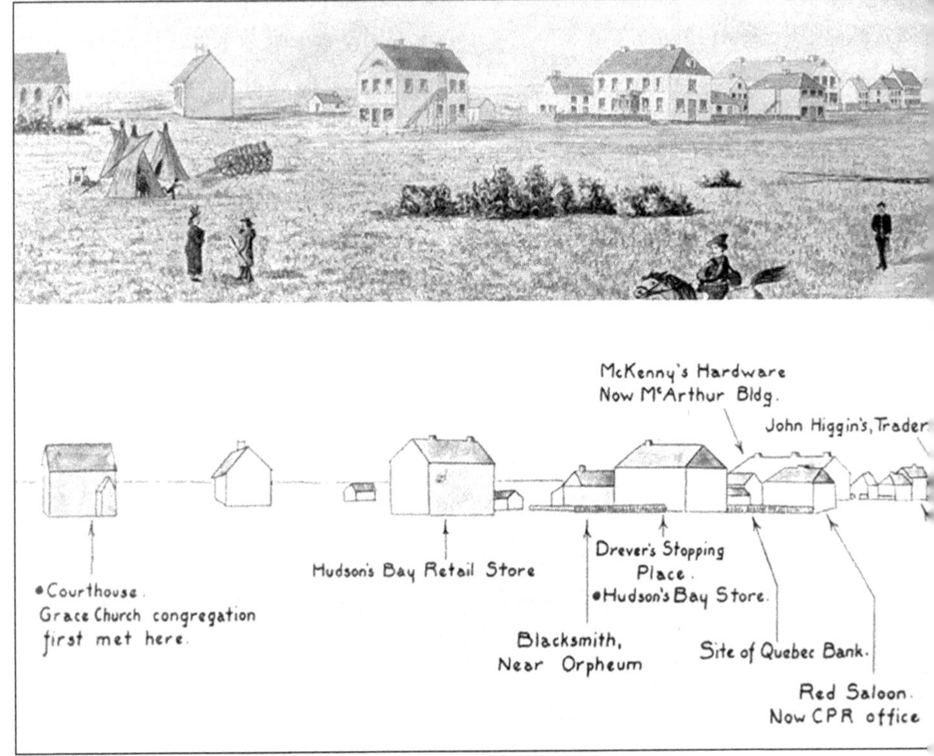

Main Street, Winnipeg, 1870.

streets were filled "with recumbent figures sandwiched in Winnipeg earth." Cunningham explained: when the drunken men fell down, "one side became a large cake of mud," and when they struggled to regain their footing, they inevitably fell over on the other side sheathing it in mud, as well. On Thursday morning, Cunningham reported the 600-hundred-yard road between Winnipeg and Fort Garry to be "fairly populated" with bleary-eyed troops and voyageurs "encased in thick, hard coatings" from which they were "with difficulty released."

On Wednesday night, Cunningham also reported the assault of Father François Xavier Kavanagh of St. Francis Xavier by "someone on horseback." Travelling from Winnipeg to White Horse Plains, the stranger asked Kavanagh, "Who the devil is out on the road so late?" Kavanagh identified himself and the "highwayman" shouted back,

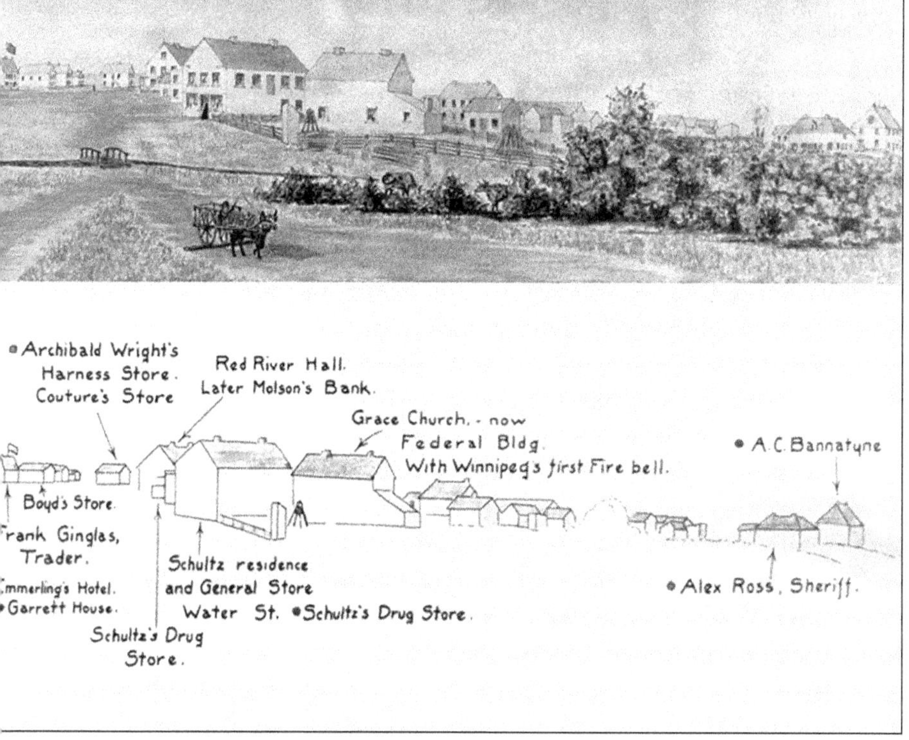

"Damn your eyes, take that!" and fired his pistol into the air, causing Kavanagh to fall off his horse and injure his arm.

The expedition men set out from Fort Garry again on Thursday afternoon to assault the taverns and saloons of Winnipeg, but Wolseley ordered guards out to bring them in. Wolseley's authority, though, extended only to the troops — Cunningham said the voyageurs, scouts, and guides persisted in being "hopelessly drunk." On Friday morning, the road between Winnipeg and the fort was again "strewn with sleeping beauties" who had "fallen by the wayside in two's and three's and there lay regardless of gibes, kicks, and in fact all mundane considerations."

While the beauties slept on Friday morning, Bishop Taché crossed the river from St. Boniface to meet with Donald Smith and Wolseley at Fort Garry. R-SJ said that Taché wanted to discuss the "great fear" the

French-speaking residents had about the impending arrival of the Ontario Volunteers and the "difficulties" they expected with them. He also wanted to discuss reports that a priest "had been shot at." Wolseley responded by issuing orders prohibiting his officers from "going out shooting." Smith responded, as well, issuing a proclamation on Monday, August 29, banning the sale of liquor between 7:00 p.m. and 6:00 a.m. and posting special constables in the village to help keep the peace. By that point, R-SJ said that prohibition wasn't necessary, since "the liquor is fortunately coming to an end, the price is high, and money is beginning to be scarce."

In Winnipeg, Cunningham reported that "utter confusion" continued on Friday night when Alfred Scott, one of the three delegates sent to Ottawa to negotiate Red River's entry into Confederation in the spring, was "taken by the heels and dragged through the mud of the principal street of Winnipeg." By Saturday, Cunningham said, the English residents of Red River had become disgusted with Wolseley. They insisted he "had no authority in the country whatever — that he had no authority even to retain prisoners taken — that he had no authority to capture Riel." The French-speaking Métis voted with their feet. According to Cunningham, "The French half-breeds have scarcely shown themselves at all in Winnipeg since the arrival of the troops." And evidently for good reason: those few who had come into town "have got soundly drubbed," making "police arrangements" for the protection of these "kindly, simple people" who were without crops, furs, or prospects for the coming winter "much called for."

DEPARTURES AND ARRIVALS

The first companies of Ontario soldiers began arriving at Fort Garry in the evening of Saturday, August 27. The next morning, the Regulars commenced preparations to leave, starting on Monday. Wolseley had the following address read to the Regulars at the church service on Sunday:

> Fort Garry, August 28th, 1870
> To the Regular Troops of the Red River Expeditionary Force:

I cannot permit Col. Feilden and you to start upon your return journey to Canada without thanking you for having enabled me to carry out the Lieut.-General's orders so successfully.

You have endured excessive fatigue in the performance of a service that for its arduous nature will bear comparison with any previous military expedition. In coming here from Prince Arthur's Landing, you have traversed a distance of upwards of 600 miles. Your labours began with those common at the outset of all campaigns — namely, road-making and construction of defensive works. Then followed the arduous duty of taking the boats up a height of 800 feet, along 50 miles of river, full of rapids and numerous portages. From the time you left Shebandowan Lake until Fort Garry was reached, your labour at the oar has been incessant from daybreak to dark every day. Forty-seven portages were got over, entailing the unparalleled exertion of carrying the boats, guns, ammunition, stores, and provisions over a total distance of upwards of 15,000 yards. It may be said that the whole journey has been made through a wilderness, where, as no supplies of any sort were to be had, everything had to be taken with you in the boats.

I have throughout viewed with pleasure the manner in which the officers have vied with their men in carrying heavy loads. I feel proud of being in command of officers who so well know how to set a good example, and of men who evince such eagerness in following it.

Rain has fallen upon 45 days out of the 94 that have passed by since we landed at Thunder Bay, and upon many occasions officers and men have been wet for days together. There has not been the slightest murmur of discontent heard from any one. It may be confidently asserted that no force has ever had to endure more continuous

> labour, and it may be as truthfully said that no men on service have been better behaved or more cheerful under their trials arising from exposure to inclement weather, excessive fatigue, and the annoyance caused by flies.
>
> There has been a total absence of crime amongst you, during your advance to Fort Garry, and I feel confident that your conduct during the return journey will be as creditable to you in every respect.
>
> The leaders of the banditti who recently oppressed Her Majesty's loyal subjects in the Red River Settlement having fled as you advanced upon the Fort, leaving their guns and a large quantity of arms and ammunition behind them, the primary object of the Expedition has been peaceably accomplished. Although you have not, therefore, had an opportunity of gaining glory, you can carry back with you into the daily routine of garrison life the conviction that you have done good service to the State, and have proved that no extent of intervening wilderness, no matter how great may be its difficulties, whether by land or water, can enable men to commit murder, or to rebel against Her Majesty's authority, with impunity.
>
> (Signed)
> G.J. WOLSELEY, Colonel
> Commanding Red River Expeditionary Force
> Fort Garry, 28th August, 1870
> (Signed) Geo. Huyshe, Captain

On Monday morning, "in the quietest manner possible," Captains Calderon and Wallace readied to depart with their companies back down the Red River. The only glitch was the reluctance of a certain black bear to board Wallace's boat. At some point, someone had given the beast to Wallace as a gift and Wallace's crew was adamant it could be harnessed to help haul the boats across the portages. R-SJ reported that the bear exhibited "the greatest disinclination" to get in Wallace's boat and "coercion being accompanied with the probability of serious personal inconveniences, no man felt any great anxiety to become bear leader." With time ticking by, a few "brave souls" tried to coax the creature aboard, but it got free and "a chase through the camp immediately ensued." Eventually, the troops cornered the bear and somehow inveigled it aboard. R-SJ said that the bear looked "very miserable and uncomfortable as the boat shoved off, but not more so than the voyageur whose duty in the bow compelled him to sit by the side of the strange passenger."

The Regulars staggered their departure over the week — the last of them left on Friday, September 2, and the Artillery and Engineers on Saturday. By this point, all the Ontario Battalion was at Fort Garry and most of the Quebec Battalion was at Stone Fort. R-SJ said that the Volunteers were "very free from serious illness, and as soldiers, are in capital order."

After September 3, the only British troops remaining in Red River were Wolseley and his staff — Lieutenant Colonel W.J. Bolton, Lieutenant James Alleyne, Lieutenant Heneage, Assistant Controller Matthew Bell Irvine, and Assistant Commissary George Alfred Jolly. They intended to stay another week to see Archibald installed and finalize winter arrangements for the Volunteers (contract for provisions, ensure construction of winter quarters was completed, instruct the Volunteers "at gun drill," et cetera). And then this last group planned to take John Snow's road to the North-West Angle and catch up with the rest of the battalion on Lake of the Woods. Bolton rode out on September 3 to see how far Snow's men had progressed. For the most part, he found the road in decent shape — "a capital prairie road" for 78 miles, but afterward, 33 miles "more of woods, mud, and brûlée that offer the most formidable obstacles to a through journey." Bolton was optimistic that the route would be "passable" in a week or 10 days after the crews "opened up with axe and spade."

On September 7, Bolton left Fort Garry with a group that included Kate Ranoe. Back in Toronto a month later, she would describe this part of the journey in an exclusive for the *Globe* (see "A Lady's Journal"). Wolseley caught up with this group on September 11.

A LADY'S JOURNAL

By the time Kate Ranoe returned to Toronto in October 1870, she was a seasoned war correspondent and deft travel writer. And yet, save for one Globe *article published on October 31, 1870, there is no record of Ranoe ever publishing again. Below are some key passages from Ranoe's account of the first portion of her journey home from Fort Garry to the North-West Angle via John Snow's road.*

FROM FORT GARRY TO TORONTO: A LADY'S JOURNAL

Having accompanied the Red River Expedition through their long and toilsome journey to Fort Garry, witnessed the many obstacles that had to be overcome, shared in the difficulties and dangers of the Winnipeg River route, its foaming rapids and rocky portages, and seeing the impracticability of the latter portion of the route for purposes of regular travel, one can imagine that it was with feelings of great interest that I listened to the various descriptions of the new road leading from Fort Garry to the North-West Angle of Lake of the Woods.... The descriptions we received of the new road were so varied and perplexing that, womanlike, I became curious and expressed a wish to make my homeward journey by the new route; for I thought that, however hazardous a journey it might prove, it was well worth the venture, and that if even I suffered a little inconvenience, so great is the charm of contemplating new scenery, and so invigorating is the Gypsy-like life one has to lead in travelling through a new country, that fatigue is easily endured.

We left the landing place on the right bank of the Red River, opposite Fort Garry, at half-past nine, having taken a long time to get the carts and horses ferried across.... After riding 15 miles, we found a pool of water and therefore camped for dinner. Two more carts had joined our party; one was driven by a French half-breed, the other contained his wife and beautiful baby, as fair as a lily. The woman seemed a little astonished to see me, but with that innate politeness so characteristic of our neighbours, she did not wait to stare, but at once came up to wish me *bonjour* and to show me her baby, of which she was evidently very proud. She seemed to pity me for not being equally fortunate. She took it for granted that madame had not any children; for if she had a family, she would certainly not ride about and travel so many miles simply for the sake of seeing the country. Evidently, not a women's rights woman — the acquisition and the establishment of a new province was nothing to her. She was, notwithstanding this drawback, a nice, intelligent, kind-hearted creature, and we were much indebted to her at nightfall.

The rule of the expedition — an excellent one — was to camp at sunset; but [next day] we were in search of a pool of water that had been much lauded, and therefore disobeyed orders, and should have suffered in consequence but for the thoughtfulness of the French half-breed's wife.... One by one the stars peeped from their hiding places, and a faint pale ray of light in the deep blue heavens gave us hope that the moon would soon rise. We were just thinking that we should be obliged to camp for the night and dig for water when we saw a bright spark and a thin column of smoke curling up in the distance. We all rode to the spot as quickly as possible and found that the French half-breed had, at his wife's request, remained behind to kindle a fire for us near the much-desired pool of water. The chosen spot seemed all we could wish, except the much-lauded water, which was decidedly muddy.

My small tent was at once pitched for me, the baggage carts were drawn up in a line, and the horses let loose.... Huge logs of wood were brought from all sides, and we were soon seated around a blazing campfire. Our home for the night was certainly most picturesque, and we forgot the fatigue of the day in the perfect beauty of the present scene.

At about half-past nine [the next morning], we reached the pretty village of Oak Point and were now 33 miles from Fort Garry. Here the various farms and cottages, with their neat gardens, had a bright want-nothing look about them. The farmers were evidently blessed with thrifty wives, for butter, milk, and eggs were to be had in plenty, and all good of their kind. After riding a few miles through the bush, we came to a large, well-built house, the property, I believe, of Mr. Snow, the surveyor of the road. The house was empty, but it had such a comfortable look about it that we all stopped to peep in at the windows. There was a nice stove in the kitchen, and had it been dinnertime, the temptation to enter the house by the window and make use of it would I fear have been irresistible. Contenting ourselves, however, with a drink of good water from a stream which flowed near the house, we cast our house-breaking intentions to the winds and continued our journey.

We camped for that night at Broken Head River, about 46 miles from Fort Garry. When I got down from my supposed place of comfort, I quietly resolved never to ride in a springless cart again if I could possibly help it; every bone in my body ached! Fortunately, a night's rest does wonders, and I was rested and ready for an early start the following morning.

[The next day we] camped at nightfall, all well satisfied with the progress we were making. We had just finished supper when Colonel Wolseley and Mr. Irvine drove up to our camp; they had left Fort Garry early that morning and driven 76 miles in one day. The same distance had taken us three. It must be remembered that the men of our party had to march, and that the pace of the cart horses was not a fast one.

....

The next morning [the road] ended at White Birch Lake. Here we had to leave the carts, the baggage they contained being placed on eight pack horses.... Whilst we were waiting, a party of Indians came up, a chief's son, some children, and two squaws.... The youngest of the two women was the only wife of the chief's son. On one occasion her husband, returning from one of his journeys, brought home a companion for his wife, doubtless in his own mind calling her Mrs. Squaw No. 2. The pretty squaw objected to this intrusion into the family circle, and on the same evening, cut her rival's fishing net into stems, tore her hair, and fairly beat her out of the camp. In mere justice, I am bound to admit that the intrusion was no fault of the intruder. Yet, as a woman, I must add that I respected my dark sister for intuitively knowing, this early, the rights which civilization would accord her, though I did not admire her manner of enforcing them.

After about an hour's ride (or rather walk), we felt that we were approaching the open swamp [at the western end of Lake of the Woods]. Each minute the ground became softer and softer, and our difficulties of progression rapidly increased. My poor horse stumbled continually and became so restive as to be almost unmanageable. Owing to the narrowness of the path, my long skirt was perpetually caught in the branches of the trees, and I expected willy-nilly to be dragged off my saddle. My hands were so fully occupied that I longed for a supplementary pair where with to protect my head and eyes from the outstretching branches. A fashionable chignon would have been in perpetual danger.

We were obliged to camp for the night on a granite island at the edge of the swamp, not more than five miles from White Birch Lake, a short day's journey indeed; but man and horse could do no more, and even the little woman of the party, though anxious to show how great were the powers of endurance of her sex, was forced to admit she was fairly tired out and would, but for the kindness of the superior beings who had promised to take care of her on the road, and who sought by every means in their power to save her each moment's fatigue, has lain down on the bare rock and, womanlike, has cried herself to sleep, too weary even to unpack a blanket.

The distance from Fort Garry to the North-West Angle has been described as 90 miles; for those following the footpath, it was over 100, and the last 30 miles undoubtedly difficult to pass; but it must be remembered that even with the disadvantage of crossing an unmade road, the journey from Fort Garry to Thunder Bay is shortened by eight days.

As we crossed Lake of the Woods [the next day], the three large boats filled with Dawson's men passed us.... The *Globe* canoe, in which I spent so many happy and eventful days when accompanying the expedition to Fort Garry, had in the kindest manner been placed at my disposal for the return journey.

- 19 -

GREAT FEAR

> I must confess that almost up till now I have had a prejudice against [John] Schultz I don't know why. Probably it was that I never met him before, but since I have met him here, he gives me the idea that he is a man, not only to lead, but to be followed. And from the influence he has with the people, and the way they look upon him as their champion, combined with his noble, manly bearing, it is little to be wondered at that Riel and his party were so anxious to put him out of the way.
>
> — Robert Cunningham, *Daily Telegraph*, September 6, 1870

> It is a great pity that the 60th are withdrawn from Winnipeg this winter.... The Volunteers are excellent men, and, it is hoped, are well-disciplined soldiers; but it is impossible to disguise the fact that very little provocation would be necessary to create a disturbance in which Ontario or Quebec Volunteers would take part, and which might end only in bloodshed.
>
> — Molyneux St. John, *Globe*, August 27, 1870

The departure of the British troops stoked "great fear" in locals about the Dominion army. R-SJ said that both English- and French-speaking residents believed the Regulars embodied the Queen's authority and as such could be trusted as they were "without any partisan feeling in local matters." The same couldn't be said of the Canadian soldiers. While the Volunteers might very well turn out to be "well-disciplined soldiers" and "excellent men," R-SJ wrote that "very little provocation" would be needed to draw the Ontario and Quebec Volunteers in and "which might end only in bloodshed."

Cunningham was also worried about provocation and bloodshed. On September 3, he wrote that he "no longer felt safe" — stores and houses were being "broken into and goods stolen," drunken revellers were "firing off their revolvers at midday on the open streets," and four fights broke out in the streets before 11:00 a.m. And to top it off, John Schultz's father-in-law, James Farquharson, offered a public reward "of twenty pounds each for the capture of Riel, O'Donoghue, and Lépine." R-SJ said that "there never was such a chaos of public sentiment, such a muddle of political affairs, as now exists in Manitoba."

Archibald's arrival on Saturday evening, September 3, proved to be little balm. In the afternoon, Wolseley had ordered the guns out and an honour guard to parade "about the hour at which he was expected." But Archibald didn't arrive until 8:00 p.m., by which point the guns and guard had long been removed. Only Donald Smith and Colonel Wolseley came down to the wharf to welcome the amiable Nova Scotian "on his safe arrival," and then they "quickly disappeared inside the fort." Except for a salute at eight the next morning, "all other ceremonies are deferred until next week."

JOHN SCHULTZ

Archibald and the Volunteers weren't the only arrivals in Red River the first week of September. On Sunday, September 4, John Schultz, James Lynch, and the other "refugees" who had spent the previous months stoking indignation across Ontario arrived home, and, in R-SJ's words, "commenced to work."

Schultz's first order of business was to attend a meeting at St. John's Cathedral that Archdeacon John McLean had convened to draft "an address to be presented to the lieutenant governor." According

Dr. John Christian Schultz, Senator.

to Cunningham, McLean opened the meeting by declaring that as a member of the clergy he had "no peculiar desire" to "mix himself up with politics" but did think "the time had now arrived when the laity ought to take political matters into their own hands." McLean then read a draft of an address to Archibald that had been "circulated round the various parishes."

R-SJ mentioned that the address was more of a "formal document intended merely to welcome the arrival of the governor" and made no reference to "the misdeeds of Riel or the expectations of the English settlers." As Cunningham reported, this prompted Schultz to the floor to tell the audience that he found the archdeacon's aphorism *ne sutor ultra crepidam* to be a "capital one" but hinted "henceforth the clergy had better mind their own business and leave politics alone." Schultz then moved to strike a committee to draw up a new, more substantial address to the lieutenant governor with respect to "affording redress to those who have been injured and protection to others who may have been compelled to act against their better judgment." He then charged the committee to meet at his house that evening and continued talking about Thomas Scott at some length, saying he wanted Scott's body disinterred and a "Christian" burial provided. The resolution carried unanimously.

Later that evening, "quite a party" turned out at Schultz's house. "The doctor" started the proceedings by calling on supporters to "demand the body from Mr. Donald Smith" and then deputized James Lynch, Michael Power, and William Farmer to deliver the following message to Smith:

> WINNIPEG, September 5, 1870
> *To Donald A. Smith, Esquire, Governor Hudson's Bay Company, and Acting Chief Magistrate of the District of Assiniboia*
>
> SIR, — A large meeting was held tonight of the comrades and loyal friends of the late Thomas Scott, who was so barbarously murdered outside the walls of Fort Garry on the 4th of March, 1870. After mature consideration they have deemed it their duty to approach you as the acting Chief Magistrate of the Province, and to ask to be allowed to receive at your hands his remains, so that they may give to them a Christian burial, which surely at least is due to him who died for his Queen and country.

A Committee appointed by the meeting will be at the Fort at 9:00 tomorrow morning to receive the remains.

(Signed) JAMES LYNCH, M.D. On behalf of comrades from Town of Winnipeg
MICHAEL POWER On behalf of comrades from Headingley
WM. A. FARMER On behalf of comrades from Portage la Prairie

THE STORY OF THOMAS SCOTT'S DEATH

At John Schultz's Sunday evening meeting, Cunningham met Reverend George Young, the Methodist minister who had ministered to Thomas Scott while he was imprisoned at Fort Garry. Cunningham said that Young — "a more kindly, warm-hearted, generous, truthful man does not live" — had promised Scott he would "give a true statement of the case to the people of Canada," and "preferring me and the paper I represent," gave the *Telegraph* reporter an exclusive. Cunningham promised "a simple story" free from "anything of rhetoric flourish, or grandiloquent misstatement."

Young began by setting the record straight. Contrary to public opinion, he told Cunningham, Scott wasn't "taken in arms" by Louis Riel and his men on December 7, 1869. He had been at Schultz's house that night when Riel's men surrounded it and marshalled the 50 or so men and women inside up to Fort Garry. Young maintained that Scott, "with that chivalrous spirit which probably cost him his life," went to the fort of his own accord to ask Riel to allow the women and children to leave, and it was at that point Scott was taken prisoner.

On January 23, Scott said that he escaped with Schultz and a few others and made it to Kildonan where they made plans to rescue the remaining prisoners and overthrow Riel. The group returned to Fort Garry on February 15 but were overtaken by Riel's forces and Scott was thrown back in jail. According to Scott, Schultz escaped capture and made his way on snowshoes to Lake Superior and eventually to Ontario.

The Sunday after Scott was re-imprisoned, Young was called to Fort Garry to pray with the prisoners "as was his usual custom." It was at this point that Young learned Scott was "in irons" and in solitary confinement. Young asked the guards to see Scott and was led to a "bare, cold room" where Scott had only "one blanket to keep him warm."

Once inside, Young asked Scott, "Why have you been placed in solitary confinement?"

"I don't know," Scott replied. "Yesterday it was very cold and I was trying to get near the stove to warm myself when one of the guards with insulting language ordered me off. I reasoned with him, and while we were talking, O'Donoghue came up and asked why I was making so much noise, I replied that I was not making much noise and said that though I was a prisoner I ought to be treated with common civility."

O'Donoghue told him, "Prisoners don't deserve to be treated with civility." Then Scott was put in solitary.

The following Thursday, Young was at home when a messenger came from the fort and told him that "a prisoner who was to be shot tomorrow at noon" wanted to see him. The minister hurried to the fort and found Scott still in solitary confinement, although moved to a room with a bed, a candle, and writing supplies.

Scott told Young that he had complained to Riel about his trial — "it had not been a fair one." He said it had been conducted exclusively in French and he didn't understand what charges had been brought against him. Scott said that Riel told him, "Five of the six counsellors concurred in condemning me."

"If I have done anything worthy of death," Scott replied, "I am willing to die, but it is hard that I should have to die for the blunders of the Canadian government."

Young then asked Scott, "Do you fully realize the perilous position you are now in?"

"I do," Scott replied. "But will they dare to do it? They have the power to do it, and they hate me enough to do it, but will they *dare* to do it?"

Young stayed for the evening and Scott told him how he wanted his personal belongings dispersed after his death. After that, Scott asked to be alone for the night, so Young went home to spend a sleepless night.

Early the next morning, Young returned to the fort resolved to find clemency for Scott. The minister talked to Donald Smith, Père Lestang, and even Riel himself. In the last conversation, Young asked Monsieur le Président if he would spare Scott's life.

"No," Riel replied, "he is a bad man and has insulted the guards. He has had a fair trial. Five out of six of the Council of War have found him guilty, only one objecting, and with tears in their eyes condemned him to die." Riel then asked Young, "Does Scott not really think he will be shot?"

Young told him, "It is hard for him to believe it."

"What, does he not believe me?"

Young said he pleaded with Riel that even if Scott's sentence couldn't be commuted, he should receive at least another day of life.

According to Young, Riel thundered in response, "What, is he not penitent? Is he not prepared? Go and tell him from me that he has got to die in an hour. Have you got a cross, Mr. Young? You should get a cross, and hold it up before his eyes. That would impress his mind."

Young went back to Scott's room and waited for the dreaded hour. At a few minutes past noon, and then a few more, the pair had "some faint hope" that Riel had agreed to Young's request. But to no avail — Riel's men entered the room shortly after twelve, tied Scott's arms behind his back, and put a white veil over his head. Young said that Scott called out, "O, this is awful."

The minister asked the guards to give them a couple of minutes to say a final prayer, and the guards agreed. The two then knelt on the floor and Young "prayed fervently." When the guards returned a few minutes later, Scott asked if he could say goodbye "to the boys." The guards consented and showed Scott downstairs to where the rest of the prisoners were held. As Scott descended, he said to Young, "This is a cold-blooded murder. Be sure and make a true statement."

After Scott said his goodbyes, the guards led him out the main south gate of the fort and a few paces along the sleigh track. Shortly, one of the guards told Scott to halt. Young asked the guards for another few moments to pray, which was granted.

When Scott and Young finished their prayers, they rose and the minister told the prisoner that he had to leave. Scott asked Young to draw the veil tighter over his eyes. The reverend did so, then said good-bye, turned back toward the gate, and asked the guards once more for clemency.

"Please, give the prisoner one more day," Young pleaded with the officer commanding the firing party.

"No," replied the officer. "His time is come. He must die."

O'Donoghue was at the gate when Young got there. The minister tried one last time. "This is a terrible thing. Try to get it put off for a day. I know your influence is sufficient if you will use it."

O'Donoghue was unmoved. All he admitted to was: "It's gone very far."

Young then heard a volley of shots. He turned and saw Scott "fallen forward on his face in the snow." Young rushed back and found the man's right shoulder "twitching violently."

One of the executioners pronounced, "He is dead."

A second said, "Put him out of his misery."

A third said the same, while a fourth took out his revolver, "pointed it close to Scott's head, and fired."

Young asked Riel to provide Scott's body for burial later in the day. At first, Riel agreed but then changed his mind and "distinctly refused." Young then asked two members of the Provisional Government (Bob O'Lone and Alfred Scott) to intervene, which they did. Riel agreed that if Young were to guarantee that "everything be done quietly," he would transfer the body. But the remains were never transferred. Young said he learned later that Ambroise-Didyme Lépine, the adjutant general, claimed the body and had his men conduct the burial in secrecy.

The next day, Young ran into Riel and asked if Scott would be the last execution. Riel told him, "I don't know. I don't know. Some of them are almost as bad as Scott. Some of them are very bad men. One of them is now before the council. He may go, too. His name is Parker."

Young thought if Bishop Taché hadn't arrived back in Red River shortly after the Scott incident, "there would have been a series of murders."

At 9:00 a.m. on Monday, September 5, John Schultz's deputies — James Lynch, Michael Power, and William Farmer — arrived at Fort Garry to formally request that Donald Smith provide the body of Thomas Scott. R-SJ said that the acting governor told the delegation he was deeply sympathetic with "the spirit which may be presumed to have prompted the request," but regretted not being in a "position to comply with their desire."

Smith then tried to bury the request in red tape. He told the delegates they first needed to "establish their claim" to Scott's body and possessions "by deposition before a magistrate." After that, they could make an application to "the authorities of the Province of Manitoba" for permission to search and, if found, recover the body. Smith told the three men he himself was "entirely ignorant of the spot in which the remains were deposited."

- 20 -

NO SELFISH OBJECT

> The fate of this country is in the hands of its own people. Let wise counsels prevail. Let the people devote themselves to the task of developing their great resources in a spirit and with an energy worthy of the mighty heritage which has fallen to them, and we may fairly hope for that blessing which a kind Providence seldom withholds from efforts well-intentioned and well-directed.
>
> — Adams Archibald, Inauguration Address, September 6, 1870

The morning of Tuesday, September 6, was "miserable wet, muddy, and unpleasant." It was particularly so for Thomas Spence, editor of the pro-Métis *New Nation* and one-time business associate of John Schultz. According to Cunningham, who got the story from Spence's landlady, Spence woke at 9:00 a.m. to a "heavy foot" on the stair leading to his room followed by a "heavy hand" on the door handle. Spence said that it opened, and Schultz, backed by two "associates," filled the frame.

Spence was startled. "Good morning, Doctor," he said nervously.

"Get up," Schultz barked, patting a dog whip under his arm.

"Ha-ha," Spence murmured, laughing uneasily. "I am glad to see you back again, Doctor. Have you been quite well since you left?"

"Get up," Schultz repeated, still patting the whip.

Spence told Schultz, "You have no right coming into my bedroom in this way and had better get out."

Schultz held his ground and told Spence to get up once more. Spence didn't move, so Schultz grabbed the bedclothes, threw them on the floor, and "administered in the coolest possible manner — one-two-three-four-five-six — lashes on the all-but-nude carcass of the editor."

Spence howled and then yelled at Schultz, "If you had come alone and I was armed, you would not have dared do such a thing."

"In the coolest manner possible," Schultz then "pitched a revolver on the mattress." Spence grabbed the gun, and Schultz told his associates to wait downstairs. When they were gone, Schultz told Spence to "get up" again. Spence froze, and Schultz once more "went 'one-two-three-four-five-six' over his loins." Finally, Spence jumped out of bed, left the gun on the pillow, pulled on his pants, and "suffered himself to be half pitched down the stairs." There, Schultz was able to force Spence to scribble out "a humble apology" for supposedly insulting Schultz's wife while Schultz was away in Ontario. In public, Schultz maintained that the whipping was entirely about the insult and had "nothing to do with politics at all" — like the fact that Spence, a one-time ally of Schultz, had become the editor of Riel's *New Nation* in late March 1870.

Wrote Cunningham: "Thus rather auspiciously was augured in the 6th of September 1870, the date marking the confederation of the Province of Manitoba with the Provinces of the Dominion."

FIRST LEVEE

Despite the inclement weather and mud on Tuesday, September 6, throngs of Manitobans from north, south, east, and west gathered with local clergy and military on the front lawn of the governor's house to celebrate Adams Archibald's swearing-in. The ceremony itself began just after 1:00 p.m. in the governor's drawing room with George Hill, Archibald's private secretary, administering the oath of office. Beside Archibald stood Wolseley and HBC Governor Mactavish's private secretary, Joseph Hargrave; on his left were Donald Smith and Bishop Taché. After Archibald took the oath, Smith read an address to Archibald "on behalf of the Members who constituted the Council of Assiniboia":

> May it please your Excellency:
>
> We, the members that constituted the Council of Assiniboia, nominated by the Governor and Committee of the Honourable Hudson's Bay Company, desire to welcome your Excellency on your arrival in this country to assume the office of Lieutenant-Governor.
>
> We would express the hope that you may personally enjoy your residency amongst us, whilst we rejoice to believe, from the general approval which your Excellency's appointment has met with, that your services are likely to be of great value to this country at the present delicate and critical juncture.
>
> Your Excellency may rely on receiving from us individually as private citizens, our best assistance in your administration of the affairs of the country; and as those who were formerly accountable under the Governor appointed by the Honourable Company, for the direction of affairs, we venture to assure your Excellency that notwithstanding the events of the past year you will find the people of this country loyal to Her Majesty, obedient to the laws, and ready to support your Excellency in the just administration of them.
>
> We look forward to a rapid change in the circumstances of this Province from the opening up of the country, and the development of its resources, and we feel sure that its union with the Dominion of Canada will greatly promote this result. We would, therefore,

> express our pleasure at this union being now happily secured, though we are not unmindful of many acts of kindness shown from time to time by the Honourable Company to this Settlement.
>
> We would, then, in welcoming your Excellency amongst us, hope that your Excellency may see a large development of the resources of the country, while it is under your charge, and we pray that, by the guidance and blessing of God, wise measures may be adopted, and peace, plenty, and prosperity be the results.

Smith then introduced the council members who were present: the Right Reverend Bishop of Rupert's Land, Robert Machray; the Right Reverend Bishop of St. Boniface, Alexandre-Antonin Taché; magistrate and justice of the peace Robert McBeath; William Fraser from Kildonan; magistrate Pascal Breland from White Horse Plains; magistrate Salomon Hamelin from St. Norbert; and Thomas Bunn, former secretary to the Provisional Government.

After shaking hands, R-SJ said that Archibald read out his reply "in such a manner that each sentence carried its intended weight and left the same impression on the hearer that would have been conveyed had the reply been made verbally, and as the impulse of unrestrained feelings":

> GENTLEMEN, — I thank you sincerely for your kind and warm welcome. Your assurance that I may rely upon your assistance in the administration of the affairs of this country, rely upon the assistance of the gentlemen who constituted the late Council of Assiniboia, an assistance the value of which I do not underrate, gives me encouragement to hope for some measure of success in the government of the country. Of this at least let me assure you, my whole time and any ability I may possess shall be devoted without reserve to the one object of promoting the best

> interests of this vast Territory; and I shall endeavour to act in such a way that the approval with which, as you have kindly reminded me, my nomination as Governor has been generally met, shall not be found to have been wholly undeserved.
>
> Now that the Province has been incorporated I am sure it will partake of the prosperity of the older communities politically joined to the other Provinces. New routes of communication will soon be opened up. The telegraph system, extended to this place, as it shortly will be, will give you hourly communication with Canada and Europe. The highway and the telegraph will remove the isolation in which you have been kept hitherto by the boundless prairies of the south and the impassable swamps and lakes of the east.
>
> I most cordially concur in your hopes that, under the guidance and blessing of God, wise measures may be adopted which may be followed by peace, plenty and prosperity.

At the end of his speech, Smith led Archibald and the group onto the front lawn for what R-SJ described as the "pump-handle ceremony." The soldiers were introduced by Wolseley, the civilians by Smith, the clergy by Taché and Machray. According to R-SJ, some of the crowd were polite, remembered "the number that were to follow," shook hands, and moved on. A few took Archibald's hand "as if they were afraid it would bite." And a not unsizable portion "took advantage of the opportunity to see what the new governor was like and only relinquished their hold as they were desired to pass on to the left."

Wolseley then showed Archibald to the parade ground at the south end of the fort to review the soldiers. As R-SJ reported, the Ontario Battalion "turned out in remarkably fine order," presented arms as they proceeded onto the ground, and then opened ranks, which Wolseley and Archibald "passed through" on their way to some assembled chairs. The battalion formed an open column with three guns at the head and "closed to quarter distance column" going by the lieutenant governor "at the double." The battalion ended by "deploying into line and advancing in slow time for the general salute." R-SJ thought that Archibald was impressed — the Volunteers' movements were "one and all executed with a regularity and precision that does infinite credit to the regiment, and every day adds to their efficiency." Cunningham felt so, as well. He overheard Archibald remark to Wolseley: "If I had not been told they were Volunteers, I would have taken them for one of the finest battalions I have ever seen in the English army."

Not everyone in Red River attended the installation ceremony. Around Winnipeg — and even down around the fort — some had been busy posting "placards of a character calculated to disquiet certain persons." One featured a "picture of a man hanging," with wording to the effect that this was the "proper fate of Thomas Bunn." Another asked: "What should be done with the consort of murderers?" A third threatened Riel's friends with "a tar barrel and a liberal supply of feathers." In response to rumours of lynch mobs and house torchings, Wolseley agreed to Archibald's request for pickets to be set up throughout town to ensure the peace. And then, in the midst of all this, reports reached Winnipeg that Riel had arrived at Pembina. Cunningham said that a messenger reported the former president had "lost his horse on the way and arrived almost bootless and with little food." Riel supposedly told them that "he who ruled in Fort Garry a few days ago is a wanderer, depending for food on two dried suckers."

SECOND LEVEE

Archibald moved quickly to establish rapport with all parts of the Red River community. On Wednesday, September 7, he crossed the river with Hill, Smith, and Wolseley to attend a second levee at Bishop Taché's "palace" in St. Boniface. Compared to the frontier ramshackle of Winnipeg and the militarism of Fort Garry, the architecture of the parish was refined, stately, elegant even. The building stood 60 feet

St. Boniface Cathedral, Red River Settlement.

wide by 150 feet long and had white alabaster-like walls and two huge spires facing west. One hundred yards south was the Grey Nuns' convent and school, an impressive, hip-roofed structure standing two and a half storeys tall.

Taché was waiting on the St. Boniface shore for the ferry to dock. When it did, the bishop greeted Archibald and the others warmly and ushered them to the gardens in front of the cathedral. A band of schoolboys struck up "God Save the Queen" and a salute was fired from a set of anvils out back as they approached. Over the entrance to the garden, an arch bore Archibald's personal motto — *Concordia Salus* and *Palma Non Sine Pulvere*. Taché took the party through the garden, up the stairs, and into the cathedral. Above the main door was a large sign declaring BIENVENUE. Cunningham said that a group of between 50 and 60 Métis crowded around the steps to hear Taché begin the proceedings in his learned French.

> *To His Excellency, A.G. Archibald, Lieut.-Governor of Manitoba and of the North-West Territories:*
>
> May it please your Excellency to permit the population of French origin of Manitoba respectfully to salute in your person the representative of our very

> gracious Sovereign, as well as the distinguished man chosen by the Government of Canada to apply in this rising Province the salutary principles of responsible Government. We are happy to take advantage of this solemn occasion, loudly to affirm our loyalty to Her Majesty and the satisfaction which our entrance into the Canadian Confederation gives us.
>
> Jealous of our rights and liberties, we desire no privileges other than those which the constitution and the laws guarantee to our compatriots of a different origin. We even wish that these distinctions of origin should only manifest themselves in their mildest and most agreeable forms, so that the whole population of Manitoba without any rivalry might form but one and the same people, ready to develop the resources of our common country, and gather the abundant fruits of prosperity which the wise administration of your Excellency shall bring to maturity in this land of our affections.
>
> May it therefore please your Excellency to receive the wishes inspired by the most cordial welcome. May your sojourn amongst us be so agreeable as to compensate in some measure for the sacrifice you incur in separation from your family. Inhabitants of a country where we are compelled to travel much, we well understand the anguish of separation. We also ardently pray for the happiness of those dear to you, and for whose absence you must have such poignant regrets.

Cunningham reported that Archibald looked pleased. When Taché finished, Archibald read his own speech — in French — which he had been working on diligently since spring:

GENTLEMEN,

I receive with great pleasure the kind address of the people of this Province of French origin. It gives me sincere gratification to be assured of your loyalty to the Crown, and of the satisfaction you feel in becoming a part of the Canadian Confederation.

The Constitution which has been conferred on the people of Manitoba places them on a footing of equality with the people of the other Provinces. You enjoy the same rights and privileges, you are governed by the same rules of administration, and you must accept the same responsibilities. Your prosperity in the future must depend mainly upon the wisdom with which you exercise the powers so liberally conferred upon you.

I entertain the strongest hope that, in the exercise of the functions devolving upon the people of the Province under that Bill, they will indicate the soundness of the policy which has tended to them, at so early a stage of their political life, all the privileges of a self-governing community. I shall look to the people of all classes, irrespective of origin or race, to unite with me in my efforts to preserve the peace and good order of the community, to maintain the supremacy of the law, and to suppress disturbances and disorder of all kinds. So far as matters of civil government are concerned I shall know no distinctions. It shall be my study to treat you all as one people — alike interested in the prosperity and development of our common country.

Give me then loyally your confidence. Let us work together for the good of the Province. With this as our aim and object, we may fairly promise

> ourselves in an era of progress and prosperity such as the country has not yet seen.
>
> Accept my thanks for your kind wishes towards those who are near and dear to me by ties of nature.

After the speeches, Taché led Archibald and the others back to the garden for musical entertainment. The band played "God Save the Queen" again followed by "Rule Britannia." The students then "executed a series of glass and catches in a style which, as regards precision and taste, considerably surprised me, and showed that at St. Boniface College there were men who knew how to teach boys." Archibald spoke to a few of the students, and Taché walked the group back to the ferry landing. A second salute from the anvils echoed throughout the late afternoon as the ferry set off and returned the new lieutenant governor and his entourage to Fort Garry.

INTERVIEW WITH BISHOP TACHÉ

After Archibald left, Cunningham hung around, hoping to get a few moments alone with Bishop Taché. The bishop was happy to oblige.

"You know, the *Telegraph* has been terribly severe on myself and the priests," Taché said.

"I'm sorry, but I cannot help that," Cunningham replied.

"You won't abuse us."

"I make it a point not to abuse any man where abuse is not merited. And as regards what I had seen at St. Boniface, I cannot discern anything wherein I could abuse anybody. On the contrary, I have seen much that surprised me and gratified me. But does this address that has been presented today accurately convey the sentiments of the French half-breeds?"

"Decidedly," said the bishop. "As regards myself, I am as loyal a man as is to be found on British territory. My grandfather and my father fought on the side of Britain, and I inherit the loyal spirit that animated them. As regards the French half-breeds, they are loyal to the core and are ready to join hand and heart in welcoming the governor and developing the resources of the country. But they cannot be trampled upon. One of my priests has been shot at. Several of them have been insulted, and I have been forced to bring my nuns who keep the school over the river."

"But why?" Cunningham asked.

"Because," Taché said, "it has been threatened that our house would be burned and murder committed."

According to Cunningham, the conversation went on for some time, with Taché continuing to maintain that "the half-breeds are loyal and that nothing might be feared from them, if they are only treated fairly."

Reflecting on the interview later that night, Cunningham admitted he was "never more disappointed in my life." He had somehow formed the impression that the bishop was "a tall, sour, sinister-looking man" but instead "found him a dapper, medium-sized Frenchman, with a good face and a grey eye, of the most genial expression, and a manner gentlemanly in the extreme." The reporter concluded that Taché was "eagerly anxious to see the history of the Red River Territory buried in oblivion."

- 21 -

VINTAGE WOLSELEY

> The departure of Colonel Wolseley this morning was characteristic of the man. He made up his mind to start at daylight this morning in order to overtake Colonel Bolton's party before they should be compelled by the marshes to abandon their carts and take to pack horses, and though various little difficulties hovered in the distance, threatening to delay his departure, as other departures had been delayed, his nervous anxiety to "get on" anticipated and frustrated what has hitherto proved themselves overpowering.
>
> — Molyneux St. John, *Globe*, September 10, 1870

Colonel Wolseley left Fort Garry early on the morning of September 10. The previous day he had ridden up to Lower Fort Garry to inspect the Quebec Battalion and ensure they were set for winter. Wolseley said he was struck by "the marked improvement in the appearance and bearing of the men," since he had last inspected them in Thunder Bay. The men seemed healthy, having filled out "under the influence of hard work, good food, and abstinence from liquor." Wolseley complemented the officers on "the efforts that must have been made by them in the interval between the two inspections." While "anything but credible" at Thunder Bay, Wolseley told the men they could now "challenge comparison with any regiment of foot in the service." Lieutenant Colonel Louis-Adolphe Casault thanked Wolseley for his kind remarks and said, "The good order of the battalion was attributable to the zeal felt by the officers and men in following an officer for whom they entertained feelings of admiration and respect."

When he got back to Fort Garry, Wolseley drafted an order relinquishing command and wrote a message to the Volunteers. In typical style, the colonel had the address read to the men after he left the next day.

> HUDSON BAY HOUSE
> FORT GARRY, 9th Sept. 1870
>
> FIELD FORCE ORDERS
>
> 1. Col. Wolseley has handed over command of the troops in the Province of Manitoba to Lieut. S.P. Jarvis [actually, Lieutenant Colonel Samuel Jarvis], 1st Ontario Rifles, who will assume command of them from this date.
>
> 2. The following address is to be published in Regimental Orders and read to the men on Church Parade next Sunday.
>
> By order,
> JAMES F. MACLEOD
> Brigade Major
>
> To the Soldiers of the Militia Regiments of the Red River Expeditionary Force:
>
> In Saying "Good-bye" I beg that each and all of you will accept my grateful recognition of your valuable services, and my best thanks for your zeal you have displayed in carrying out my orders. I congratulate you upon the success of our Expedition, which has secured to this country a peaceable solution to its late troubles.

The credit of this success is due to the gallant soldiers I had at my back; upon you fell the hard labour in which officers and men vied as to who should do the most.

Nothing but that "pluck" for which British soldiers, whether born in the Colonies or in the Mother Country, are celebrated, could have carried you so successfully through the arduous advance upon this place.

From Prince Arthur's Landing to Fort Garry is over 600 miles, through a wilderness of forest and water, where no supplies of any description obtainable. You had to carry on your backs a vast amount of supplies over no less than 47 portages, making a total distance of upwards of seven miles, a feat unparalleled in our military annals. You have descended a great river, esteemed so dangerous from its rapids, falls, and whirlpools that none but experienced voyageurs attempt its navigation. Your cheerful obedience to orders has enabled you, under the blessing of Divine Providence, to accomplish your task without, I may say, any accident.

Although the banditti who had been oppressing the people fled at your approach without giving you an opportunity of proving how men capable of such labours could fight, you have deserved as well of your country as if you had won a battle.

Some evil-designing men have endeavoured to make a section of this people believe that they have much to dread at your hands. I beg of you to give them the lie to such a foul aspersion upon your character as Canadian soldiers by continuing to comport yourselves as you have hitherto done.

I desire to warn you especially against mixing yourselves up in party affairs here: to be present at any political meeting, or to join in any political procession, is strictly against Her Majesty's Regulations — a fact which I am sure you have only to know to be guided by.

I can say, without flattery, that although I have served with many armies in the field, I have never been associated with a better set of men. You have much yet to learn of your profession, but you have only to attend as carefully to the orders of the officer whose command I now hand you over, as you have done to mine, to become shortly a force second to no corps in Her Majesty's service.

My best thanks are especially due to Lieut.-Cols. Jarvis and Casault for the punctuality with which they have executed their orders.

I bid you all "Good-bye" with no feigned regret. I shall ever look back with pleasure and pride to having commanded you; and, although separated from you by thousands of miles, I shall never cease to take an earnest interest in your welfare.

G.J WOLSELEY
Commanding Red River Expeditionary Force

At daybreak the next morning, Archibald and a group of Ontario Battalion officers came down to the river to see Wolseley off. As the "first streaks of dawn" rose in the east, and the stars "still visible," the boat "pulled down the Assiniboine, and the colonel and Irvine turned to wave their last goodbye to those on shore."

WOLSELEY EXIT INTERVIEW

Colonel Wolseley reached Thunder Bay on September 22 and had to wait 36 hours for the *Chicora* to arrive. (One can only imagine the consternation.) He made Collingwood on Tuesday, September 27. Waiting for him there was a telegram from Lieutenant General James Lindsay with instructions to report post-haste to Montreal to join him on a steamer bound for England on Saturday, October 1. Fearing he would miss the last train to Montreal, Wolseley had the managing director of Northern Rail requisition "one of the best engines in the rolling stock" to take him to Toronto. The *Telegraph* reported the trip was made "in exceedingly short time, the spin from Aurora [Ontario] being accomplished in 50 minutes."

On board the 7:30 p.m. Grand Trunk Express to Montreal, Wolseley agreed to talk with a *Daily Telegraph* reporter who stayed on "as far as Whitby for the purpose of obtaining information of the expedition." The conversation was reported as follows:

> Reporter: The public here have been very anxious to know from some good authority how the Volunteers conducted themselves on the way up. Can you oblige me with the information, Colonel?
>
> Wolseley: I can, and I shall only be too glad to let the Canadian public know through the columns of your popular journal the high opinion I hold of the Volunteers of Canada. From the day of our departure from Collingwood, I never heard a murmur of disgust. Nothing but the pluck, for which British soldiers, whether born in the colonies or at home, are proverbial, could have carried us through the fearful arduous task. The road, as you know, from Prince Arthur's Landing to Fort Garry is upwards of 600 miles long, one huge wilderness of forest and water. There were no facilities for obtaining supplies. We had to carry our kit and rations on our backs, and carry them we did with the most unflinching ardour. We crossed 47 portages, making a total distance of seven miles, and that is a feat which I believe no military expedition ever performed before.

The obstacles that lay in our way were formidable, but as the Scotch say, "We set a stout heart to a strait brae," and arrived at our destination without any accident of any account. Although I was delighted at the conduct of the Volunteers from first to last, I had expected that some of them would get discontented when the excitement and novelty of the first few days' march had died out. But, no, they kept up their pluck and portaged, canoed, and trudged through wilderness and bush with a cheerfulness that took me by surprise. They were all anxious to measure bayonets with the banditti at the fort, and that made them overcome the difficulties that mightily and daily beset them. As they neared Riel's capital, they grew at times feverish, just as I have seen soldiers when they expected to come across the enemy. On the morning that we sighted the fort, they were in the brightest spirits.

It would have been a sorry day for Masters Riel, O'Donoghue, and company if they had offered resistance. There would have been no holding my men back. When we found the horses gone and the stable empty, a general feeling of disappointment pervaded all ranks, but there was no help for it. We were enthusiastically received by the English settlers, the French hanging back as if ashamed of the part they had played. I had little time to look around me while at the fort, but things seemed to be in a muddled state. However, we worked hard, and after a few days' relaxation, matters settled down quietly.

Reporter: Did the Volunteers conduct themselves well on entering the fort? I mean, did they refrain from putting their animus against the half-breeds in a practical shape?

Wolseley: Yes, they behaved better than I expected. A few got drunk and were put down in the "black" book, but they kicked up no ungainly rows. We had a couple of fights or so, but they originated in drink, and the other spectators quickly interfered and stopped them.

Reporter: Did you see a dispatch in this morning's *Telegraph* giving particulars of the death of the French half-breed Goulet, who was an active abetter in the murder of Scott?

Wolseley: Yes, I read that coming down from Collingwood. I am persuaded in my own mind that he was neither insulted nor driven to death by any of the expeditionary force. My predecessor, Lieutenant-Colonel Jarvis, keeps up a rigid discipline, and I don't think such a sad mistake could have been committed by the Volunteers. I imagine that it was the result of a drunken brawl with the Indians or voyageurs.

Reporter: Do you think the peace of the territory is now perfectly secured?

Wolseley: I think so. Governor Archibald is taking the right steps to bring about a general reconciliation of all parties, and everyone will say that it is to his own advantage to keep quiet and live contentedly. The Indians are perfectly satisfied with what has been done for them so far, and Bishop Taché is doing his best to crush any dissatisfaction that may still exist among some of the French settlers.

> Reporter: Will Fort Garry require a permanent garrison?
>
> Wolseley: No, I should think not. Fifty policemen would be force enough to preserve order. The only difficulty now is that of creating an amnesty to those concerned in the insurrection, and that will soon be remedied.
>
> Reporter: Do you think, Colonel, that the territory is likely to draw immigrants?
>
> Wolseley: I am certain of it. It is really a magnificent country, well adapted in every way for supporting an immense population, and I am sure that it will someday be one of the richest and most populous districts, not only in Canada but in the known world.

....

The Red River Expedition marked the end of Garnet Wolseley's official duties in Canada, which proved formative to the rest of his career. In 1873, he was promoted to major general and led a British campaign to victory against Ashanti forces during the Third Anglo-Ashanti War in present-day Ghana. His officer corps included many from the Red River Expedition, including William Francis Butler. Five years later, Lieutenant General Wolseley led British forces in the final stages of the Anglo-Zulu War in southern Africa. In 1882, Adjutant General Wolseley led 31,000 British troops in putting down a revolt in British-controlled Egypt. Wolseley's last field campaign was in 1884 when, as general, he led an expedition to rescue Major General Charles George Gordon from the besieged Sudanese capital of Khartoum. Recalling the success of Canadian voyageurs in 1870, Wolseley arranged for 390 Volunteers to convey the force's boats and supplies up the Nile

River "as we sent the little expeditionary force from Lake Superior to Fort Garry on the Red River in 1870." While Wolseley finished his career as commander-in-chief of the British Army, many remember him immortalized as "the very model of a modern major-general" in Gilbert and Sullivan's *The Pirates of Penzance.*

- 22 -

CHINESE PUZZLE

> It is pretty evident that Governor Archibald has by no means come to a bed of roses in coming to Manitoba.
>
> — Robert Cunningham, *Daily Telegraph*, September 15, 1870

> It is unfortunate that the inauguration of the new Province is attended by the Chinese puzzle which the Dominion Cabinet devised, and called the Manitoba Bill.... What between an Executive Council, a Legislative Assembly, a Legislative Council that may or may not be continued, and the locking up of 1,400,000 acres of land, the framers of the constitution of Manitoba have contrived to add as many difficulties as possible to the situation.
>
> — Molyneux St. John, *Globe*, September 10, 1870

Three hours after Colonel Wolseley left Fort Garry on Sunday, September 10, St. John reported hearing a "strange, loud noise" coming from outside the south gates. Upon inspection, the noise turned out to be from a group of 40 "Saulteaux engaged in some type of noisy performance." The men, women, and children were "painted and decorated with feathers, beads, thimbles, and similar articles." When the group finished, it marched round the fort to the north gate and sought permission to enter and meet with Lieutenant Governor Archibald.

The delegation was led into the fort by a man on a small pony "who had eschewed his clothing in favour of brightly coloured paints." Proceeding with obvious knowledge of the place, the leader headed for the small garden in front of the governor's house, dismounted, and planted in the middle a brightly painted long staff decorated with hawks' feathers and a "broad band of parti-coloured cloth." The leader mustered the members of the troupe into their proper places — four men in the centre on drum duty, behind them a dozen or so, including five young boys. In between, the leader had the dancers and orators form up.

The painted leader inspected the group, gave a shout, and the drummers began a steady beat followed by the orators and their chants. As these settled into syncopation, the leader had the dancers begin their movements, marked off at intervals by a "synchronized series of shouts." The troupe continued for 20 minutes or so until the paint on the dancers' faces began to run and the musicians "were out of breath." And then, of a sudden, "everybody stopped," gave a "yell of self-congratulation," sat down, and smoked their pipes.

A few minutes later, the leader had the drummers drumming and the dancers dancing again, this time as a prelude to an oratory series. Speaker followed speaker, with frequent interruptions of a loud "Ho," which St. John said was "the Indian" for "Hear, Hear." While there were a lot of them, the length of the speeches was made short by all the "strenuous dancing." St. John was inspired: "If members of some parliaments could be made to perform a mazurka or waltz upon the floor of the house, continuing until the speaker ordered them to stop, how much might be spared to those who are compelled to read the debates?" Throughout the ceremony, the troupe leader walked and clapped and shouted, encouraging everyone to have their best say.

With some predetermined gesture or shout unknown to the observers, the group let out a collective "Ho!" and the formal discussions with Archibald — the grand powwow — began. St. John provided no coverage, except to note "sometime later" that the lieutenant governor brought the meeting to a close with the presentation of "some tobacco, molasses, and flour."

....

"Establishing friendly relations" with Indigenous Peoples was just one piece of the "Chinese puzzle" the Dominion had tasked Archibald with solving. According to the instructions of John Young, the Canadian governor general, Archibald was to "open communications" with First Nations between Thunder Bay and Fort Garry to "secure year-round passage" and "facilitate settlement" on those lands. He was also tasked with figuring out how to administer section 31 of the Manitoba Act, which granted 1.4 million acres to Métis residents. St. John said that uncertainty over property title was the key obstacle holding back "waves of settlers anxious to settle in the province." According to him, "No one can take up land until this question is settled, for no one knows what land will be given away, and no one will run the risk of being turned off his claim."

In the North-West Territories, Archibald was responsible for laying the groundwork for future treaty-making. His tasks there included: describing "the state of Indian Tribes now in the territories; their numbers, wants, and claims"; developing recommendations for their protection and improvement of condition; and figuring out the best method ("by treaty or otherwise") for removing "any obstructions that may be presented to the flow of population into the fertile lands that lie between Manitoba and the Rocky Mountains."

Another piece of Archibald's Chinese puzzle was unravelling the *Manitoba Act* into some semblance of functional government. Archibald's first challenge here was appointing an Executive Council ("the governor cannot constitutionally act without advisers") from a candidate pool drained shallow by the effective disqualification of most capable individuals. St. John said that most people with direct experience in government — either under the Hudson's Bay or the Provisional Government — were regarded by "large sections of the people with distrust" and their appointment would likely "alienate the confidence and support of a large body." On top of this, Archibald had to administer a census, "parcel out the country into electoral districts," and hold elections so "the voice of the country" could be heard. Manitobans didn't wait for such constitutional niceties to voice their opinions on how Archibald and the new government should proceed.

PRETTY STIFF KIND OF STUFF

Since returning from the second levee in St. Boniface on September 7, Archibald was besieged by a steady stream of advice on priorities for the new government. Cunningham said that the Anglican bishop, the Right Reverend Robert Machray, told Archibald they had worked hard to develop a network of missions throughout the province and territories and had made "considerable bodies of Indian converts in connection with them." This gave the Anglican Church "a deep interest in the future of these tribes." The bishop "ventured to express hope" that Archibald's government would take measures "at the earliest convenience" for "entirely preventing the carrying of intoxicating liquors into the interior for traffic with the Indians." In the past, free-flowing liquor had proven to be "a fruitful source of misery and degradation for that people, and a chief obstacle in the way of missionary exertion."

According to St. John, members of St. James parish claimed "no wish to dictate any policy" but were clear with Archibald that they expected the "English-speaking portion of the province — the larger and more influential portion, they said — to be fully and fairly represented in the new government." They were also clear about their "express wish" for a "full and impartial investigation to be made into the disastrous proceedings of the past few months" during which many of "Her Majesty's loyal subjects were seized and imprisoned, the life of one of them cruelly taken, and a large amount of property stolen and made away with."

On Monday, September 12, Archibald met parishioners from St. John's — "the Canadians in the settlement" — including John Schultz. The meeting was fuelled with "the feeling of indignation that has swept over the whole settlement," as Cunningham reported. The delegation told Archibald that it was they who had personally been "subjected to every species of indignity, imprisonment, and losses by men who had no cause of justification; whose sole aim was plunder and indiscriminate robbery; [and] whose political and social influence were of the lost type." They expressed "alarm and indignation" that the "very murderers of the martyr Scott have been released without even the semblance of inquiry" and no steps had yet been taken by either Wolseley or Archibald to "bring to punishment the parties implicated in these treasonable practices." "Pretty stiff kind of stuff," wrote Cunningham. St. John said that Archibald responded by "expressing his determination to preserve order and enforce a compliance with the law" and told Schultz specifically "that on him depended much whether peace and harmony could not be restored."

GRAND POWWOW

About the time the parishioners from St. John's were meeting with Archibald on September 12, news reached Fort Garry of a smallpox outbreak at Carleton House in the future Province of Saskatchewan. According to St. John, "An Indian woman, sick with the smallpox, went into the fort, and numbers of the people residing there caught the disease." The Plains and Woods Cree encamped there vacated "in great fear, and the [Hudson's Bay] Company's hunter being ill the supply of buffalo meat will not be forthcoming, and great privation is expected." St. John said there were also reports of an outbreak at Portage la Prairie, "a place distance about 60 miles from here, and as there are many Indian camps in the neighbourhood of this place, some little alarm has been created." The Anishinabe in and around Winnipeg were prompted to ask for vaccinations "and for vaccine matter to carry to their friends." Cunningham added a week later that "the greatest anxiety" exists in the settlement regarding the smallpox epidemic. He had heard reports that it was "spreading with fearful rapidity and carrying off the Indians by the thousands," and said the authorities had stopped all traffic between the infected localities and those not infected and that American authorities had "stopped the transport of furs."

Prompted in part by news of the outbreaks, Archibald rode out to Indian Mission at St. Peter's on September 13 to meet with Chief

Henry Prince and about 200 of his Saulteaux. Owing to heavy rains, the meeting was held in the parish school.

Through an interpreter, St. John said that Archibald opened the proceedings by thanking Prince and his people for their loyalty to the Great Mother during the recent troubles and then explained his authority as lieutenant governor of Manitoba and the North-West Territories. On the question of settling their land claims, Archibald told Prince that these would be "duly considered at a later period" in light of the more pressing matters at hand, namely the smallpox outbreak. Archibald encouraged Prince to take his people and "make a speedy departure to their hunting grounds" to avoid catching the disease. To that end, he encouraged the chief to tell his people not to visit liquor stores in town "visited by Indians from Portage la Prairie," and for that matter "against the admission of liquor among them at all."

Prince began his reply by saying how glad he was to see the lieutenant governor, whose "appearance, manner, et cetera, assured him that the real representative of the Queen had at length arrived." He assured Archibald that his people were "most loyal" and they "entirely disapproved" of the bad conduct of the men behind the "recent unpleasantness in the settlement." Prince agreed about the "pernicious influence of liquor" and supported Archibald's recommendation that none be sold in their countryside. The chief also agreed that his people should soon leave for their hunting grounds but said it would be useless, since they had no ammunition: they were, in fact, "the poorest people in the territory" despite all the talk about all the land that supposedly belonged to them.

Archibald told Prince he would leave orders at Lower Fort Garry on his way back "for certain quantity of ammunition to be placed at Mr. Prince's disposal." At this point, the meeting concluded and Archibald and his party returned to Fort Garry — only to find it in chaos once more.

- 23 -

ELZÉAR GOULET

> Since I have been connected with the press, I have never sat down to write with a grave feeling of responsibility, feeling a greater necessity for extreme caution, and having as it were a stronger personal interest in what I am about to write, than now.
>
> — Robert Cunningham, *Daily Telegraph*, September 18, 1870

On Monday, September 12, Cunningham rose early "to hire a horse" so he could ride out to Indian Mission to cover the meeting between Adams Archibald and Chief Henry Prince. He crossed the river to St. Boniface and went to the stables of his "old friend Marionne" — the blacksmith he had met back in January. Cunningham ran into "Captain Gay," Riel's cavalry head who was boarding there; Louis Schmidt (undersecretary to Riel's Provisional Government); and Elzéar Goulet, whom Cunningham claimed he "had never seen before" and "knew nothing of his history or the part he had played in the late rebellion."

Schmidt recognized Cunningham from the previous winter and came over to shake his hand. "Ah! And you are Monsieur Cunningham? I know you wrote bad things of us last winter — very bad things."

At first, Goulet didn't say anything, but "latterly came up" and joined the conversation. "I wish, Monsieur Cunningham, that I could speak good English. I wish to say something to you. I wish I could speak to the people of Canada. They say I cut Scott's throat. That is

Elzéar Goulet (1836–70).

a lie. They say I shot Scott through the head. That is a lie. They say I tortured Scott. That is a lie. For after Scott was condemned, I went to Riel and said, 'You must not shoot Scott,' and again and again I urged him not to carry out the sentence, but Riel said it must be done."

Cunningham asked Goulet if he could arrange an interview with Riel.

Goulet told him, "Come with me to Pembina and I will take you to Riel and see you safe back."

"When are you going to Pembina?"

"Now. My horse is ready."

Cunningham said he couldn't go right at that moment. "I have to go and see the meeting between the governor and the Indians at Stone Fort so that I can't by any possibility start before Wednesday morning."

"Well, I shall wait for you. I shall go over to the town on your representation of safety." Goulet then changed the topic. "When is the amnesty coming?"

"Why, I do not know of any amnesty," Cunningham replied. "I do not see the use of an amnesty for such as you. Go to your home, work your farm, and nobody will trouble you. I think you are better without an amnesty than with one."

"But I want to go over to the other side of the river. I have business to do. Then, when I go over, they will insult me and probably attempt to beat me."

"Who?" Cunningham asked.

"Why, the soldiers."

"By no means, any French half-breed ought not to harbour any such ideas," Cunningham insisted. "There should be no 'cross the river' at all. I am sure that not one of the soldiers would molest you in any way if you were to go over."

"Well, then, shall I go over?"

Again, Cunningham dismissed "the idea of any danger of insult or harm in the town." Then he mounted his horse and left for Indian Mission.

POINT OF IMPORTANCE

Cunningham returned to Winnipeg later the next day and learned that "a man had been drowned in the river." He asked around and found out it was Elzéar Goulet. Cunningham was shocked: "I don't know how a murderer feels," he admitted, "but somehow when I heard of Goulet's death, I underwent symptoms the like of which I never experienced before, and the like of which I hope I shall never experience again, for I saw at a glance, that had he and I not met, he might have been safe at home with his family in Pembina."

The first version of Goulet's death that Cunningham pieced together went like this: Goulet went into Winnipeg on Tuesday despite friends urging him not to go, assuring them, "Cunningham said there was no fear and I go now on his word."

After having a drink at one of the local establishments, Goulet made his way to the porch of another tavern and was sitting with the proprietor when an older gentlemen — "a Canadian" — came up, pointed, and asked, "Are you not Goulet who shot Scott?"

Goulet denied that he was, then jumped up and fled with "some eight or a dozen set after him." He "ran along the bank of the river, his pursuers dropped off one by one, until only three were left, and at last he took to the water. But, poor man, he had not swam many yards when he threw up his arms, sank, and never rose again until he was fished up by his friends next morning." According to Cunningham, at least two soldiers were "mixed up in the affair."

Writing a few days later, St. John uncovered a few more details that strongly suggested Elzéar Goulet had been murdered:

> Mr. Cunningham, the special correspondent of a Toronto paper, not aware of Goulet's complicity in the murder of Scott, had engaged him as a charioteer for a trip he was about to take, and told him that he could cross the river without danger of being molested in town. Goulet came over, and while at the door of a house was recognized by a relative of one of the winter prisoners, and pointed out as the man who had bandaged Scott's eyes. From words that passed, Goulet became alarmed for his personal safety, and ran. He was immediately followed, and amongst his pursuers were two men belonging or attached to the Ontario Battalion. Captain McDonald [actually, Alexander Macdonald], of that regiment, seeing what

> was going on, and recognizing one of the men as his own, called him back, told him not to interfere in quarrels amongst the citizens, and sent him [to] bring back the other soldier. Before he reached his comrade, however, Goulet had turned to the river, and seeing men still after him, plunged into the stream, and sank whilst attempting to cross. One of the soldiers followed him, but what then followed forms the subject of two different accounts. It is alleged on one side that the civilian and one of the soldiers threw stones and sticks at Goulet as he was swimming, and that one hit him on the head; whilst the soldier who followed him into the water denies the charge, and says that, seeing the man in the water, he followed in order to save him.

RUMOURS AND RECRIMINATIONS

By Tuesday night, September 13, rumours swirled in the settlement that Robert Cunningham had "decoyed" Goulet over to the Winnipeg side of the river where he "fell into the snare set for him." Cunningham vehemently denied the charge, claiming not to have been aware "in the slightest degree that he was connected with Scott's death." He denounced "lynch law" outright, "whether in Winnipeg or San Francisco," and denied the right of "any man to go standing about barrooms and edging on half-drunken fools to do their dirty work, and avenging their private wrongs, and setting law at defiance, and all the time keeping themselves nicely under cover."

On Thursday morning, news of Ontario soldiers being mixed up in Goulet's death prompted Lieutenant Colonel Jarvis to "parade the whole battalion." When finished, Jarvis "addressed them in the most severe style, forbidding them in the most emphatic way to mix themselves up, in any way whatever, with political matters." He also initiated "drill three times a day" and barred the soldiers from visiting town "without a pass." St. John thought the latter was "a wise order," since even though "the behaviour of the men as soldiers is excellent, the sale of liquor — and liquor of the worst description — looses all the worst passions of the men, and having lost the ability to exercise judgment they are liable to be led by any national or party cry into excesses the consequences of which would be most disastrous."

News of Goulet's death spread through the new province as fast as the wildfires burning across the prairie that week. Rumours of Métis soldiers rising to avenge Goulet's death were also rife. On September 17, Cunningham said that Riel and his supporters held a "mass meeting at Stinking River," while St. John described a large number of Métis "arming, mustering, and drilling at St. Joseph." On September 18, Cunningham reported that 400 men were allegedly on their way from St. Joseph to Fort Garry "to avenge the death of Goulet" and that Bishop Taché told him he was supposedly "no longer responsible for the conduct of the French half-breeds." St. John noted the "alarm" in Portage la Prairie of armed Métis soldiers "coming across to vent their spite on those parts of the settlement beyond the protection of the troops." On September 22, St. John added that "large parties of Métis men" were "mustering about St. Joseph and Pembina, threatening the boats descending Red River." And the next day, Cunningham wrote about the presence of "50 men, known to be Riel's most ardent supporters, well armed and well mounted" being "seen near Scratching River yesterday." The *Telegraph* reporter further maintained that Goulet's death accelerated "the great migration that is going on among the French half-breeds — for they are going off by the hundred."

FORCED TO ACT

The precariousness of Lieutenant Governor Archibald's authority was brought home on Thursday, September 15. Goulet turned out to be an American citizen, and just as Jarvis was tearing a strip off his soldiers, Henry Robinson, the American vice-consul, visited Archibald to request a formal investigation into Goulet's death. The lieutenant governor agreed, but in the absence of a coroner — or any other component of a functioning judiciary — he was forced to establish a "magisterial examination" led by two civilians sworn in under the former Assiniboia laws for the purpose.

Goulet's death forced Archibald to act. On Friday, he appointed a bare-bones executive council with Alfred Boyd as provincial secretary and Marc-Amable Girard as treasurer. Boyd's initial task was to draft and issue Archibald's first proclamation on Saturday, September 17, entreating "faithful subjects" to "return to and engage in their usual occupations and pursuits," "keep and maintain the peace," and "aid and assist" magistrates and peace officers "in the suppression of disorders and riots of all kinds." According to St. John, it wasn't "helpful at all" to have the new government threatening such punishment.

Next, on Tuesday, September 20, Archibald appointed Captain Frank Villiers, quartermaster of the Quebec Battalion ("an old cavalryman, 13th Hussars," said St. John), to head up a police force consisting of 10 mounted and 20 foot policemen at first, with more to be appointed at a later date "if circumstances require them." Archibald also made a number of appointments to get the census under way. And to deal with the threat of insurrection at St. Joseph and from across the border, Archibald ordered Jarvis to send a company of soldiers to garrison at Pembina. St. John visited Pembina on September 26 and witnessed the company "encamped on the west bank of the Red River at a point lying about a mile north of the old boundary post that marks the 49th parallel, north latitude." The reporter used the word *old* because a survey made during the early part of the summer had thrown back the position of the 49th parallel nearly a mile behind the line agreed upon by the British and American governments 30 years earlier.

On September 24, Boyd issued a second proclamation on Archibald's behalf, this one prohibiting the sale of liquor to Indigenous Peoples in order to quell the "quarrelling and rioting" among the "bands of Indians resorting to Winnipeg and the neighbourhood, resulting in the deaths of an Indian woman and child." According to the proclamation, "If any person, without distinction of race, supply or sell to any person popularly known as an Indian, or any member of an

Indian nation, the means of intoxication, he shall, on being convicted before a petty court, on the oath of one or more witnesses be fined."

A VERY PROTRACTED INVESTIGATION

Five days into the hearings Archibald established to look into the death of Elzéar Goulet, Cunningham was shocked at "the most ludicrous performance I ever saw in a court of justice." According to him, the Crown attorney appointed by Archibald (a solicitor recently arrived from Montreal) couldn't compel key witnesses to give evidence. One such witness, a young man who swore he saw "a party of eight or ten pursing Goulet," refused to provide the names of any of them. The *Telegraph* reporter added that the man "objected to the question — objected to the court — denied their right to put such a question — denied their right to sit at all, and quoted most extensively and safely from a pamphlet, which, so far as I could make out was of no authoritative value whatever." And the two magistrates appointed to administer the proceedings were no help. Cunningham said they seemed "scared almost out of their wits" that if they did anything "illegally, the consequences might be something serious." Cunningham wasn't even sure whether they were magistrates at all.

Eventually, "after a very protracted investigation," a warrant was issued on September 30 "against a certain party in grey clothes who was seen to chase Goulet into the river and to throw something at him while he was struggling." Cunningham maintained that it was a "remarkable fact" that even though "at least a dozen of the witnesses knew perfectly who this man in grey clothes was — not one of them, either by coaxing or forcing, could be brought to divulge his name." According to St. John, everyone in the settlement knew the man had come with the expedition and was one of the voyageurs. No one would name him, though, the warrant was never executed, and justice for Goulet's murder was never meted out.

THOMAS SCOTT AGAIN

Calls for justice weren't limited to Elzéar Goulet. "Canadians" in Red River continued their pursuit of justice for Thomas Scott, as well.

During September, Cunningham said that Archibald received at least six petitions seeking retribution for the "foul murder" as well as delivery of Scott's body "for Christian internment." As Cunningham reported, Boyd responded on Archibald's behalf on October 4: he was frustrated with the failure of English-speaking members of the settlement to help "preserve peace and order," particularly their failure to "share in the indispensable work of protecting the public peace." And even with offers of "a rate of wages higher than given in any of the older provinces," Boyd wrote that "not a man in any one of the parishes from which the petitions have come — not a man among those who have signed the petitions — has offered himself, in terms of the appeal, to take his share in the indispensable work of protecting the public peace." With respect to Scott's remains, the government considered "the right to dispose of these remains, and take direction of their sepulchre, belongs strictly to the relatives and friends of the deceased." But because the requests were coming from "so large and so respectable a body of men" and they were clear they would assume "responsibility of disinterring the remains of the deceased without authority from his relatives," Boyd said the government wouldn't interfere in any search for Scott's remains being conducted "with a view to their being buried according to the rites and ceremonies of the church to which the deceased may have belonged."

On October 17, Cunningham closed this chapter of the Red River Rebellion: "On Thursday last a committee of petitioners presented themselves at Fort Garry to exhume the remains of the late Thomas Scott. The spot where the hole was dug having been pointed out, the men began to dig. Down they went, and when about six feet from the surface they came upon a coffin but it was empty. Where Scott's remains are no one can tell."

THE VOLUNTEERS

Newspapers, both domestic and American, weren't kind to the Ontario Volunteers, with reports that some might have been involved in the murder of Elzéar Goulet. St. John, though, was strident in their defence: "Whether the buglers did or did not take an active part in the pursuit or pelt the man in the water, the worst possible light will be cast over the matter by Goulet's associates." St. John insisted that most of the French-speaking settlers had "made up their minds" even before the expedition arrived that "the Ontario Battalion was composed of Orangemen thirsting for their blood, and the fact that these soldiers being mixed up in the matter, however free from blame they may be, will confirm them in their opinion." Even the fact that no member of "the Orange Nemesis" was involved in Goulet's murder (the two soldiers purported to be involved in Goulet's death were "both Roman Catholics") was "surely to be forgotten when the story is told throughout the country."

St. John was particularly incensed with a story published in the *St. Paul Daily Press* that described how "nearly a thousand Canadian Volunteers," "bigoted partisans" who "thirsted for the blood of the French half-breeds," overran the settlement in full militaristic force. According to this story, after being paid off, the troops and voyageurs "let loose" on Winnipeg for three days, "seeking out the partisans of Riel; bullying and insulting them; threatening them with violence; and in one case shooting a priest in the shoulder." St. John, however, claimed that no Ontario Volunteers had "laid hands" on any "half-breed, French or English," nor had he "yet heard of a revolver being fired in the settlement since their arrival."

By the end of September, both St. John and Cunningham reported that Manitoba had become "as quiet and dull as it was before." "The Volunteers at both Fort Garry and Stone Fort," St. John wrote, "were busy helping Simon Dawson's carpenters prepare barracks suitable for the harsh prairie winter on its way. And when they weren't working, the Volunteers were "making good use of the fine weather" and bats and stumps "discovered in the fort" for cricket, which "goes on every afternoon." Down at Stone Fort, the Volunteers with the Quebec Battalion had "organized a dramatic troupe" and were preparing a second performance, which the lieutenant governor attended. But this was just busywork. Cunningham said that most of the enlisted men were "beginning to weary for home," the excitement of the past five months having "died out among them," since they felt their "mission has not been fulfilled." He ventured, "If officers and men were polled, 19 out of every 20 would vote for home." To stress his point, Cunningham relayed a conversation he had with a non-commissioned officer on the parade grounds at Fort Garry one evening in late September.

"Mr. Cunningham," the unnamed Volunteer said, "I want to speak to you." He led the reporter to a secluded spot and then all at once struck a log with his clenched fist. "I could cry!"

"My dear fellow, what's the matter?" Cunningham asked.

"The matter — why, everything's the matter. What did we come here for? Did we not come to see tyranny abolished, wrongs redressed, and murderers punished, but when is this to be done? Or is this to be done at all? Or is it not? Or were we sent here to be made hewers of wood and drawers of water? Since we left Toronto, we have been wrought like slaves, and the slavery still continues and grows every day. We ask for a furlough and we are told we must apply to Ottawa, while officers are going one after the other without applying to Ottawa."

Cunningham tried to encourage the young man "to go on, do his duty, and in the end would have his reward."

"Reward!" the man snapped. "My reward — but where are the rewards going? One comes with a letter from Sir George and another comes with a letter from Sir George, and the one gets a snug berth and the other gets a snug berth — and we, the young educated men from Ontario, are left out in the cold to be browbeaten and left to do navvy work. No, sir, offer a discharge to this battalion now, and there are not three men in it but would receive it gladly and go home disgusted."

Cunningham left the conversation at that point, with the Volunteer "cursing his folly for ever having connected himself with the expedition."

To himself, Cunningham thought it was

> rather a painful process to get mingled up with such lamentations. No doubt these young men started from home with the noblest motives — tired, it may be, with an enthusiasm which for the time being blinded their better judgments and prevented them from weighing dispassionately the probable results of the undertaking in which they were about to engage, and it is a sad thing to see them fretting and making themselves miserable, because they have discovered that after all a soldier's life is just what it has always been, and is little relieved by these things called motives, let them be what they may. They are kindly fellows the Rifles.

By October 10, the Ontario Volunteers started to move into their new barracks. Even though they weren't quite finished, "and the windows are in most cases to be put in yet," St. John said the men "speak of the change as being definitely for the better. The nights are now pretty cold."

A RETROSPECT

Covering the Red River Expedition changed Robert Cunningham, especially his connection to the murder of Elzéar Goulet. The change is evident in one of the last pieces he filed for the *Telegraph* in which he provides "a retrospect" on "the events of the past five months." Cunningham admits that he had been "a spectator to a great solemn, expensive farce."

Back in the spring, Cunningham witnessed the "mighty storm of indignation" that swept over Ontario in the wake of Scott's death and saw how it fuelled preparations for a campaign to "crush disloyalty and insurrection" and "carry vengeance on the head of the murderers." At Sault Ste. Marie, along Dawson's road and the Kaministiquia River, and all along the old canoe route from Shebandowan Lake to Fort Frances to Red River and on to Fort Garry, Cunningham saw first-hand the "toiling and moiling," the "men engaged in it sweating and groaning and almost dying in the cause of their country." He said that he listened "over and over again" to the "congratulatory speeches made to the brave soldiers for their indomitable perseverance and their noble bearing amid unparalleled hardships."

And yet, despite all this, Cunningham couldn't help thinking there was "a good deal of the farcical" about the whole adventure. And what made it farcical was the failure of the English-speaking residents in Red River to "do their duty either to the governor, the government, or their country." True, "bells rang out, and guns were fired, and handkerchiefs were waved, and school children sung welcomes" as the expedition rowed up the Red River, but Cunningham maintained that he hadn't witnessed "much gratitude." The reporter wrote: "Somehow the tears seem to have been very easily dried." Even the adulation and loyalty claimed in the "countless addresses" parishioners made to the new lieutenant governor "seems to have been a good deal of essential lip service."

Instead of working to help Archibald "organize the whole machinery of the constitution," Cunningham felt the "English people" continued to do "everything in their power to weaken [Archibald's] hands and impede his work," like "harping on about Scott's murderers and Scott's body" and "demanding the capture of the pillagers and so on." For Cunningham, all this amounted to nothing more than "very much a merely private revenge."

Cunningham said that a "clergyman of the Church of England" summed up the attitude of most English inhabitants succinctly: "If we cannot have justice for the past, we won't allow justice to have any sway with the present." For Cunningham, this was "most lamentable," particularly since Canada had "spent millions of dollars to bring law and order and protection to these people, and all the thanks she gets is something very like impudent ingratitude." He thought the situation was particularly acute for Archibald who "came into the province resolved to govern it without reference to creeds at all." Had he "snubbed Bishop Taché; ignored the French half-breeds altogether;

opened wide his arms and received the Protestant clergy alone into his councils," the English would have been happy. But Archibald's more liberal approach had set the English inhabitants "at defiance" with his authority.

Cunningham judged Canada's newest province to be "in a very abnormal condition altogether." He entreated "every right-thinking citizen, instead of throwing every possible impediment in the way, lend every possible assistance toward the consolidation of the wants of the constitution." Cunningham then heeded his own advice: he quit the *Daily Telegraph* and became co-publisher of *The Manitoban*, a pulpit he used to support Archibald's administration and advocate passionately for conciliation in his newly adopted home.

- 24 -

SELKIRK

> The Indians are difficult people to deal with, for they are very sensitive, and abide by their own notions of right and wrong. Those who have remained in about the settlement have behaved themselves very well; and the remark made by one of them, that they had injured no man's property, although when hungry they might have, without any danger or difficulty, killed bullocks on the prairies, was quite true.
>
> — Molyneux St. John, *Globe*, September 22, 1870

At Fort Garry on September 19, Lieutenant Governor Archibald held another grand powwow with about 200 delegates from the "Saulteaux and Cree" who wanted to discuss the terms of the Selkirk Treaty signed in 1817. In St. John's words, even though the tract ("comprising about two miles" along both banks of the Red and Assiniboine Rivers) had been "bought and paid for years ago," the delegates were seeking "'a consideration' for the remainder of the country."

According to Cunningham, the meeting started about noon, with the mostly male participants adorned in war paint and profuse feathers making their way into the fort. As they assembled on the main parade grounds, "four great chiefs" arranged themselves at the front, each displaying their "George the Third Medal," an award bestowed upon Indigenous allies of King George III in the War of 1812.

At about 1:00 p.m., Archibald came down to the grounds accompanied by Lieutenant Colonel Samuel Jarvis, Alfred Boyd, and Marc-Amable Girard. The leader of the delegation, a chief Cunningham identified as Long Ears, opened the ceremonies by taking an "enormous pipe" from a cloth sack and lighting it. He took a half-dozen puffs and handed it to Archibald, who made a "wry face at the sight of the formidable instrument." The lieutenant governor soldiered on and managed three puffs that sent a "cold shudder through his whole frame." A few minutes later, Archibald turned around "quite pale" and said, "That confounded pipe has made me sick."

At this point, Long Ears rose and addressed Archibald through an interpreter. "The good God gave us the land. The good God wishes nothing but the truth. These are my chiefs and my big family." He waved to the crowd. "I don't like to speak for nothing. I demand something today for myself and my children. The Queen always speaks the truth, and we put her words in our heart. If nothing is given us today, we will all freeze in the plains."

Archibald replied, "I have given you presents already and asked that you go away to your winter hunting grounds and not come back till spring."

"The Queen told us not to go," the chief insisted.

"I want you all to go away to your hunting grounds," Archibald repeated. "Go away and come back in the spring and I will make a treaty with you."

On this point, St. John said the delegates were skeptical and jealous of the influence they believed Henry Prince had over the lieutenant governor owing to the "favours that had been shown him." They asked that "no treaty with any individual chief" be signed but rather only "with all the chiefs in council assembled." According to St. John, Archibald agreed to this.

Cunningham wrote that the conversation continued.

"We had not enough last time," the first chief said to loud applause.

"If I give you some ammunition and flour now, will you all go away?" Archibald asked.

"It all depends on how much you give us," the chief said to further applause and "ho-ho-ho's."

A second chief then rose and began to speak. His face "was painted of a bright ochre colour, streaked with vermillion." "I am very glad to see the governor," the chief said, making his way over to Archibald to shake his hand. "I am perfectly willing to regard Your Excellency as a kind of distant relation, but by no means can I look upon you as a father. Fathers take care of their children and give them plenty of things. Your Excellency has given us nothing at all, and whenever you come down handsomely, I will call you father and embrace you. There are 530 of us altogether, and all require food to eat and powder to shoot. If the governor would only give us what we want, we will go away and not come back anymore till spring." The second chief assured Archibald, "There are plenty of cattle all about the plains that we can go and shoot and eat, but we will not."

"What exactly do you want?" Archibald asked.

Cunningham said the chiefs presented a list of material "to the value of some thousands of pounds." Archibald refused, and so began "a great deal of higgling." The result was an accepted offer of 600 pounds of powder, 1,200 pounds of shot, 1,600 pounds of flour, 30 pounds of tobacco, and 30 pounds of rice.

The agreement was ratified by smoking the chiefs' pipe, which the leader of the group lit and passed, one delegate smoking after the other. St. John said that Archibald went last, "gallantly put the pipe in his mouth, and followed the example that had been set. The most hardened smoker might have hesitated before complying with this custom."

Like Cunningham, St. John left his correspondent duties in October 1870 to support Archibald and his administration. Within weeks of reporting on the September 19 grand powwow, Archibald hired St. John to help lay the groundwork for future treaty-making and colonization in the West, including resolution of the Selkirk Treaty dispute. The appointments launched St. John on a very remarkable and varied career in his new home.

- 25 -

EMBEDDED THEREAFTER

Although differing from him on many questions of public policy, we must acknowledge the energy and ability [that Cunningham] brought to bear on all questions that he took in hand, and the consistency of his courses in dealing with them. He did not allow the exigencies of a party or the necessities of a political leader to divert him from the course he had laid out for himself; and to this may perhaps be attributed much of the opposition that he encountered in his political career.

— *Manitoba Free Press*, July 1874

"Sweet Kate Ranoe" was a toast, a theme for many a callow muse, the goddess at whose feet the habitués of box, pit, and gallery worshipped, the good fairy of the box office.... Pretty, petite, shapely, graceful, charming in every mood and action, blessed with a sweet voice of rare flexibility, she was the incarnation of comedy.

— *Victoria Home Journal*, August 1893

The late Mr. St. John was a man of versatility, and his career was an eventful one.

— *Globe*, February 1904

Robert Cunningham, Molyneux St. John, and Kate Ranoe were early pioneers of embedded journalism. They canoed over the same rapids, traversed the same portages, ate the same pork and tack, were bitten by the same sandflies and mosquitoes, faced the same diplomatic and military threats, and experienced first-hand the repercussions of military action on a local population. But while these challenges provided great content for coverage of the expedition, the experience did something more — it embedded them directly and significantly into the lifeblood of their adopted country.

THE MANITOBAN

In one of his last posts for the *Telegraph*, Cunningham said that a new paper called *The Manitoban* had started up — "the first number displays talent." The talent, in part, was his. In October 1870, Cunningham and William Coldwell, a former colleague from the *Globe*, formed a partnership and purchased the printing plant previously used to produce the *Nor'-Wester* and *New Nation.*[1]

The inaugural edition of *The Manitoban* hit the two streets of Winnipeg on October 15, 1870. Cunningham and Coldwell told readers that their "course" would be "plain and decided. We shall yield to none." As for the "remarkable interlude" in the recent history of Red River, they condemned "the conduct of the men who usurped authority lawlessly to imprison loyal British subjects and ruthlessly committed murder" but stressed *The Manitoban* wouldn't dwell on those events. Rather, the editors promised to consider it "in the light of history" and vowed to do all in their power "to strengthen the hands of the new government in these endeavours to secure law and order, to consolidate the institutions of the country, and to develop the resources of the province."

It is unclear if Archibald intended to curry *The Manitoban*'s support when he gave Cunningham and Coldwell the contract as Queen's Printer in October 1870. If the lieutenant governor did, he accrued significant return on his investment. Over the fall of 1870, Cunningham and Coldwell worked hard as part of Archibald's "central committee" of supporters, travelling throughout the English-speaking parishes to get a slate of like-minded candidates elected in Manitoba's first election in December. Cunningham, together with moderates such as James Ross,

Alexander Begg, and Andrew Bannatyne, urged electors to co-operate with French-speaking parishes and support Archibald's policy of "letting bygones be bygones." Their message was simple: "Archibald's policy deserved approval, and the united people of the new province should look to the future and elect only men with a stake in the country's future."[2] Of Archibald's committee, only James Ross attended more campaign meetings that fall — eight versus Cunningham's seven.[3]

MON VRAI CUNNINGHAM

By the summer of 1871, Cunningham's — and *The Manitoban*'s — support for Archibald's conciliation efforts extended to strong and loud avocation for Riel's amnesty and the fair and prompt settlement of Métis land claims under the Manitoba Act. In May 1871, *The Manitoban* published this:

> There are no rebels properly so-called in this Province, and there never were above half a dozen, even in the palmiest days of Riel's rule. The few who were disloyal were newcomers who had brought their anti-British feelings with them, and joined in Riel's movement for reasons peculiar to themselves. Riel himself, it is well known, never pronounced against British supremacy, he always hoisted the British flag, but objected to Canada taking possession of this country without giving its people the right to pronounce on the intended absorption. How was it then, it might be asked, that, having only this object — which is legitimate in itself — he went on to rob, imprison and murder? Our belief is that these half-dozen rascals had the principal hand in these excesses, their intention being to create such a breach between this country and England as could not be healed without a big row, in the course of which the United States might find occasion to step in and have a say.[4]

Quite a change from Cunningham's first reports of Riel in January 1870.[5]

Cunningham's commitment to conciliation and advocacy of Métis rights earned him broad support from both English and French moderates in Manitoba — enough to run in the federal riding of Marquette in the 1872 election. *The Manitoban*, not surprisingly, backed Cunningham, declaring he had "almost immediately after settling in this country devoted himself to securing the rights of the half-breeds and old settlers as against those who in Canada would have deprived them, if they could, of what had been promised."[6] By this time, Louis Riel was one of Cunningham's friends and supporters: he came out of hiding to serve as a returning officer. That poll went solidly Cunningham, 339 to 10. Not all were happy with the election results. According to Coldwell, after news of the results hit the streets, *The Manitoban*'s office "was wrecked by a mob who (intending perhaps to be quite impartial) also wrecked the offices of the *Nor'Wester* and *The Métis*."[7]

In the spring of 1873, Métis leaders — Bishop Taché, Abbé Ritchot, Louis Riel, and others — sought Cunningham's help with fixing how lands were being disbursed to Métis families under section 31 of the Manitoba Act. By that time, the Dominion government was using a lottery system. Unfortunately, the prospect of quick cash encouraged many adult Métis to sell their and their children's rights to participate in the lottery.[8] To discourage the practice, Métis leaders asked Cunningham to move a motion in Parliament[9] to have the Dominion government follow the strict wording of section 31, which granted lands only to children of the family heads and not the heads of families.[10] The motion moved Prime Minister Macdonald to make the change via order-in-council.[11]

In Parliament, Cunningham continued to advocate for amnesty for Riel. In a speech given in March 1873, he said:

> Riel had been pronounced a murderer. He might be so and he might not, but this everyone knew that no

> man had a right to be called a murderer until he was proved to be. Louis Riel had given every opportunity to be tried, but no sworn information had ever been made before any magistrate in Red River charging Riel with murder. He himself at a public meeting was accused of having refused to grant a warrant for Riel's arrest. He offered on the spot to sign a warrant if any man would step forward and swear to an information, but no man did so neither then nor since.
>
> With regard to the amnesty, he firmly believed that amnesty was promised. He believed that on various grounds. The Government had given no indication on this point; everything was quiet respecting it; but he had authority which he could not dispute and which he could not question that that amnesty was promised by more members of the Government than one, by Lord Lisgar, and by Sir Edward Thornton at Washington. As the amnesty was granted he held it ought to be acted on, in order that the honour of Canada and England might be maintained. The honour of both countries was involved, and if it had been promised something decisive ought to be done to remove the cloud which continued to hang over the Province in consequence of this matter.
>
> If something were done one way or the other, the wranglings, bickerings, quarrels and listlessness which prevailed in that country would disappear; and these people who before had lived so happily, so peacefully and so undisturbed, would once more enjoy the comfortable existence they had enjoyed before Canadian connection commenced.[12]

Again, quite a difference from Cunningham's first reports from Red River.

The Métis community relied on Cunningham in private matters, as well. In correspondence with Cunningham in the spring of 1873, Bishop Taché told the Marquette MP: "I this morning had the visit of Mrs. Goulet who is confident that you will be kind enough to plead before the government the cause of the unfortunate orphans left destitute by the murder of the late Goulet. I know your appreciation of the sad occurrence, so I had no hesitation in assuring Mrs. Goulet that you will have spared no efforts in this matter."[13]

In June, Cunningham telegraphed Taché from Ottawa to suggest that he persuade Riel to run in the by-election triggered by the surprise death of Sir George-Étienne Cartier.[14] Riel "seized on the idea" and began his campaign in Provencher with broad support from moderates such as Cunningham, Marc-Amable Girard, Joseph Royal, Andrew Bannatyne — and even Donald Smith.

The Métis were appreciative of Cunningham's efforts. When he returned home in July 1873, the community in St. Vital thanked him for his work and told him his name was "written for ever in our grateful memory." Riel also bid Cunningham "a hearty welcome home" and thanked him for "your manly stand in the House of Commons, your successes, as well as what you have done for the country in general, and the Métis population of the province.... In devoting your energy to the cause of the Métis children you have earned the general approval of the Métis heads of families."[15]

Riel was elected to the House of Commons on October 11, 1873.[16] His supporters, including Cunningham, contributed funds to defray Riel's costs of travelling to Ottawa to take his seat. Riel did travel to Ottawa, but fearing arrest only took the oath of allegiance and signed the roll in the clerk's office in March 1874. In a vote immediately after, Riel was expelled from the House of Commons by a majority of 56.

STOUT DEFENDER

Back in Ottawa after an easy re-election in January 1874, Cunningham promoted a number of local causes: construction of a rail line between Pembina and Fort Garry, construction of a rail bridge over the Assiniboine River, and incorporation of the City of Winnipeg. And then, in April, he was appointed to the Council of the North-West Territories.[17] The *Manitoba Free Press*, a persistent critic of Cunningham's, wondered what qualified him — "certainly not any peculiar fitness for the position; not as a complement to the old settlers, because he is not one; and we are very certain that the new settlers that esteem it such cannot be found." The *Press* could only surmise that "perhaps it is because he is the stout defender of the rebels of murderers of '69–'70; or because he has laboured to the utmost of his ability to do injustice to the English-speaking people of the province, particularly the new settlers."[18]

En route from Ottawa to attend his first council meeting, Cunningham died suddenly at St. Paul, Minnesota, on Saturday, July 4, 1874. According to the *St. Paul Daily Press*, on Friday morning, July 3, Cunningham "was taken with a severe hemorrhage of the lungs, which was so prolonged, and the loss of blood so great, that notwithstanding the kindest care and the most skillful medical attention, he sank very rapidly and expired Saturday morning." The *Globe* wrote that while Cunningham would be remembered by his friends "as having possessed many amiable and genial qualities," his public career was "marred by a certain infirmity of purpose that placed him at times in positions his better instincts would have avoided."[19] Alexander Begg and Walter Nursey were more charitable. They said news of Cunningham's death "was received alike by all classes of the community, independent of politics or creed, with sincere manifestations of regret. Mr. Cunningham was a brilliant journalist, and the newspaper world sustained in his early demise, an acknowledged loss."[20] At his family's request, Robert Cunningham was buried in Oakland Cemetery in St. Paul.

To his dying day, Cunningham advocated for his friend, Louis Riel. In an interview for the *New York Herald* published just a couple of weeks before he died, Cunningham said the death of Thomas Scott "was an unfortunate act," but when the "whole circumstances" of that period were considered, "there is not a single case in the history of the world that can be instanced where a people went through such a crisis

Robert Cunningham, Member of Parliament for Marquette, Manitoba.

with less bloodshed than what is called the Red River Rebellion of 1869. Notwithstanding all that, the cry for vengeance is more intense in Canada today than it was three years ago."[21]

The feelings between the two men were mutual. In a poem he wrote three years after Cunningham's death, Riel told his good friend, Joseph Dubuc, that the former *Telegraph* reporter was *mon vrai Cunningham.*[22]

In 1874, Louis Riel left for exile in the United States, eventually settling in Montana with a wife and family and where he worked as a teacher. Ten years later, Gabriel Dumont convinced Riel to return to Saskatchewan to help resolve a long list of Métis and settler grievances against the Canadian government. Many of these echoed the grievances that had sparked the Red River Rebellion 15 years earlier. Frustrated with the federal government's inaction, Riel and his supporters announced the creation of a provisional government on March 19, 1885. One week later, the North-West Rebellion broke out with a skirmish between Métis forces and the North-West Mounted Police (NWMP) at Duck Lake. The rebellion ended after three days of fierce fighting near Batoche on May 12. "Cold and forlorn," Riel surrendered to NWMP scouts on May 15. Riel was charged and convicted of the crime of high treason in the summer of 1885. After two unsuccessful appeals, he was hanged at the NWMP barracks in Regina on November 16, 1885, "meeting his death with dignity, calmness, and courage."

A SHOWER OF OFFICES

Like Robert Cunningham, Molyneux St. John owed Adams Archibald much in building a life and career in post-expedition Manitoba. Days before his last article for the *Globe* appeared on October 22, 1870, St. John was contracted by Archibald to examine and report back on issues key to his gubernatorial mandate, including the state of titles to land in Manitoba and the disputed terms of the Selkirk Treaty, how best to appropriate lands for the Métis grant under section 31 of the Manitoba Act, and an assessment of "factors bearing on land settlement" in the new province. In his spare time that fall, St. John also ran for office as a government candidate in Manitoba's first provincial election in the riding of St. James. He lost 35 to 21 to Opposition candidate Edwin Bourke.

St. John reported back to Archibald in January 1871[23] and evidently the lieutenant governor was pleased enough to appoint him clerk of the Manitoba Legislative Assembly in March 1871, and then in July, secretary to newly appointed Indian Commissioner Wemyss Simpson.[24] That appointment came just in time for St. John to accompany Archibald and Simpson to Stone Fort to negotiate Treaty 1 with the Anishinabe and Swampy Cree. On August 3, 1871, St. John affixed his signature to Treaty 1 as witness. Later that month, St. John accompanied the team to Manitoba Post on the northwest shore of Lake Manitoba to negotiate Treaty 2 with the Chippewa and Cree. Treaty 2 was completed on August 21, 1871, with St. John again signing as witness.[25]

Archibald continued to shower patronage on St. John throughout 1871 and 1872. Appointments included member of Manitoba's first Board of Education, superintendent of Protestant Schools and secretary of the Protestant Section of the Education Board, attorney-at-law for Manitoba, justice of the peace for Selkirk County, and Chair of the Manitoba Agricultural Association.[26] At these, the *Manitoba Liberal* — a harsh critic of Archibald's — asked: "Now, will anyone wonder that the duties of some of these offices must be neglected? We can see no earthly reason why all the offices in this country should be showered on one or two individuals, while we have dozens of men better capable of discharging the duties of some of them."[27]

A VERSATILE MAN

Adams Archibald's resignation in 1872 caused St. John to search for a new patron, and in July of that year, he found one — Wemyss Simpson appointed him Indian agent and assistant to himself as Indian commissioner. St. John retained the position when Joseph-Alfred-Norbert Provencher replaced Simpson in early 1873.[28] In September, St. John accompanied Provencher, Manitoba Lieutenant Governor Alexander Morris, Robert Pither (still Indian agent at Fort Frances), and Simon Dawson (now Member of Parliament for Algoma) to the North-West Angle on Lake of the Woods to begin negotiation of Treaty 3 with the Saulteaux.[29] After lengthy and at times difficult discussions, Treaty 3 was concluded on October 13, 1873, with St. John once more signing as witness.

Provencher and St. John didn't see eye to eye; St. John supposedly "expressed some resentment at being passed over for the position himself."[30] In July 1874, he resigned as Indian agent and in November became managing editor of a new paper in Winnipeg, *The Standard*.[31] There was speculation that the new owners included Donald Smith, who wanted a newspaper to advocate passage of the Pacific Railway through Winnipeg and construction of a north–south Pembina Branch to connect Winnipeg to the Northern Pacific south of the border.[32] Smith got a good return on his investment: *The Standard* campaigned strongly for both initiatives, as did St. John personally when he ran in the 1874 provincial election (he lost again) and in his role as co-chair of the Manitoba Railway Committee in the winter of 1875.[33]

St. John's tenure with *The Standard* didn't last long. In April 1875, the paper was merged with the *Manitoba Free Press*, and St. John moved back to Toronto where he rejoined the *Globe*.[34] A year later, he was appointed special correspondent again, this time to cover Governor General Lord and Lady Dufferin's trip to British Columbia. The point of Dufferin's mission was to assure British Columbians that the Dominion government intended to follow through on its commitment to build a transcontinental rail line as per the Terms of Union. St. John left Ottawa with Dufferin and his party on July 31. They travelled by rail to Chicago and then on to San Francisco where they boarded a Pacific Mail Company steamer to Esquimalt. After spending a few days in Victoria, they sailed up the coast to Haida Gwaii, crossed to Fort Simpson (near present-day Prince Rupert), came back down to the Fraser River, and proceeded inland as far as Kamloops. Dufferin and his entourage returned to Victoria in mid-September, where Dufferin addressed Government House on September 20. Dufferin and his party returned to Ottawa in October.[35]

Between July and October 1876, St. John filed 25 stories for the *Globe* and later published them as *The Sea of Mountains: An Account of Lord Dufferin's Tour Through British Columbia in 1876*. In one of the more outstanding passages, St. John described a Haida village on Skidegate Bay, Graham Island:

> The village consists of about forty houses, each of which contains several families, as we found to be the

case in most of these Indian settlements, and these houses are built in one continuous line, some little distance above high water mark. There are a few smaller houses or storehouses behind the others, but that which attracts the eye and rivets the attention at once, is the array of carved cedar pillars and crested monuments that rise in profusion throughout the length of the village. In the centre of the front face of every house was an upright pillar of cedar, generally about forty feet high, and from two to three feet in diameter. From base to top these pillars had been made to take the forms of animals and birds, and huge grotesque human figures, resembling somewhat the colossal figures recovered by the excavation at Nineveh. The birds and reptiles, curious and unlike as they were any that the Indians themselves see, one could understand; but there were griffins and other fabulous animals represented, that one would have imagined the carvers thereof had never heard of. The carvings were in some places elaborate, and in many places coloured. Some of the pillars a few yards in front of the houses were surmounted by life-size representations of birds or animals, the token of the family, coloured in a fanciful manner. In one or two instances there were outline carvings on a board surmounting a pillar, as a picture might be set on the top of a post. The main and tallest pillars, however, were those of which one formed the centre of each house, and through which entrance was had into the interior. Many of the rafters of the houses protruded beyond the eaves, and terminated in some grotesque piece of carving. The Indians could not tell the age of this village, nor had they any tradition on the subject, so far as we could discover. The village must, however,

> be some hundreds of years old, for the cedar rafters in some houses were crumbling to pieces, and cedar lasts for centuries. Many of the pillars bore signs of being very old, but they are usually sound. Indian villages are usually so essentially only places of shelter against inclement weather, that the appearance of an Indian town of such indisputable age and with such evidences of dexterity in a branch of art, gave rise to endless wonderment and surmise. Whence did the Hydahs obtain the models from which they have copied, since they never could have seen what they carved about their dwellings? One of the party purchased a walking-stick with a small piece of workmanship on the handle, but the Indians passed it about amongst themselves, and none could tell what animal it was intended to represent. It seemed as if the parentage of the carving may have been in China, for one or two of the squatting figures had the same leer on their countenances that one sometimes sees on the figures in a Chinese Joss House.[36]

In the fall of 1876, St. John left the *Globe* for the last time and moved back to Winnipeg where he was made sheriff of the North-West Territories. Twelve months later, he was appointed interim Indian superintendent of the Manitoba Superintendency after Provencher was dismissed for administrative incompetence, fraud, corruption, and dereliction of duty.[37] St. John resigned in July 1879 when John A. Macdonald's Conservatives returned to power and undertook a wholesale reorganization of the Department of Indian Affairs under Edward Dewdney.[38]

Over the next 15 years, St. John continued to churn through appointments and contracts. In 1880, he moved to London to work for fellow Winnipegger Alexander Begg at the Canadian Pacific Syndicate office promoting immigration to the Canadian Prairies. One estimate had the volume of literature produced by Begg's office amounting "to over a million pieces within a period of six months. Through the London office, the company advertised regularly in 167 journals in Great Britain and in 147 continental papers.[39] Two years later, St. John moved to Montreal to become the director of the Land Corporation of Canada (LCC), one of a couple of dozen companies that had received charters from the Dominion government to purchase land from the Canadian Pacific Railway and resell it for colonization. In 1884, shares in LCC went bust, and St. John offered himself as scapegoat to the board; a majority of directors agreed and voted down St. John's re-election bid 11 votes to 9. In 1887, St. John returned to the newspaper business as editor of the *Montreal Herald* and president of the Ottawa Press Gallery in 1889. Two years later, he returned to the Canadian Pacific Railway as superintendent of advertising.

"THE GREAT NORTH-WEST"

After returning to central Canada in the fall of 1870, Kate Ranoe turned up only a couple of times in the newspapers. One story had her in Winnipeg in January 1871, attending the inaugural session of the Manitoba Legislative Assembly and Winnipeg's "first great ball." In the fall of 1871, another had her taking over the lease of the Theatre Royal in Montreal and attracting "large audiences" during what one writer called "the Ranoe season." In 1873, Ranoe was reported back in Winnipeg; three years later, she was starring in productions in Toronto, Hamilton, and Washington, D.C.; and in 1877, she topped the bill in "a new drama written by her husband" at the Opera House in Toronto. The last record of Ranoe and St. John's theatrical partnership is from March 1878 when "a dramatic performance of some pretensions took place at Pelly [Manitoba] and achieved a most complete success." The play was *Estranged*, its author "our Mr. Sheriff St. John," and the production was "under Mrs. St. John's directions, and thus her own experience and the author's intentions were happily united."[40]

Ranoe gained most attention for a lecture she delivered around Southern Ontario in 1871. It was called "The Great North-West" and

RDAY. MAY 27. 1871.

LECTURE.

THE GREAT NOR'-WEST.

MUSIC HALL, MAY 30th,

MISS KATE RANOE,

(MRS. MOLYNEUX ST. JOHN.)

Will Lecture on the

RED RIVER EXPEDITION

AND

MANITOBA.

810-tfTThS

ST. ANDREW'S SOCIETY

Advertisement for "The Great North-West" lecture.

premiered at Toronto's Musical Hall in May. According to reviews in the *Globe* and *Telegraph*,[41] the evening went as follows.

Shortly after 8:00 p.m., Samuel Harman, the former mayor of Toronto and long-time alderman for St. Andrew's Ward, took the stage and introduced himself as chair for the evening. Harman welcomed the "fashionable audience" and complimented the "courage and spirit" that Ranoe exhibited in accompanying her husband on the "Abyssinia-like" expedition to Red River.

Ranoe then rose and walked to the podium at centre stage. She was "handsomely attired in a lemon-coloured silk dress, with tulle over-skirt, and with a coronet of gold wheat on her head." The crowd offered "hearty applause," and Ranoe waited a moment to begin her three-part lecture.

When the applause subsided, she launched in, starting with the "early history of the Red River Settlements" in which she explained the differences between the English and French to be "on account of their nationality and religion." She described the period of "benevolent and paternal" rule by the Hudson's Bay Company, an "anomaly" that she said stood in the way of "opening up settlement in the Great North-West." The actress followed with an exposition on the "events connected with the recent insurrection," maintaining that the death of Thomas Scott had to be "ascribed chiefly to the evil influence of [William] O'Donoghue" and was "generally disapproved by the French population." Ranoe "expressed satisfaction" with the fact that the "only sentiment which survived that period of disturbance and trouble was expressed in a demand for justice upon the murderers of one man instead of vengeance upon many."

The second part of "The Great North-West" dealt with the expedition itself. Ranoe discussed her reasons for joining her husband on the trip and the difficulties she encountered "overcoming the objections raised against her accompanying the expedition." While not documented by the reviewers, Ranoe described these "with humour." She then sought to enlist "the sympathy of her auditors in her adventures as one of the voyagers in the *Globe* canoe." She took the audience on the trip up the Kaministiquia River and from Shebandowan Lake to Winnipeg and relayed in graphic detail "the picturesque scenery of the route." Ranoe also recounted the enthusiasm and "readiness of the Volunteers to undertake the difficult expedition" and the many "difficulties overcome by the troops." The actress ended her account of the expedition with the final approach to Fort Garry and testified to the "order and tranquility which had rapidly succeeded to the period of disorder and passion."

In part three, Ranoe specified the "natural advantages" that Manitoba boasted "for the purposes of settlement," enumerated the alternative routes for getting to the province, and offered "many shrewd and practical suggestions to those who might contemplate making it their future home," including "high tribute to the comforts of married life."

Ranoe concluded "The Great North-West" with a call for justice. The *Globe*, said Ranoe, "demanded justice be done to the Indian, and that in the future there may be no cause for reproach of conscience, and that when what is now a prairie and a wilderness, becomes the garden and the wheat field, the flowers will bloom over no grave of oppression, nor hamlet be built upon land wrenched from the Indian but the Dominion will grow, based on justice, and truth and prosperity will flourish over the land." This "generous appeal on behalf of the Indian tribes, for whom no settlement had yet been made," was met with "continued applause."

Harman retook the stage at this point and said he could "only interpret the continued and hearty applause as a vote of thanks to the fair and talented lecturer," which inspired another ovation. The former Toronto mayor concluded the evening by offering Ranoe "the thanks of the audience."

Ranoe delivered "The Great North-West" in Hamilton and St. Catharines in the following weeks, and the *Globe* and *Telegraph* said she planned additional readings, as well.

THE END

In March 1893, the sad news of the "accidental death of Mrs. Molyneux St. John, a lady well known and highly esteemed by the older residents of Winnipeg," reached Canadians across the country. The *Victoria Home Journal* wrote: "survivors of an older generation" would remember Mrs. St. John "as Miss Kate Ranoe."[42] Ranoe was killed while crossing St. Catherine Street in downtown Montreal. An eyewitness said she was "leaning on her husband's arm" when a runaway horse "with nothing on it except a few bits of harness" caromed down Peel Street and knocked her down. The witness said Ranoe was kicked "on the breast, which must have killed her instantly, for when picked up she was dead."[43] Ranoe was 49. The *Globe* said that "an immense number

Kate Ranoe, Montreal, 1868.

Molyneux St. John.

of prominent citizens" attended her funeral in Montreal, and her husband "received many messages of condolence."[44]

Six months later, Molyneux St. John moved to Winnipeg to assume duties as editor of the *Winnipeg Free Press*, a position he held until July 1895. The *Winnipeg Daily Tribune* said that St. John "proved himself to be a gentleman of sterling and most amiable character. In conducting the paper, personalities were most rigidly eschewed, and while many may have differed from the strongly partisan tone of the paper from a political standpoint, all must have respected its cleanness and desire to be fair."[45] It wasn't long until St. John was on the move again, though, this time to work for the Department of the Interior in Ottawa. Seven years later, in January 1902, Prime Minister Wilfred Laurier appointed him Gentleman Usher of the Black Rod.

On January 30, 1904, St. John died of uremic poisoning. An obituary in the *Globe* tells of the painful, protracted ordeal:

> A fortnight ago Mr. St. John was attacked with grippe, which induced a return of kidney trouble, from which he had been a sufferer. He was removed to St. Luke's Hospital, where it was thought that with skillful nursing and good medical care he might recover. He grew gradually worse, however, and on Friday evening his physician called in for consultation with two specialists. At this consultation, Mr. St. John's recovery was pronounced hopeless. The patient then continued to sink rapidly, and passed away in a state of unconsciousness.[46]

Molyneux St. John, "one of the best-known newspapermen in Canada,"[47] was 67. He was buried next to the love of his life in Montreal's Mount Royal Cemetery.

Remains of Colonel Wolseley's transports, 1870.

APPENDIX 1: THE EXPEDITION VESSELS

The *Globe* provided the following commentary on the vessels under contract to the Red River Expedition.

Arctic: "The American propeller *Arctic* has just arrived and is waiting for orders. She is under charter to the Government for 25 days at $400 dollars per day, in gold. She has a carrying capacity of 600 tons, which is more than sufficient to clear everything the Government have here — hay and lumber included" (June 7, 1870).

Clematis and *Union*: "The *Clematis* carries all the ammunition and a company of troops. The *Union* carries the remainder of the Regulars who came up by the *Prince Alfred*.... The *Clematis* gets $250 and the *Union* $350 a day" (June 1, 1870).

"Capt. Wilson, the Custom House officer of this place [Collingwood], and Mr. Hamilton, the County Attorney, had started for Marquette, with a view to chartering two boats, and the result of their negotiations was the arrival of the *Union*, a propeller about the size of the *Brooklyn*, on Saturday night. On Saturday afternoon, Col. Bolton also chartered the *Clematis*, a very powerful tug, at a rate of $250 per day" (June 2, 1870).

Clifton: "The *Chicora* will also have in tow a barge laden with forage. George Smith of this place [Collingwood] has received instructions to charter a barge for the purpose. He is negotiating for the barge *Clifton*, one of the largest vessels of the kind on Lake Huron. The *Clifton* was built at Chippewa, and was used for some time as a steamer, and was one of the swiftest vessels of the lake, but the engine was taken from her and transferred to the steamer *Francis Smith*, which now plies between here and Owen Sound, and the *Clifton* was converted into a barge" (May 21, 1870).

Robert Cunningham was less kind: "It is currently rumoured, though some think the statement must be a canard, that the barge *Clifton* is likely to be chartered for the conveyance of military stores. If such tubs as the *Clifton* are employed to any extent, it will be easy to foresee what will be the dismal fate of the present expedition. Formerly a trader between this port and Owen Sound, she was condemned years ago as unseaworthy, and her engines were taken out of her. To accept such a thing would be proof of disgraceful incompetence or something worse" (*Daily Telegraph*, May 23, 1870).

Francis Smith: "It was announced that the Government intended to charter the *Francis Smith*, the most capacious and one of the swiftest steamers on Lake Huron, to take the place of the *Chicora* in forwarding supplies from Collingwood to the Sault.... [She] is the largest Canadian vessel on the upper lakes. She will carry, her owners say, twice as much as the *Chicora* fully laden, with 40 boats and 500 men to boot. Her accommodation, however, is not so good, she having no upper cabins, but for a quick transport — the thing needed — she is invaluable" (May 20, 1870).

Orion: "The large three-masted schooner *Orion*, Captain Zeland, has now on board 15 of the boats built at Kingston, from whence she came here to load with 40,000 feet of lumber, she will then proceed to Hamilton to take in four more boats and start on her voyage at once" (May 4, 1870).

Pandora: "The fine schooner *Pandora*, Captain Harrison, has now almost completed her loading. When our reporter visited her yesterday afternoon, the hands were busily employed in taking on board the remainder of the boats built here for the expedition, and she had already in her hold 500 barrels of pork, 40,000 feet of lumber, and 90 tarpaulins to be used as coverings for the boats. The *Pandora* is really a handsome, weatherly looking craft, and judging from her trim appearance, ought to make a rapid passage to her destination" (May 4, 1870).

Prince Alfred: "The *Prince Alfred* carries four guns, of which two are steel Armstrong 12-pounders, one brass howitzer 24, and one 14. She was originally built for a tug for the Grand Trunk to ply between Sarnia and Green Bay, and was converted into a gunboat during the course of last winter, under the superintendence of Mr. Wyatt. She is 170 feet in length overall, and has two masts to enable her to sail as well as steam. She is fitted with an engine of 259 horsepower for propeller; another of 60 horsepower, used as a fire engine, having four different hose attached capable of pumping 45,500 gallons per hour; and a donkey engine, for pumping the boilers and bilge. Her two boilers are each 30 feet long and five feet in diameter, and protected by bunkers of four feet, in solid thickness of coal. The engine, which is a fine piece of mechanism, was built by Bartley & Gilbert, of Montreal. She was fitted at Goderich with a new wheel nine feet three inches in diameter, and steams at a rate of 14 miles per hour. Her wheelhouse is iron-plated, besides which she carries portable armour for her sides. She can accommodate 60 men in the forecastle, and 11 officers in the cabin" (May 27, 1870).

Rescue: "On Monday last, Capt. Murray received orders to send up a squad of eight men from the Clinton Company to man the gunboat *Rescue*, which was passing Goderich on her way to Sault Ste. Marie, in order to frustrate alleged Fenian manoeuvres. The Clinton boys were ready and willing as usual.... Accordingly, on Tuesday afternoon, the squad passed up to Goderich" (May 25, 1870).

Shickluna: "The new propeller *Shickluna*, of the North Shore Transportation Company, was chartered by Mr. Gilbert for the Government last Saturday morning, and left Port Stanley the same evening for this city [Toronto], where she will take in stores for the Red River expedition, and steam at once for Fort William" (May 3, 1870).

Waubuno: "The *Waubuno* is a small but compactly built steamer, built in 1865, at Thorold, for carrying passengers between Collingwood and Sault Ste. Marie. Inspector Weatherly pronounces the vessel to be seaworthy, and 'the best-appointed vessel I have been on board of in my own district, as regards requirements of safety.' Every precaution has been taken to guard against accidents. The vessel is under the management of Captain Campbell, an experienced officer on the upper lakes" (May 17, 1870).

"The *Waubuno* left the Sault at 4 p.m. on Wednesday. When a little below the American channel, where it is not more than five miles wide, the vessel ran aground at 9 o'clock, the night being very dark. Every effort was made to get the vessel off, but finding it impossible to do so, she blew a whistle at intervals all night.

"A little after daylight, the American tug *J.C. Morrison*, with two schooners in tow, passed down the channel within two miles of the stranded vessel. The tug answered the signal, and promised to return leaving the schooners above the Neebish rapids, about two miles distant; but she never returned.

"The American tug *Peck* passed up soon after, and took no notice of the signals. During the afternoon the American tug *Annie Dobbins* passed down with tow, without taking notice of the signals. Another tug passed by, and the Captain of the *Waubuno* sent out a boat to ask assistance. The tug did not even slacken her speed, but passed on nearly swamping the boat which had been sent to ask for assistance. The *Waubuno* remained on the rocks all night. In the morning the *Shickluna*, with the *Orion* and the *Pandora* in tow, passed up the Canadian channel and gave every assistance to help off the vessel.

"The tug *Okonra*, of Owen Sound, passed up soon afterwards, with freight for the Sault, and helped the *Shickluna* till the *Waubuno* was got afloat. This was not accomplished till 2 p.m. on Saturday. The vessel is uninjured by accident, owing to the great strength of her hull" (May 24, 1870).

APPENDIX 2: THE EXPEDITION ARTISTS

In the spring of 1870, the Red River Expeditionary Force drew huge crowds — at the Crystal Palace in Toronto, at the wharf in Collingwood, at Camp Sault, and at Prince Arthur's Landing. Among those who came out "to see the troops" were three artists whose photographs, sketches, and paintings represent the bulk of the expedition's visual documentation.

DUNCAN FRASER MACDONALD

On June 10, the *Globe*'s Sault Ste. Marie correspondent said the *Waubuno* arrived from Parry Sound with "a photographer from Guelph" named D.F. Macdonald. According to the reporter, Macdonald took a general survey of the area and then some specific "views" of the grounds, the tents, and other "objects of interest." One "view," the reporter judged "particularly capital," was of a group of officers gathered in front of Major Acheson Gosford Irvine's tent.

Macdonald was born in West Flamborough, Canada West, and moved to the Parry Sound district in 1867. There he worked for the Crown Lands Department as a wood ranger, timber cruiser, and eventually Crown timber agent. Much later, he was appointed local Indian agent for the district. Macdonald was also an avid diarist and photographer. The Archives of Ontario contain a small trove of his records, including photographs of the expedition taken at Sault Ste. Marie: the "capital view" of the officers in front of (presumably) Major Irvine's tent, two views of the camp, one shot of expedition teamsters at breakfast, another (presumably) of their camp, and one of an unnamed soldier enjoying a pipe. With one exception, Macdonald's are the only known pictures of the expedition from Sault Ste. Marie.

The *Globe* said that Macdonald intended to accompany the expedition "at least to Fort William," and the "views" and sketches he planned to take "will no doubt command a large sale throughout the country." There is no record of Macdonald proceeding to Thunder Bay.

FRANCES ANNE HOPKINS

For decades a woman was rumoured to have accompanied Colonel Wolseley and his expedition to Red River. Most assumed it was British painter Frances Anne Hopkins, given her legendary travels through Rupert's Land in the 1860s with her husband, HBC superintendent Edward Hopkins. Based on personal diary entries, Alice Johnson, longtime archivist of the Hudson's Bay Company and assistant editor of its Record Society, says Hopkins was back in Britain with her husband and children by the middle of July 1870. Nevertheless, Johnson maintains that Hopkins did travel to Prince Arthur's Landing in June 1870 with her friend, Louisa Wolseley, the colonel's wife. It was during this trip, Johnson says, that Hopkins most likely visited the portage around

The Red River Expedition at Kakabeka Falls (1877) by Frances Anne Hopkins.

Lower Kakabeka Falls on the Kaministiquia River, which is depicted in one of the most famous paintings of the expedition, *The Red River Expedition at Kakabeka Falls.*[1]

Perhaps Louisa Wolseley and Frances Anne Hopkins were the "two ladies" St. John said arrived at Prince Arthur's Landing aboard the *Chicora* on June 3, 1870. According to him, "There is little or no accommodation here for ladies, and those are venturesome who come up unless on invitation." On June 9, St. John (and presumably Ranoe) boarded the *Okonra* with the ladies and "a large party of officers" and "steamed over to the Kaministiquia." St. John described the day like this in the *Globe* of June 15, 1870:

> It was a bright, clear summer afternoon, and the river, with its banks of variegated green and silver beech — its dark reaches, from which no opening could be seen — and its great grim neighbour Mount McKay, towering above and frowning over the stream.... Mile after mile was passed as the *Okonra* steamed on; and there, where to preserve the harmony of the scene, only noiseless canoes and silent Indians should have been found, our noisy little tug lashed the river into foam, and spirited streams of water from her side, while her living freight laughed and talked, waking the echoes of the mountain with the ring of their voices, mingling expressions of admiration for the scene, with congratulations at the absence of mosquitoes.
>
> We all landed at Point Muro, the *Okonra* going alongside the bank of the river, and walked across to see the rapid. I don't think any of the party saw it, for we kept too far down; but instead of the rapids we came across a colony of mosquitoes and blackflies.

Cunningham reported ladies at Prince Arthur's Landing, as well. At the June 25 boat race between the Ontario Battalion's Company

Kakabeka Falls on the Kaministiquia River (1871) by William Armstrong.

No. 5 and the Royal Engineers, "all the ladies" for 10 miles around were invited. "There are not very many ladies about," wrote Cunningham in the *Telegraph* of July 1, 1870, "but those that are, are very pretty and exceedingly interesting."

Johnson says Hopkins and Louisa Wolseley returned to Montreal with Lieutenant General James Lindsay in early July 1870.

WILLIAM ARMSTRONG

On board the *Chicora* on June 3, 1870, was a photographer whom St. John said proposed to "accompany the expedition and take a series of views along the route." The man was still in camp on June 11, but by then "everyone about the place" was asking "when is he going to begin? We all want photographs of the camp, the bay, the Indians, and of everything in general, to send to our friends." By June 15, the photographer was gone, prompting St. John to ask: "Is there not in Toronto a photographic establishment sufficiently enterprising to send an artist up who will take views of the camp and Thunder Bay, and accompany the expedition to Red River?"

The photographer could have been Toronto-based painter and photographer William Armstrong, the most prolific documenter of the expedition. At least 13 of his expedition sketches appeared in *Canadian Illustrated News*, including *Kakabeka Falls and Portage*, which served as the basis for his most famous expedition rendering, *Kakabeka Falls on the Kaministiquia River*. For years there had been rumours that Armstrong had served with the expedition. His obituary said he was "chief engineer" with the "63rd Regiment" in charge of getting "the troops to negotiate the rivers and lakes of northwestern Ontario."[2] While Armstrong might have been the photographer St. John reported in Prince Arthur's Landing in June 1870, the *Globe* had Armstrong back in Toronto by June 18 selling paintings.[3]

One of Armstrong's most intriguing works from this period is *Mr. and Mrs. St. John Running the Rapids, Sturgeon River*. In November 1871, the *Canadian Illustrated News* published one of Armstrong's drawings to commemorate "a daring adventure on the part of a lady who pluckily accompanied her husband throughout the Red River expedition" and helped promote Ranoe's lecture tour for "The Great North-West." The drawing was entitled *Mr. and Mrs. St. John Running*

Kate Ranoe and Molyneux St. John running the rapids on the Sturgeon River in Northern Ontario.

the Rapids, Sturgeon River and was the basis for Armstrong's 1871 painting of the same name.

What inspired Armstrong to make the drawing? In the absence of any hard evidence, I suggest the following: If Armstrong travelled to Thunder Bay to visit the expedition in June 1870, there is a good chance he met St. John and Ranoe — and was charmed by them and their story. And given the popularity of "The Great North-West" and Armstrong's interest in the expedition, there is an equally good chance that Armstrong attended Ranoe's lecture in Toronto in May 1871. Who knows exactly, but Ranoe did write one particularly dramatic account of running rapids on the Maligne River just past Sturgeon Lake (*Globe*, August 15, 1870), recounted in chapter 13, "Intellectual Characters." It certainly would have added suspense and excitement to her lecture, perhaps enough to inspire Armstrong.

NOTES

INTRODUCTION

1. Canada. House of Commons. Address by the Governor General John Young, in *Journal of the House of Commons of the Dominion of Canada* 3 (May 12, 1870): 356.

CHAPTER 1: BLAWSTED FENCE

1. Quoted in J.M. Bumstead, *The Red River Rebellion* (Winnipeg: Watson & Dwyer, 1996), 45.
2. Quoted in George F.G. Stanley, *The Birth of Western Canada: A History of the Riel Rebellions* (Toronto: Longmans, Green, 1936), 70.
3. Captain Donald Cameron was a frequent target for scorn in the Canadian press around this time. In April 1870, the *Globe* reported this: "When Captain Cameron was at Pembina using the eye-glass, which it is his misfortune to require, and wearing a pair of long boots, that the rigorous climate necessitated, the Postmaster of the town, who was doubtless an average representative of the intelligence of the place, said to another gentleman —

   "'I say, mister, is your Queen Victoria so almighty hard up as that?'

   "'What do you mean?' was the reply.

   "'Wal, look here now — whatever do you call that critter there?'

   "'That gentleman is Captain Cameron, who accompanies the Hon. Mr. McDougall.'

"'Wal,' said the American official, interrupting his companion, 'if you took off them boots, and that prospecting glass, and let the gas out, I'll be gol-darned if you couldn't weigh him on our letter scales!'" (*Globe*, April 30, 1870.)

4. George F.G. Stanley, *Louis Riel* (Toronto: McGraw-Hill, 1963), 65, 71.
5. Quoted in Stanley, *Birth of Western Canada*, 72.
6. Ibid., 80.
7. Ibid., 81–82.
8. Ibid., 84.
9. Ibid., 88–89.

CHAPTER 3: ERRAND OF PEACE

1. Quoted in Stanley, *Birth of Western Canada*, 130.

CHAPTER 4: TWO CORRESPONDENTS AND A BURLESQUE STAR

1. Quoted in Reed Turcotte, *When Canadian Newspaper Publishers Were King* (Greenwood, BC: BCP Publishing, 2017), 41.
2. St. John Point on the eastern tip of Hornby Island in the Strait of Georgia is named after Molyneux St. John. According to him, the point was "so called from the fact that in days when it had no name, your correspondent used to hide there for wild fowl." See also knowbc.com/limited/Books/The-Encyclopedia-of-Raincoast-Place-Names/S/St-John-Point.

CHAPTER 7: CAMP SAULT

1. Garnet Wolseley, *The Soldier's Pocket-Book for Field Service* (London: W. Clowes and Sons, 1869). There is no record in official correspondence of Wolseley approving either Cunningham or St. John to accompany the expedition, and Wolseley had full authority over all expedition operations. In Lieutenant General Lindsay's "Instructions for the Guidance of Colonel Wolseley," he told Wolseley, "I shall not interfere with your arrangements, relying on, and having the greatest confidence in your discretion."

CHAPTER 9: DECEITFUL APPEARANCES

1. See Eugene H. Cropsey, *Crosby's Opera House: Symbol of Chicago's Cultural Awakening* (Madison, NJ: Fairleigh Dickinson University Press, 2000), 270.
2. For the 60th Rifles, see Nesbit Willoughby Wallace, *A Regimental Chronicle and List of Officers of the 60th, or the King's Royal Rifle Corps, Formerly the 62nd, or the Royal American Regiment of Foot* (London: Harrison, 1879). For the 1st (Ontario) and 2nd (Quebec) Battalions, see Fred Shore, "The Canadians and the Métis: The Re-Creation of Manitoba, 1858–1872" (Ph.D. diss., University of Manitoba, 1991); and Surgeon-Major E.W. Young, "Medical History of the Red River Expedition, in the Months of May–October 1870," *Army Medical Department Report for the Year 1870 and Supplement to Report for 1869*, vol. XII (London: Harrison and Sons, 1872), 448–73.

CHAPTER 25: EMBEDDED THEREAFTER

1. In point of fact, the plant was originally Coldwell's; he had owned it with the *Nor'-Wester* between 1860 and 1865. Louis Riel and his Provisional Government purchased the plant in January 1870 to produce the *New Nation* under the management of Thomas Spence. Cunningham and Coldwell took a $2,800 loan from Donald Smith to do so. See Donna McDonald, *Lord Strathcona: A Biography of Donald Alexander Smith* (Toronto: Dundurn, 1996).
2. Neil Ronaghan, "The Archibald Administration in Manitoba — 1870–1872" (Ph.D. diss., University of Manitoba, 1986), 587. On this point, see also David Burley, "The Emergency of the Premiership," in *Manitoba Premiers of the 19th and 20th Centuries*, ed. Barry Ferguson and Robert Alexander Wardhaugh (Regina: Canada Plains Research Centre, 2010).
3. Ronaghan, 587.
4. "Ontario vs. Manitoba," *Manitoba and Northwest Herald*, November 14, 1871.

5. Cunningham's support for Archibald included a small role in the Fenian Raid of September 1871. According to Gilbert McMicken, Prime Minister Macdonald's intelligence officer dispatched to the scene, Cunningham had organized a Home Guard company to help guard Winnipeg from the Fenian threat rumoured to be massing at the border under William O'Donoghue, Louis Riel's ex-lieutenant. In the "great excitement" that prevailed, Cunningham on his authority as justice of the peace issued warrants to arrest several suspicious suspects. As McMicken remembered, "In Mr. Cunningham's eyes an Irish name, especially if the person who bore it was a Roman Catholic, was a strong ground for suspicion and a justifiable cause of arrest."

   McMicken said Archibald was "very anxious" about the "scores of arrests" made on Cunningham's orders, so he volunteered to go to the police station and see what could be done. McMicken found six prisoners and said he had the following conversation with the officer in charge, a Mr. Barton.

   "Who ordered this man's imprisonment?" McMicken said he asked.

   "Mr. Cunningham," replied Barton.

   "By what authority did you receive him or retain him in custody?"

   "Mr. Cunningham's order."

   "A written order?"

   "No."

   "Have you no written order or warrant of commitment?"

   "No."

   And so on through the list.

   McMicken then invoked his authority "as an officer of the Dominion specially charged with matters within the criminal jurisdiction of the General Government, and the sanction of His Honor the Lieutenant-Governor of the Province, to set the prisoners at liberty."
6. "Marquette," *Manitoban and Northwest Herald*, September 14, 1872.

7. Coldwell said the mob was made up of recently arrived citizens from Upper Canada who, since the election lists were two years old, had no votes. It took months to get the press up and running again. See mhs.mb.ca/docs/transactions/3/norwester.shtml.
8. See Thomas Flanagan, "The History of Métis Aboriginal Rights: Politics, Principle, and Policy," *Canadian Journal of Law and Society* 5 (1990): 71–94.
9. "Mr. CUNNINGHAM — On Monday next — The House in Committee of the Whole to consider the following resolutions: — 1. That by the 31st clause of the Manitoba Act of 1870 it is enacted that one million four hundred thousand acres of the ungranted lands of the Province of Manitoba is appropriated for the benefit of the families of the Half-breed residents, to be divided among the children of the Half-breed heads of the families residing in the said Province at the time of its transfer to Canada. 2. That by the said clause the children of the Half-breed heads of families alone have a right to a share in the distribution of the said one million four hundred thousand acres of land. 3. That in the opinion of this House the Government should strictly abide by the spirit and the letter of the law, and reserve all such lands to be divided among the said children of the Half-breeds, and that any lands that may be granted to such Half-breed heads of families, or to any other old settlers in the Province, to be so granted out of the ungranted Crown lands in the Province."
10. House of Commons Proceedings, March 12 and 24, 1873, NAC, RG 14 D 4, P-58, 16, 35.
11. Canada subsequently passed legislation to clarify the grant and to define the recipients not by age but as "all those of mixed blood, partly white and partly Indian, and who are not heads of families": an act to remove doubts as to the construction of section 31 of the Act 33 Victoria, chapter 3 and to amend section 108 of the Dominion Lands Act, S.C. 1873 (36 Vict.), c. 38.28.
12. Cunningham also advocated for fair treatment of Indigenous Peoples in the treaty-making processes then occurring across the

Prairies. In March 1873, he spoke to a motion in the House of Commons concerning the "dissatisfaction prevailing among the chiefs, head men, and Indians treated with in Manitoba and adjacent territories in the year 1871." Early that season, Cunningham said Archibald had told 15 chiefs located along the Saskatchewan River that the Indigenous Peoples commissioner would meet them at Fort Edmonton in August. But the commissioner never arrived. "Forced by sheer starvation," Cunningham told the legislators, "they left for their hunting grounds, thoroughly convinced that no faith was to be relied in Canadian pledges or promises and with a full determination to have nothing to do in the way of treaty with a nation on whom no reliance could be placed." This was unfortunate, for "if there was one thing more than another that should be attended to in dealing with that people, it was carefulness in making promises and, secondly, in rigidly adhering to those promises when made." Cunningham said the treaty with the Swampies signed in 1871 was yet another example of a "great blunder" committed by the Dominion government as "today these very Swampies were as discontented as ever, and all but repudiated the Treaty entirely." The reason? "The terms of the Treaty, meagre as they were, had not been complied with." As for future treaties, Cunningham said it was imperative for the Dominion to "get the assistance of intelligent men, acquainted with their language, habits, and prejudices." Such men, said Cunningham, were available in Manitoba, "men who had lived almost their whole lives with the Indians, and would be of great service to the Commission trading with the Indians."

13. Letter of A.A. Taché, St. Boniface, to Robert Cunningham, March 28, 1873, Robert Cunningham fonds, F-69, box B294026, Archives of Ontario.
14. Stanley, *Louis Riel.*
15. 1-170 Draft of an Address to the Inhabitants of St. Vital to Robert Cunningham, St. Vital, July 24, 1873.
16. Louis Riel's election campaign was complicated when a warrant for his and Ambroise-Didyme Lépine's arrest was issued and executed

in September. Riel escaped, but not before the sheriff searched Bannatyne's and Cunningham's houses, believing Riel to be hiding there. The deputies eventually arrested Lépine at his farm. The day before pretrial motions were to begin, Cunningham and Bannatyne, together with Marc-Amable Girard and Abbé Ritchot, lobbied Alexander Morris, the new lieutenant governor of Manitoba, that Lépine's arrest was illegal, claiming he had been issued amnesty by the Dominion government. Morris deferred to the courts. See Alexander Begg, *History of the North-West* (Toronto: Hunter, Rose, 1894), 137–39.

17. Cunningham joined a collection of Manitoban leaders on the council, including Marc-Amable Girard, Donald Smith, Pascal Breland, Andrew Bannatyne, Joseph Royal, and John Schultz.
18. Editorial, *Manitoba Free Press*, April 18, 1874.
19. "Death of Mr. R. Cunningham, M.P.," *Globe*, July 13, 1874.
20. Alexander Begg and Walter Nursey, *Ten Years in Winnipeg* (Winnipeg: Times Printing and Publishing House, 1879), 99.
21. "The Interview," *Manitoba Free Press*, June 13, 1870.
22. George F.G. Stanley, ed., *The Collected Writings of Louis Riel/Les écrits complets de Louis Riel* (Edmonton: University of Alberta Press, 1985).
23. St. John's appointment was published in *The Manitoban*, October 21, 1870. With respect to the Selkirk Treaty, St. John confirmed Henry Prince's and the Peguis' perspective that the original Indigenous signatories believed they weren't agreeing to the sale of land to the Crown but rather were entering into a 20-year lease in exchange for an annual rental payment. See Canada, Public Archives, MG12, Al, No. 164a, Molyneux St. John to Adams Archibald, January 3, 1871. Quoted in Ronald C. Maguire, *An Historical Reference Guide to the Stone Fort Treaty* (Ottawa: Department of Indian and Northern Affairs, 1980).

    On the question of allocating Métis lands, St. John advised Archibald against using scrip as it would "inevitably lead to chicanery and fraud, the spoliation of ignorant men, and the accumulation of land in the hands of speculators." While the Dominion government ultimately adopted the scrip system, history would agree with St. John, that it "is calculated to be more mischievous than beneficial." See Report, Molyneux St. John, January 3, 1871, to Adams Archibald, Exhibit 1-0557, 11. Cited in Gerhard J. Ens and Joe Sawchuk, *From New Peoples to New Nations: Aspects of Métis History and Identity from the Eighteenth to the Twenty-First Centuries* (Toronto: University of Toronto Press, 2015).

Regarding St. John's report on settlement lands, a future scholar judged it a "remarkable document because it is one of the few government efforts to afford local environmental conditions a key role in Manitoba settlement." See Shannon Bower, "Wet Prairie: An Environmental History of Wetlands, Flooding and Drainage in Agricultural Manitoba, 1810–1980" (Ph.D. diss., University of British Columbia, 2006).

24. Canada, Indian Claims Commission, Roseau River Anishinabe First Nation Medical Aid Claim (Ottawa: The Commission, 2001).
25. By February 1872, both the Swampy Cree and Anishinabe Nations began registering complaints that the terms of Treaty 1 weren't being fulfilled, specifically a number of items that were agreed to verbally but not included in the text of the agreement. Luckily, St. John had documented the verbal agreements and attached them as a signed memo to the original treaty. In 1875, the Dominion government used the memo in resolving the complaints by directing it to be considered as part of Treaties 1 and 2 and instructing the Indigenous Peoples commissioner to "carry out the promises therein contained." See Department of the Interior, Annual Report of the Department of the Interior for the Year Ended 30th June 1875 (Ottawa: Maclean, Roger & Co., 1875). Also see Wayne E. Daugherty, *Treaty Research Report: Treaty One and Treaty Two (1871)* (Ottawa: Department of Indian and Northern Affairs Canada, 1983), aadnc-aandc.gc.ca/DAM/DAM-INTER-HQ/STAGING/texte-text/tre1-2_1100100028661_eng.pdf.

26. *Manitoban and Northwest Herald*, June 24, 1871, 2.
27. *Manitoba Liberal*, July 26, 1871.
28. Brian Titley, *The Indian Commissioners: Agents of the State and Indian Policy in Canada's Prairie West, 1873–1932* (Edmonton: University of Alberta Press, 2009), 18. Wemyss Simpson was only doing the job on a part-time basis, as he had other business interests in Sault Ste. Marie. When he was asked to take up duties full time in January 1873, he resigned. Joseph-Alfred-Norbert Provencher was appointed in January 1873 and took up his new position on June 2 of that year.
29. See Wayne E. Daugherty, *Treaty Research Report: Treaty Three (1873)* (Ottawa: Department of Indian and Northern Affairs Canada, 1986), rcaanc-cirnac.gc.ca/eng/1100100028671/1564413174418.
30. Cited in Titley, *The Indian Commissioners*, Molyneux St. John to W. Spragge, deputy superintendent general of Indian Affairs, May 30, 1873, LAC RG10, vol. 3603 f1987, 215.
31. *The Standard*, December 12, 1874. Ironically, *The Standard* was Cunningham's old newspaper, *The Manitoban*, rebranded by the new owners.
32. According to the *Nor'Wester*, the *Standard* "has a new name and heading but otherwise it is in the plumage, a little ruffled, of the old *Manitoban*.... The proprietorship is in 'other hands,' meaning the Hudson's Bay Company." *Nor'Wester*, November 11, 1874. See also McDonald, *Lord Strathcona*, 276–77.
33. See, in general, "Report of Mayor Kennedy and Mr. St. John," *Manitoba Free Press*, April 17, 1875.
34. *Manitoba Free Press*, May 29, 1875, 2.
35. There is no evidence that Kate Ranoe accompanied St. John on this trip, though it is curious that the *Manitoba Free Press* reported in September 1876 that "Miss Kate Ranoe (Mrs. St. John), whose friends in this city are very numerous, will shortly return to the stage."
36. This passage was reprinted as Molyneux St. John, "Description of a Village of the Hydah Indians, Near Skedigate Bay in Graham

Island, One of the Queen Charlotte's Islands, Off British Columbia," *Journal of the Anthropological Institute of Great Britain and Ireland* 8 (1879): 426–27. Excerpted from Molyneux St. John, *The Sea of Mountains: An Account of Lord Dufferin's Tour Through British Columbia in 1876* (London: Hurst and Blackett, 1877).
37. See Titley, *The Indian Commissioners.*
38. Indian [superintendent], Manitoba — [Minister of the Interior], October 5, 1878 [recommends the appointment] of Molyneux St. John as Order-in-Council Number: 1878-0891. On the investigation into Provencher, see Titley, *The Indian Commissioners.*
39. In London, St. John kept up his interest in the theatre, as well, co-writing *Under the Mistletoe*, a "comedy-drama in a prologue and five Tableux." It was produced at the Imperial Theatre in December 1881; the reviews weren't kind. Said Austin Brereton in *The Theatre*: "It is a most miserable play, lacking plot, construction, and good dialogue. Only that as a slave of duty I was obliged to remain in my seat until the close of the piece, I should have left long before the conclusion." *The Theatre* 5, no. 25 (January 1882): 49.
40. "Theatricals at Pelly," *Manitoba Free Press*, March 30, 1878, 1.
41. "The Great North-West," *Globe*, May 31, 1871, 1; "The Great North-West," *Daily Telegraph*, May 31, 1871, 4.
42. *Victoria Home Journal*, August 26, 1893, 7.
43. "News from Montreal," *Globe*, March 30, 1893, 5.
44. "News from Montreal," *Globe*, April 1, 1893, 13.
45. *Winnipeg Daily Tribune*, July 24, 1895, 2.
46. "Usher of the Black Rod Dead. Special Despatch to the Globe," *Globe*, February 1, 1904, 6.
47. "Well Known in the West: Molyneux St. John, Former Newspaperman of Winnipeg, Dies at Ottawa," *Winnipeg Tribune*, February 2, 1904, 3.

APPENDIX 2: THE EXPEDITION ARTISTS

1. Alice Johnson, "Edward and Frances Hopkins," *The Beaver* (Autumn 1971): 15–16.

2. Repeated in Henry C. Campbell, *Early Days on the Great Lakes: The Art of William Armstrong* (Toronto: McClelland & Stewart, 1971), 9. "In 1870, William Armstrong embarked on an adventure that was to become one of the epics of Canadian history. He joined the military expedition under Colonel Garnet Wolseley that was sent to subdue Louis Riel and his followers, then in open rebellion at Fort Garry. His help in engineering was needed to enable the troops to negotiate the rivers and lakes of northwestern Ontario. He was given the rank of captain in the 63rd Regiment and was made chief engineer."
3. See Thorold Tronrud, "William Armstrong: Art and Enterprise," in *William Armstrong, 1822–1914: Watercolour Drawings of New Ontario — from Georgian Bay to Rat Portage*, ed. Janet E. Clark (Thunder Bay, ON: Thunder Bay Art Gallery, 1996).

SOURCES

Except for specific references made in the Notes, sources by chapter are as follows.

INTRODUCTION

Ranoe, Kate, and Molyneux St. John. "The Red River Expedition." *Globe*, August 15, 1870.

CHAPTER 1: BLAWSTED FENCE

Bowsfield, Hartwell. "Snow, John Allan." *Dictionary of Canadian Biography*. biographi.ca/en/bio/snow_john_allan_11E.html. Accessed July 8, 2019.

Bumsted, J.M. *The Red River Rebellion*. Winnipeg: Watson & Dwyer, 1996.

Clark, Lovell. "Schultz, Sir John Christian." *Dictionary of Canadian Biography*. biographi.ca/en/bio.php?BioId=40542. Accessed July 8, 2019.

Dawson, Simon James. *Report on the Line of Route Between Lake Superior and the Red River Settlement*. Ottawa: Queen's Printer, 1868.

Dorge, Lionel. "Thibault (Thibaud, Thebo), Jean-Baptiste." *Dictionary of Canadian Biography*. biographi.ca/en/bio/thibault_jean_baptiste_10E.html. Accessed July 8, 2019.

Latham, David. "Mair, Charles." *Dictionary of Canadian Biography*. biographi.ca/en/bio/mair_charles_15E.html. Accessed July 8, 2019.

Morton, W.L. "Irumberry de Salaberry, Charles-René-Léonidas d'." *Dictionary of Canadian Biography*. biographi.ca/en/bio

/irumberry_de_salaberry_charles_rene_leonidas_d_11E.html. Accessed July 8, 2019.

Rea, J.E. "Scott, Thomas." *Dictionary of Canadian Biography*. biographi.ca/en/bio/scott_thomas_1870_9E.html. Accessed July 8, 2019.

Read, Colin Frederick. "Dennis, John Stoughton." *Dictionary of Canadian Biography*. biographi.ca/en/bio/dennis_john_stoughton_1820_85_11E.html. Accessed July 8, 2019.

Reford, Alexander. "Smith, Donald Alexander, 1st Baron Strathcona and Mount Royal." *Dictionary of Canadian Biography*. biographi.ca/en/bio/smith_donald_alexander_14E.html. Accessed July 8, 2019.

Stanley, George F.G. *The Birth of Western Canada: A History of the Riel Rebellions*. Toronto: Longmans, Green and Co., 1936.

———. *Louis Riel*. Toronto: McGraw-Hill, 1963.

Zeller, Suzanne. "McDougall, William." *Dictionary of Canadian Biography*. biographi.ca/en/bio/mcdougall_william_13E.html. Accessed July 8, 2019.

CHAPTER 2: OUR SPECIAL CORRESPONDENT

Cunningham, Robert. *Christmas Eve on Stanley Street*. Napanee, ON: S.T. Hammond, 1869. As published, this short book is bibliographically attributed to "a Globe Reporter," but it's widely thought to be by Cunningham.

———. "The Insurrection in the North-West." *Globe*, January 13, 1870.

———. "Latest from Red River." *Globe*, January 15, 1870.

———. "The North-West: From Pembina South Again." *Globe*, February 8, 1870.

———. "The North-West: Interview with Riel." *Globe*, February 3, 1870.

———. "The North-West: Over the Line." *Globe*, February 2, 1870.

———. "The North-West: Winter on the Prairie." *Globe*, February 4, 1870.

———. "Travelling to the North-West." *Globe*, January 15, 1870.

Rea, J.E. "Cunningham, Robert." *Dictionary of Canadian Biography*.

biographi.ca/en/bio/cunningham_robert_10E.html. Accessed July 8, 2019.

CHAPTER 3: ERRAND OF PEACE

Anonymous. "Indignation Meeting: Immense Crowd Immense Enthusiasm." *Globe*, April 7, 1870.

———. "Indignation Meetings: Brantford, Walkerton, Windsor, St. Catharines." *Globe*, April 13, 1870.

———. "Indignation Meetings: Hamilton, Oshawa, Listowel." *Globe*, April 12, 1870.

———. "Indignation Meetings: Princeton, Brockville, Kingston, Cookstown." *Globe*, April 14, 1870.

———. "Large and Enthusiastic Indignation Meeting at Kingston." *Globe*, April 16, 1870.

———. "Latest from Ottawa: Great Indignation Meeting." *Globe*, April 12, 1870.

Bumsted, J.M. *The Red River Rebellion*. Winnipeg: Watson & Dwyer, 1996.

Cooke, O.A. "Wolseley, Garnet Joseph, 1st Viscount Wolseley." *Dictionary of Canadian Biography*. biographi.ca/en/bio/wolseley_garnet_joseph_14E.html. Accessed July 8, 2019.

St. John, Molyneux. "The Red River Expedition: Embarkation at Collingwood." *Globe*, May 14, 1870.

Stanley, George F.G. *The Birth of Western Canada: A History of the Riel Rebellions*. Toronto: Longmans, Green and Co., 1936.

———. *Louis Riel*. Toronto: McGraw-Hill, 1963.

CHAPTER 4: TWO CORRESPONDENTS AND A BURLESQUE STAR

Anonymous. "Benefit." *Daily Telegraph*, January 18, 1869.

———. "Canada." *Globe*, January 1, 1869.

———. "Celebration of the Queen's Birthday." *Globe*, May 25, 1869.

———. "City News." *Globe*, January 18, 1869.

———. "City News." *Globe*, March 16, 1869.

———. "City News." *Globe*, April 27, 1869.

———. "City News." *Globe*, May 11, 1869.

———. "City News." *Globe*, May 26, 1869.

———. "City News." *Globe*, May 29, 1869.

———. "City News." *Globe*, June 7, 1869.

———. "Editorial." *Globe*, May 4, 1870.

———. "Miss Kate Ranoe." *Globe*, March 2, 1869.

———. "Miss Kate Ranoe," in *The Musical World*, vol. 38. London: Boosey and Sons, 1860.

———. "Plymouth," in *The Musical World*, vol. 39. London: Boosey and Sons, 1860.

———. "Royal Lyceum." *Daily Telegraph*, January 18, 1869.

Brown, Thomas Allston. *A History of the New York Stage from the First Performance in 1732 to 1901*. New York: Dodd, Mead and Company, 1903.

Egerton, Mrs. Fred. *Admiral of the Fleet, Sir Geoffrey Phipps Hornby G.C.B: A Biography*. Edinburgh and London: William Blackwood and Sons, 1896.

Goldsborough, Gordon. "Memorable Manitobans: Frederick Edward Molyneux St. John (1838–1904)." Manitoba Historical Society. mhs.mb.ca/docs/people/stjohn_fem.shtml. Accessed July 8, 2019.

Gough, Barry M. "British Policy in the San Juan Boundary Dispute, 1854–72." *The Pacific Northwest Quarterly* 62, no. 2 (April 1971): 59–68.

Harte, Walter Blackburn. "Canadian Journalists and Journalism." *New England Magazine: An Illustrated Monthly* 5 (September 1891–February 1892): 411–41.

Maynard, Walter. *The Light of Other Days Seen Through the Wrong End of an Opera Glass*, vol. 1. London: Richard Bentley and Son, 1890.

The Peerage. "Person Page – 8325." thepeerage.com/p8325.htm#i83245.

Planché, James Robinson. *The Fair One with the Golden Locks: An Original Fairy Extravaganza in One Act Founded on the Popular Nursery Tale by the Countess D'Alnois*. London: T.H. Lacy, 1879.

Robertson, John Palmerston. *A Political Manual of the Province of Manitoba and the North-West Territories*. Winnipeg: Call Printing Company, 1887.

Senelick, Laurence. *Jacques Offenbach and the Making of Modern Culture*. Cambridge: Cambridge University Press, 2017.

St. John, Molyneux. "The Gov.-General's Tour on the Coast of British Columbia." *Globe*, September 19, 1876.

———. "The New York Theatres," in *The Broadway Annual: A Miscellany of Original Literature in Poetry and Prose*. New York: George Routledge and Sons, 1869.

———. "New York Theatres, Part I: Wallack's Theatre." *Watson's Art Journal* 8, no. 21 (March 14, 1868): 273–75.

Vouri, Mike. *Outpost of Empire: The Royal Marines and the Joint Occupation of San Juan Island*. Seattle: Northwest Interpretive Association, 2004.

CHAPTER 5: COLLINGWOOD

Cunningham, Robert. "Manitoba in the Distance." *Daily Telegraph*, May 4, 1870.

———. "Sault Ste. Marie." *Daily Telegraph*, May 10, 1870.

St. John, Molyneux. "The Red River Expedition: Embarkation at Collingwood." *Globe*, May 14, 1870.

———. "The Red River Expedition: Thunder Bay Road." *Globe*, May 4, 1870.

CHAPTER 6: ISOLATED BACKWOODSMEN

St. John, Molyneux. "The Red River Expedition: The *Chicora* at Thunder Bay." *Globe*, May 30, 1870.

CHAPTER 7: CAMP SAULT

Cunningham, Robert. "The Fenians at the Sault: An Invasion Anticipated." *Daily Telegraph*, June 7, 1870.

———. "Manitoba in the Distance." *Daily Telegraph*, May 4, 1870.

———. "The Northwest: Excitement at the Sault." *Daily Telegraph*, May 13, 1870.

———. "The Northwest: The People of the Settlement Expecting the Troops." *Daily Telegraph*, May 14, 1870.

———. "On the War Path." *Daily Telegraph*, May 10, 1870.

———. "Our Sault Special: Arrival of the Volunteers." *Daily Telegraph*, May 24, 1870.

———. "Sault Ste. Marie." *Daily Telegraph*, May 10, 1870.

———. "Sault Ste. Marie: The American Fort." *Daily Telegraph*, May 20, 1870.

———. "Sault Ste. Marie: The Canal Declared Open." *Daily Telegraph*, May 23, 1870.

———. "Sault Ste. Marie: The *Chicora* Refused Passage Light." *Daily Telegraph*, May 19, 1870.

———. "Sault Ste. Marie: The Expected Arrival of the Chicora." *Daily Telegraph*, May 18, 1870.

———. "Sault Ste. Marie: A Glimpse at the Camp." *Daily Telegraph*, May 24, 1870.

———. "Sault Ste. Marie: Preparing for the Journey." *Daily Telegraph*, June 4, 1870.

———. "Sault Ste. Marie: Something About the Place." Daily *Telegraph*, May 17, 1870.

———. "Sault Ste. Marie: Sunday in the Camp." *Daily Telegraph*, May 28, 1870.

———. "Sault Ste. Marie: The Trip of the *Algoma*." *Daily Telegraph*, May 14, 1870.

———. "Thunder Bay: Arrival of the *Chicora*." *Daily Telegraph*, June 8, 1870.

CHAPTER 8: CONDITIONS ON THE GROUND

Cunningham, Robert. "Thunder Bay: Arrival of the *Chicora*." *Daily Telegraph*, June 18, 1870.

———. "Thunder Bay: A False Alarm." *Daily Telegraph*, June 9, 1870.

———. "Thunder Bay: Pages from a Diary." *Daily Telegraph*, June 15, 1870.

Huyshe, George Lightfoot. *The Red River Expedition*. Toronto: Adam, Stevenson, 1871.

St. John, Molyneux. "The Red River Expedition: Affairs at Fort William." *Globe*, June 2, 1870.

———. "The Red River Expedition: Affairs at Thunder Bay." *Globe*, June 15, 1870.

———. "The Red River Expedition: The *Algoma* at Fort William." *Globe*, June 1, 1870.

———. "The Red River Expedition: Prince Arthur Landing." *Globe*, June 9, 1870.

———. "The Red River Expedition: Working on the Road." *Globe*, June 3, 1870.

CHAPTER 9: DECEITFUL APPEARANCES

Cunningham, Robert. "Red River: Prince Arthur's Landing." *Daily Telegraph*, June 27, 1870.

———. "Thunder Bay: Weariness of Inaction." *Daily Telegraph*, July 1, 1870.

St. John, Molyneux. "The Red River Expedition: Affairs at Fort William." *Globe*, June 2, 1870.

———. "The Red River Expedition: Check to the Passage of Boats." *Globe*, June 25, 1870.

———. "The Red River Expedition: Latest from Thunder Bay." *Globe*, June 18, 1870.

———. "The Red River Expedition: The Situation at Thunder Bay." *Globe*, June 23, 1870.

CHAPTER 10: HARRY WITH THE ROAD

St. John, Molyneux. "The Red River Expedition: From Prince Arthur's Landing." *Globe*, June 27, 1870.

———. "The Red River Expedition: From Prince Arthur's Landing." *Globe*, July 1, 1870.

———. "The Red River Expedition: From Prince Arthur's Landing." *Globe*, July 5, 1870.

———. "The Red River Expedition: From Prince Arthur's Landing." *Globe*, July 7, 1870.

CHAPTER 11: UP THE KAMINISTIQUIA

Cunningham, Robert. "Kaministiquia: A Romantic Situation." *Daily Telegraph*, July 8, 1870.

CHAPTER 12: AND THEY'RE OFF

Cunningham, Robert. "Matawan: Moving Forward." *Daily Telegraph*, July 19, 1870.

———. "Matawan: One Stage Further." *Daily Telegraph*, July 15, 1870.

———. "Shebandowan: A Startling Incident." *Daily Telegraph*, July 26, 1870.

Ranoe, Kate, and Molyneux St. John. "The Red River Expedition: The First Detachment." *Globe*, August 15, 1870.

———. "The Red River Expedition: From Lake Shebandowan." *Globe*, July 29, 1870.

———. "The Red River Expedition: From Rat Portage." *Globe*, September 8, 1870.

———. "The Red River Expedition: The Road to Manitoba." *Globe*, August 29, 1870.

St. John, Molyneux. "The Red River Expedition: The Forward Movement." *Globe*, July 15, 1870.

CHAPTER 13: INTELLECTUAL CHARACTERS

Cunningham, Robert. "Barrie Portage: The Crimea and Red River." *Daily Telegraph*, August 9, 1870.

———. "Deux-Rivières: The Indians." *Daily Telegraph*, August 16, 1870.

———. "Kadgaskag Lake: The Force of Example." *Daily Telegraph*, August 10, 1870.

———. "Red River: A Storm." *Daily Telegraph*, August 15, 1870.

———. "Shelter Island: Provisions Running Short." *Daily Telegraph*, August 6, 1870.

Ranoe, Kate, and Molyneux St. John. "The Red River Expedition: The First Detachment." *Globe*, August 15, 1870.

———. "The Red River Expedition: From Lake Shebandowan." *Globe*, July 29, 1870.

———. "The Red River Expedition: From Pickerel Lake." *Globe*, August 9, 1870.

St. John, Molyneux. "The Red River Expedition: From Rat Portage." *Globe*, September 8, 1870.

———. "The Red River Expedition: The Road to Manitoba." *Globe*, August 29, 1870.

CHAPTER 14: RIGHT-OF-WAY

Cunningham, Robert. "Fort Frances: Arrival of Colonel Wolseley." *Daily Telegraph*, August 19, 1870.

Ranoe, Kate, and Molyneux St. John. "The Red River Expedition: The First Detachment." *Globe*, August 15, 1870.

St. John, Molyneux. "The Red River Expedition: The Road to Manitoba." *Globe*, August 29, 1870.

CHAPTER 15: ON TO FORT GARRY

Cunningham, Robert. "Manitoba: On the Way to Fort Garry." *Daily Telegraph*, September 7, 1870.

———. "Manitoba: Winnipeg River." *Daily Telegraph*, September 8, 1870.

St. John, Molyneux. "The Red River Expedition: From Rat Portage." *Globe*, September 8, 1870.

CHAPTER 16: CHIEF HENRY PRINCE

Cunningham, Robert. "Fort Garry: Arrival of the Expedition." *Daily Telegraph*, September 6, 1870.

———. "Manitoba: On the Way to Fort Garry." *Daily Telegraph*, September 7, 1870.

St. John, Molyneux. "The Red River Expedition: Arrival at Fort Alexander." *Globe*, September 6, 1870.

CHAPTER 17: TAKING FORT GARRY

Cunningham, Robert. "At Last: The Union Jack over Fort Garry." *Daily Telegraph*, September 1, 1870.

———. "Fort Garry: Arrival of the Expedition." *Daily Telegraph*, September 6, 1870.

———. "Fort Garry: Arrival of the Troops." *Daily Telegraph*, September 10, 1870.

St. John, Molyneux. "Latest from Fort Garry: Arrival of the Expedition." *Globe*, September 1, 1870.

———. "Latest from Fort Garry: The New Rulers." *Globe*, September 9, 1870.

———. "The Red River Expedition: From Fort Alexander to Fort Garry." *Globe*, September 6, 1870.

CHAPTER 18: INTERREGNUM

Anonymous. "Young and Archibald at Collingwood." *Globe*, August 11, 1870.

Cunningham, Robert. "Fort Garry: The Ontario Men." *Daily Telegraph*, September 14, 1870.

———. "Fort Garry: Outrages and Murder." *Daily Telegraph*, September 16, 1870.

St. John, Molyneux. "Affairs in Manitoba: Endurance of the Troops." *Globe*, September 13, 1870.

CHAPTER 19: GREAT FEAR

Cunningham, Robert. "Fort Garry: Arrival of the Expedition." *Daily Telegraph*, September 6, 1870.

———. "Fort Garry: Full Details of Scott's Murder." *Daily Telegraph*, September 22, 1870.

St. John, Molyneux. "Affairs in Manitoba: The Body of the Murdered Scott." *Globe*, September 22, 1870.

———. "Latest from Fort Garry: Arrival of Lieut.-Gov. Archibald." *Globe*, September 14, 1870.

CHAPTER 20: NO SELFISH OBJECT

St. John, Molyneux. "Affairs in Manitoba: The Body of Murdered Scott." *Globe*, September 22, 1870.

———. "Affairs in Manitoba: Col. Wolseley's Last Orders." *Globe*, September 28, 1870.

———. "Latest from Fort Garry: Arrival of Lieut. Gov. Archibald." *Globe*, September 14, 1870.

———. "The Red River Expedition: Return of the Regulars." *Globe*, September 19, 1870.

CHAPTER 21: VINTAGE WOLSELEY

Anonymous. "Col. Wolseley." *Daily Telegraph*, September 28, 1870.

Cunningham, Robert. "Fort Garry: Col. Wolseley's Farewell Address." *Daily Telegraph*, September 28, 1870.

———. "Fort Garry: Full Details of Scott's Murder." *Daily Telegraph*, September 22, 1870.

———. "Fort Garry: The Indians Excited." *Daily Telegraph*, September 24, 1870.

St. John, Molyneux. "Affairs in Manitoba: Col. Wolseley's Last Orders." *Globe*, September 28, 1870.

CHAPTER 22: CHINESE PUZZLE

Cunningham, Robert. "Fort Garry: Death of a Miscreant." *Daily Telegraph*, September 27, 1870.

———. "Fort Garry: The French and the Governor." *Daily Telegraph*, September 27, 1870.

Maguire, Ronald C. *An Historical Reference Guide to the Stone Fort Treaty*. Ottawa: Department of Indian and Northern Affairs, 1980.

St. John, Molyneux. "Affairs in Manitoba: The Body of Murdered Scott." *Globe*, September 22, 1870.

CHAPTER 23: ELZÉAR GOULET

Cunningham, Robert. "Fort Garry: Dearth of News." *Daily Telegraph*, October 25, 1870.

———. "Fort Garry: The Death of Goulet — A Reign of Terror." *Daily Telegraph*, October 5, 1870.

———. "Fort Garry: Digging for Scott's Remains." *Daily Telegraph*, October 29, 1870.

———. "Fort Garry: Goulet's Death." *Daily Telegraph*, October 4, 1870.

———. "Fort Garry: Goulet's Death." *Daily Telegraph*, October 11, 1870.

———. "Fort Garry: Lépine Shot." *Daily Telegraph*, October 8, 1870.

———. "Fort Garry: Petitions and Prayers." *Daily Telegraph*, October 26, 1870.

———. "Fort Garry: The Political Outlook." *Daily Telegraph*, October 13, 1870.

———. "Fort Garry: Review of the Past." *Daily Telegraph*, October 18, 1870.

St. John, Molyneux. "Affairs in Manitoba: Death of Goulet." *Globe*, October 5, 1870.

———. "Affairs in Manitoba: Getting Out of Chaos." *Globe*, September 30, 1870.

———. "Latest from Fort Garry: Gathering of French Half-Breeds." *Globe*, October 8, 1870.

CHAPTER 24: SELKIRK

Cunningham, Robert. "Fort Garry: The Elections." *Daily Telegraph*, October 21, 1870.

St. John, Molyneux. "Affairs in Manitoba: Death of Goulet." *Globe*, October 5, 1870.

———. "Affairs in Manitoba: A Police Force." *Globe*, October 5, 1870.

CHAPTER 25: EMBEDDED THEREAFTER

Cunningham, Robert. "Fort Garry: Digging for Scott's Remains." *Daily Telegraph*, October 29, 1870.

"Editorial." *Manitoban and Northwest Herald*, October 15, 1870.

Ronaghan, Neil. "The Archibald Administration in Manitoba — 1870–1872." Ph.D. diss., University of Manitoba, 1986.

IMAGE CREDITS

2 Historical Maps, Library and Archives Canada

5 Library and Archives Canada C-002048

7 Toronto *Daily Telegraph*, May 19, 1870

12 Library and Archives Canada e010970748

15 Archives of Ontario, Toronto, 69 Series, Robert Cunningham fonds

17 Library and Archives Canada C-001074

27 Hudson's Bay Company Archives, Archives of Manitoba, Winnipeg, HBCA P-449

31 Archives of Manitoba, Personalities, N16492 CT65

32 Photograph by William Notman. McCord Museum, Montreal, I-23764.1

36 Archives of Manitoba, Personalities, Winnipeg, ca. 1890, N91

39 Photograph by William Notman. McCord Museum, Montreal, I-36185.1

46 *Canadian Illustrated News* 4, no. 11, 165. Library and Archives Canada C-056475

48 Courtesy of Thunder Bay Public Library

51 *Canadian Illustrated News* 2, no. 2, 20. Library and Archives Canada C-050311

53 *Canadian Illustrated News* 2, no. 3, 36. Library and Archives Canada C-050320

54–55 From George Lightfoot Huyshe, *The Red River Expedition* (London: Macmillan, 1871)

63	*Canadian Illustrated News* 1, no. 32, 508. Library and Archives Canada C-048850
65	Archives of Ontario, 273 Series, Donald B. Smith fonds
74	*Canadian Illustrated News* 2, no. 1, 8. Library and Archives Canada C-050305
87	*Toronto Star* Photograph Archive. Courtesy of Toronto Public Library
98–99	From George Lightfoot Huyshe, *The Red River Rebellion* (London: Macmillan, 1871)
106	*Canadian Illustrated News* 4, no. 16, 244. Library and Archives Canada C-056531
113	*Canadian Illustrated News* 6, no. 7, 101. Library and Archives Canada C-058751
119	*Canadian Illustrated News* 6, no. 7, 100. Library and Archives Canada C-058570
133	Library and Archives Canada PA-031570
134	Archives of Manitoba, Stoval Advocate Collection, Item 209
140	Library and Archives Canada fonds C-011344
142–43	Archives of Manitoba. Winnipeg Streets–Main 1870 Collection, Item 11, Negative ID N13034
155	Library and Archives Canada 3220937
168	Library and Archives Canada C-1065
189	Archives of Manitoba, Personalities — Goulet, E.1 N21685
212	Courtesy of Glenbow Archives Special Collections, University of Calgary NA-1406-217
219	*Daily Telegraph*, May 27, 1871
222	McCord Museum I-33088.1
223	Library and Archives Canada 3337438
224	Courtesy of Thunder Bay Public Library
231	Library and Archives Canada e011154374
233	McCord Museum M2003.145.13
234	*Canadian Illustrated News* 4, no. 21, 328–29. Author's Photograph

INDEX